AMBIVALENT
ZEN

AMBIVALENT ZEN

A Memoir

LAWRENCE SHAINBERG

Pantheon Books
New York

Copyright © 1995 by Lawrence Shainberg

All rights reserved under International and Pan-American Copyright
Conventions. Published in the United States by Pantheon Books, a
division of Random House, Inc., New York, and simultaneously in
Canada by Random House of Canada Limited, Toronto.

Grateful acknowledgment is made to the following for permission to
reprint previously published material:

Grove/Atlantic, Inc.: Excerpt from *Worstward Ho!* by Samuel Beckett.
Copyright © 1983 by Samuel Beckett. Used by permission of
Grove/Atlantic, Inc.

HarperCollins Publishers, Inc.: Excerpts from *Zen Comments on the
Mumonkan* by Zenkei Shibayama, English language translation
copyright © 1974 by Zenkei Shibayama. Reprinted by permission of
HarperCollins Publishers, Inc.

Library of Congress Cataloging-in-Publication Data

Shainberg, Lawrence, 1936–
    Ambivalent Zen: a memoir / Lawrence Shainberg.
        p.   cm.
    ISBN 0-679-44116-6
    1. Shainberg, Lawrence, 1936-   .   2. Spiritual life—Zen Bud-
dhism.   I. Title.
BQ986.A42A3   1996
294.3'927'092—dc20
    [B]   95-21450

BOOK DESIGN BY DEBORAH KERNER

Manufactured in the United States of America

9 8 7 6 5 4 3 2

For

KYUDO NAKAGAWA ROSHI

with love and gratitude

I discovered that it is necessary, absolutely necessary, to believe in nothing. That is, we have to believe in something which has no form and no color—something which exists before all forms and colors appear. . . . No matter what god or doctrine you believe in, if you become attached to it, your belief will be based more or less on a self-centered idea. You strive for a perfect faith in order to save yourself. But it will take time to attain such a perfect faith. You will be involved in an idealistic practice. In constantly seeking to actualize your ideal, you will have no time for composure. But if you are always prepared for accepting everything we see as something appearing from nothing, knowing that there is some reason why a phenomenal existence of such and such form and color appears, then at that moment you will have perfect composure.

—**Shunryu Suzuki Roshi**

CONTENTS

A
C
K
N
O
W
L
E
D
G
M
E
N
T
S

My great debt to all teachers mentioned herein—even those who showed themselves to be less than I expected—is evident in these pages. Without their insight and example, I would not have been blessed with the experiences here described or the courage to record them honestly. I pray that this memoir does justice to them and to the practice they embody.

Also evident, I trust, is the debt I owe to Andra Samelson. Her friendship and unequivocal faith in the spiritual point of view sustained me through much that I've reported here, and the report itself was nurtured at every turn by her recollections as well as her considerable gifts as an editor.

My late brother, David Shainberg, was a constant source of strength, clarity and, in spite of himself, since he remained a skeptic with regard to spiritual practice, encouragement. No words can express my gratitude to him or my sorrow at his passing.

So many readers helped me that I cannot mention them all. I am particularly indebted to Steve Shainberg, Nancy Baker and Michael Flanagan, who patiently read, corrected and cheered me throughout this lengthy process; to Peter Gamby and Sasha Meyerowitz, who offered me the benefit of their experience in the Dharma; and to Irini Spanidou, Gary Clevidence, Eleanor Munro and Bill Webb for generous and perceptive criticism when I needed it most.

Certain books have been invaluable to me and are heartily recommended to the reader who would pursue these matters further: *A History of Zen Buddhism,* by Heinrich Dumoulin; *Buddhism: Its Essence and Development,* by Edward Conze; *Zen and Beckett,* by Paul Foster; *Zen Comments on the Mumonkan,* by. Zenkei Shibayama; *Nine-Headed Dragon River,* by Peter Matthiessen. Helen Tworkov's *Zen in America* was particularly helpful for material on Bernard Glassman, and my glossary owes much to the work of Dr. Louis Nordstrom, the editor of *Namu Dai Bosa: A Transmission of Zen Buddhism to America.* For Dharma inspiration, *Zen Mind, Beginner's Mind,* by Shunryu Suzuki, remains, in my view, the finest introduction to Zen practice; and for a rigorous presentation of the spiritual point of view, I always return to *I Am That,* by Sri Nisargadatta.

Deepest thanks to my agent, Jane Gelfman, whose devotion to this memoir, and my work in general, goes far beyond the call of duty, and my editor, Dan Frank, who helped me see the book with a clarity that far exceeded what I had managed on my own.

Finally, immeasurable gratitude to Vivian Bower for her wisdom and patience, her impolite criticism, the example of her steady, unsentimental commitment to sitting meditation and, most of all, our love.

AUTHOR'S NOTE

With the exception of those teachers whose names
are matters of public or historical record, all other names
herein have been changed for reasons of privacy.

AMBIVALENT ZEN

1   *Nothing removes man further from God than desire for*
union with him.   —IMAM ABU'L-HASAN ASH-SHADHILI

K yudo Roshi wears his Yankee cap to breakfast, doesn't remove it even after we sit down. He has a large collection of
hats, but he has worn this one exclusively since I bought it for
him last week at Yankee Stadium. Slightly self-conscious about
his shaved head, he never goes out without a hat, but the Yankee cap has the added advantage of making him look, if not like
an American, at least at home in the culture. Like any Zen master, he aims to walk the streets as if invisible, attract no atten-

tion, leave no trace of himself in anyone's mind. The robes he wears in the zendo are seldom worn outside it. He favors flannel shirts and khaki pants, Saucony running shoes, a Yankee jacket in the fall and, when the weather turns cold, a parka and a black woolen watch cap purchased through the L. L. Bean catalogue. In addition to hats, he collects watches and seems to wear a different one every day. He has no money (his only source of financial support being the dues we pay in the zendo), but he owns at least a dozen watches, and none are inexpensive. The fact that I wear a Timex even though I can afford a better one strikes him as a flaw in my character, even perhaps—as he sometimes hints—an elemental shortcoming in my understanding of Zen.

On the street, he walks very fast and purposefully, as if he knows his way around the city. Unfortunately, he doesn't. He has been in New York for more than six years, but outside his own neighborhood, the only one he knows is Chinatown, which he calls "my territory." As we walk, he talks incessantly, asking questions he's asked me dozens of times, grabbing my arm and turning toward me so that, since I cannot help but do likewise, both of us are virtually walking sideways. I have bumped into fire hydrants and stumbled off curbs while walking with him. "Larry-san—this Greenwich Village? Side street? Avenue? Those people over there—they artist? Homosexual? Why so many standing around?" Yankee cap or not, he is not, most definitely, at home in the culture. He reads Japanese newspapers, watches the Japanese station on cable TV, and despite the fact that he studied English in high school, speaks as if he did not encounter the language until a few months ago. An expectant woman in our zendo is "four months president." "Vagina"—a word that frequently occurs

in his lectures—is "pajama." He says "minimum" for "maximum" and vice versa. One of his favorite foods is "penis butter." Last week, in order to obtain a license to perform
marriages and funerals, one of his students took him down to
"shitty hall." The idea of English lessons, constantly suggested
by one or another of his students, strikes him as absurd. "Study
English? What you talking about, Larry-san? I grown man! I
learn myself!" If asked how his studies progress, his reply is
always the same: "Wonderful! One new word a year!" He
finds this funny, but I don't. His condescension toward language has lately been wearing thin on me. He seems to resent
the fact that he has to speak, but this does not prevent his giving incomprehensible lectures in the zendo that can last as long
as an hour and a half. Is the anger I feel at such moments the
logical response of a mind that is being tormented or proof that
my commitment to Zen is insufficient?

We went up to the Stadium to see the Yankees play the
Red Sox. In addition to the hat, I bought him two hot dogs and
a quart-sized Pepsi, which he forced himself to finish because
he is after all a monk and, serious to the point of fanaticism
about his vow against waste, cannot throw anything away. He
lives in a sort of dread of the gifts his students bring him. Soon
after he came to New York, I brought him a quart of lentil soup
I had made, not knowing that the taste of lentils makes him
nauseous. Only after eating it all did he beg me, "Please, Larry-
san, don't bean soup anymore."

For days before the Yankee game, he had been working
me over on the subject of bravery and cowardice. Ever since we
met, he has remarked on the frequency with which I speak of
fear, how many of my sentences begin with phrases such as
"I'm afraid that . . ." or "What I'm worried about is. . . ."

Whether this is because I am actually consumed with fear or because the shape of my relationship with him requires that I present myself in terms of certain assumptions of inadequacy, I never know for sure. Lately, we have rarely had a conversation in which he has not scolded me for my cowardice or timidity and today, as we wait for the subway that will take us to Yankee Stadium, he brings it up again. "Larry-san, why you always afraid? Forty-five years old talk like baby! What you think? Zen about quiet mind? Relaxation? No! No! Zen about bravery! Zazen mind bravery mind! Must bravery, Larry-san! Must sincere!" I know this, of course, have heard it from him before, but even so, my mind becomes alert with that particular combination of self-criticism, excitement and defensiveness that makes me, so often in his presence, annoyed with him and annoyed with myself for being so. Reminding myself that Zen masters become more brutal with students the more they like them, I tell myself that I should be thankful for his criticism, but who wants to be lectured in a subway station, on his way to a ball game, like a six-year-old? It does not help that before and after this outburst, giggling and asking his silly questions, he has been acting like a six-year-old himself. It is easy to forget that he is a Zen master, and most of the time he seems to forget it himself. Even so, he never strays too far from what is after all the only subject that concerns him, and in my case, at this moment, that means instructing me on the subject of fear. Later, in the seventh inning, when Willie Randolph, the Yankee second baseman, lays down a bunt, and I explain to him that another word for "bunt" is "sacrifice," he snaps, "Larry-san, if you sacrifice everything, you won't be afraid of anything."

The admonition, of course, is a quick summation of Buddhist logic: the source of my anxiety is not the succession of objects to which it attaches itself but that volatile heap of memory and habit I have come to call "myself." Give it up and you give up your fear; cling to it, and fear will haunt you always. There is nothing unfamiliar about these ideas, but at this moment, in the grandstand behind first base at Yankee Stadium, their effect on me is, like so much of what he says, neurochemical. I feel undermined and I feel exhilarated, free of my self entirely, and I cannot believe that it will ever return again.

Is the insight for him as remarkable as it is for me? Two years later, I have occasion to remind him of it. We are on a plane headed for Israel, where I am to assist him at a retreat with his students in Jerusalem, and we've both of us had a bit too much to drink. As usual, alcohol has made him silly and me a little maudlin. I am overcome with love for the practice, love for him, love for the ultimate truth that always seems to be just beyond my grasp when I am sitting in meditation, staring at the wall. "Roshi, do you remember that day we went to the Yankee game and someone laid down a bunt and I told you that the word for 'bunt' was 'sacrifice'? Remember what you said to me?"

Sipping his drink (his favorite: Scotch and Coca-Cola), he shakes his head. He is always a little annoyed when pressed for memory, either because this particular neurological function is not one of his strengths or because the very act of remembering interferes with his desire to jettison the past. When once I used the word "amnesia" in conversation with him, he looked it up in his English-Japanese dictionary. "Ah!" he cried, repeating the Japanese word several times. "Ahm-nee-jah! That's me!"

"You told me that if I sacrificed everything I wouldn't be afraid of anything. I've never forgotten that! It was one of the best things you ever said to me."

He stares at me blankly, rattles his drink and takes another sip. For a moment, I'm convinced he hasn't heard me. Watching him shift his lips from side to side, I know that he is engaged in the practice he claims to offer surefire protection against hangover, holding alcohol in one's mouth for fifteen seconds before swallowing. "Nothing to sacrifice," he says.

"What?"

"You don't have anything, Larry-san. How you sacrifice?"

.   .   .

"Who is Alan Watts?" my mother says.

My father points his fork at the book he has brought to the table and taps it sharply with the prongs. It's a small thin book with a turquoise cover and several pages folded at the corners: *The Wisdom of Insecurity*. "Alan Watts," he says, "is the wisest man who ever lived."

"But who is he?"

"Well, I guess you'd call him a philosopher. A teacher of Zen."

Mother looks at him quizzically. After all, this is 1951, nearly two decades before Zen will become a buzzword of the "Human Potential" movement; before the publication of *Zen Buddhism and Psychoanalysis, Zen in the Art of Archery, Zen and the Art of Motorcycle Maintenance, The Zen of Running* and dozens of other such books; before the Beat Generation has made Zen its rallying cry; before there is such a thing as Zen perfume; and long before anyone other than those who practice with him is aware that Nyogen Senzaki, the only Zen master now in the United States, has begun to teach the meditation

practice around which, in Japan and China, for nearly fourteen
hundred years, the vision of Zen has been centered. "Zen?" she
says. "What's that?"

This is October in Memphis, the leaves turning but not
yet beginning to fall, the overlap of the football and basketball
seasons, which are the only chronology I know. I am fifteen, my
brother, David (a freshman at Columbia), nineteen, our parents both forty-one. For the last hour and a half, I have been
playing basketball on the court in our driveway, shooting
alone. This is what I do—alone or with friends who come over
to play two-on-two or three-on-three—with most of my afternoons. Now I have washed and changed my clothes, but my
mind remains in the driveway. As always after playing, I can
still feel the ball on my fingertips. I can also feel the agitation
and disappointment with which basketball almost always
leaves me. In one sense, I am never so happy as when I am playing, but for the most part the game leaves me depressed, as if I
have failed or undermined myself, sabotaged my chances to improve. I am not a bad ballplayer, but I brood on my mistakes,
curse myself on the court and, worst of all, have a habit, even in
the midst of the game, of heeding and pursuing almost every
thought that passes through my head.

To answer Mother, Dad leaves the room and returns a
moment later with another book by Watts. Opening to a pas-
sage he has marked, he reads:

> "Zen Buddhism . . . is not religion or philosophy; it is not
> a psychology or a type of science. It is an example of what
> is known in India and China as 'a way of liberation'
> . . . a way of liberation can have no positive definition. It

has to be suggested by saying what it is not, somewhat as
a sculptor reveals an image by the act of removing pieces
of stone from a block."

He looks at Mother to see if she is satisfied. Her smile is
almost imperceptible, but I know what she is thinking. As long
as we can remember, he's been subject to these infatuations.
He quit school when he was fifteen and did not read a book
until he was thirty-five, but ever since then he's been racing to
catch up. Nowadays, he reads every morning from six until he
goes to work at eight-thirty, and every evening after dinner
until he goes to bed. Not infrequently, a book becomes tran-
scendent for him, the answer to all his questions. And since he
is by nature a proselytizer, convinced beyond a doubt that what
is good for him is good for others, the book of the moment
quickly appears at our dining table. Riding the waves of his enthusiasms, we have been through *The Story of Philosophy* by
Will and Ariel Durant, *The Importance of Living* by Lin Yu-
tang, Hendrik van Loon's *Story of Mankind* and in recent
months, now that he's interested in psychoanalysis, books by
Freud, Karen Horney and Erich Fromm. His passion is books
that diagnose the human condition and suggest an all-embrac-
ing cure. Though chronically depressed himself, he is a man
who believes that human beings are not meant to be unhappy.
Anything broken can be fixed. If you're unhappy, you've made
a mistake. Pull yourself together. If you suggest that your problems are not so tractable as he imagines, he'll offer you one of
his favorite dismissals: "You're making a mountain out of a
molehill" or "Aw, Larry, that's a lot of who-shot-John!"

Despite his reading and his philosophical inclinations, he
has little interest in classical philosophy. The only philosopher

he has read is Spinoza, and that is because, like him, Spinoza was a disaffected Jew. What he likes about Spinoza is that he resigned from his local synagogue. My father was once observant, going to the synagogue every Saturday, and he had an older brother who went to Palestine to become a rabbi and was killed in Hebron, in the Arab riots of 1931, but these days he despises organized religion and cannot forgive himself for his participation in it. "Why do I go to *shul?* For the same reason anyone else does! Because I'm superstitious. Neurotic. Because I'm a coward. Afraid of public opinion." There are close to 8,000 Jews in Memphis at this time, but among his generation, he is one of the few who was actually born here. He is also one of the wealthiest. Together, these two facts make him a sort of aristocrat, a man, as he views it, with a position to uphold. Memphis Jews are a small town hiding in a big one, a cliquish, self-created ghetto without walls. If you go to the Orthodox synagogue, you look down on members of the Reform temple. If you were born in Memphis, you are ever-so-slightly condescending to those who were not. You do not, of course, associate with the Gentiles. Like any other white, you look down on blacks. Dad is disgusted with himself for being an upright and timid member of this community, but he is either powerless to change or less than wholehearted in his self-criticism. Though he first read Spinoza when he was forty, and had formed his antireligious sentiments at least five years earlier, he will continue going to the synagogue until he is fifty-one. That adds up to sixteen years of ambivalence. At thirty-eight he served a two-year term as president of the synagogue, and even as he scoffs at Jewish ritual, he will fast on Yom Kippur, avoid meat and shellfish in restaurants, and support my mother when she insists that my brother and I waste precious afternoons, and de-

velop a hatred for religion that surpasses even his, at a Hebrew
school where we are taught—by a teacher looming over us with
a stopwatch—to speed-read Hebrew but not to understand it.

He takes up *The Wisdom of Insecurity* again and reads
aloud in a solemn voice:

> *"I have always been fascinated by the law of reversed
> effort. Sometimes I call it the 'Backwards Law.' When
> you try to stay on the surface of the water, you sink; but
> when you try to sink you float. When you hold your
> breath you lose it—which immediately calls to mind an
> ancient and much neglected saying, 'Whosoever would
> save his soul shall lose it.' "*

The reading continues for several minutes, but I hear nothing
more. Indeed, the fact that I have heard this much is a kind of
miracle. I am none too alert at the best of times, but usually,
when Dad begins to read, I don't hear words but pounding, a
droning sound, like the hum you get with defective loudspeak-
ers. But this time is different. The odd, reverse reasoning of the
Backwards Law permeates my mind before I actually understand it. It is less a matter of thought than ventilation. Like a
window has opened and a breeze is circulating in my brain. In a
sudden, blinding flash, it seems to me, I have been offered my
diagnosis and my cure. How can I doubt that the Backwards
Law is the story of my life? Isn't it obvious? Why else do I miss
so many easy shots! I try too hard to make them!

Dad's eyes are riveted on me. "Well?" he says. "What's
your response to that?"

"To what?" I say.

"Shall I read it again?"

Without waiting for my reply, he points the book at me, crying, "For God's sake, Larry, wake up! What is Watts talking about? Effort! Compulsion! Tension! Anxiety! Doesn't it ring a bell for you? Don't you realize how anxious and confused you are? How much you need to be liked, please everybody, no, don't turn away, you know what I mean. All these hours you spend on the basketball court. Are you enjoying yourself? Having fun? Hell, no! Anyone can see that! You're tortured! Driven by insecurity! But why? I'll tell you why! You're trying to make yourself secure! And it's just that need that Watts is getting at. The need that defeats you right from the start! Don't you see? The need for security makes you insecure!"

. . .

Watts's ideas had begun their circuitous route to our dinner table twenty-five hundred years earlier with the spiritual realization of a prince named Siddhartha Gautama. There are those who say of course that an infinite number of Buddhas preceded him, but for better or worse the Buddhist narrative is usually thought to begin with this one man—no less flesh and blood than my parents and I and Alan Watts. Since most of what we know of Siddhartha, or Shakyamuni, as he is known, by Buddhists, after his enlightenment, derives from tales collected two hundred years after his death, it is not always easy to separate his myth from his history, but most accounts agree that he was the son of the great king Suddhodana, who ruled over the city of Kapilavastu in northern India. He was a contemporary of Socrates, Confucius and Lao Tzu. As a child, he seems to have been rather spoiled, more than a little decadent. At the insistence of his father, who had been warned by prophecy of his son's spiritual destiny, he lived a life of privilege and extreme insulation until he discovered, almost by accident, the realities of illness, old age and death. His response to this discovery was both defiant and unselfish. How was it possible, he asked, that human beings persisted in their pursuit of pleasure while the shadow of decay hung over their lives? How could they be so oblivious to the nightmare in which they lived? "You cling to sense-objects among the most frightful dangers, even while you cannot help seeing all creation on the way to death. By contrast, I become frightened and greatly alarmed when I reflect on the dangers of old age, death and disease. I find neither peace nor contentment, and enjoyment is quite out of the question, for the world looks to me as if ablaze with an all-consuming fire. If a man has once grasped that death is quite inevitable, and if nevertheless greed arises in his heart, then he must surely have an iron will not to weep in this great danger, but to enjoy it."

Clearly, Shakyamuni himself was lacking in such will. So excruciating was his pain that ordinary life became impossible for him. His father's castle seemed "a burning house," his relationships "like the baited hook which draws a fish toward death." Abandoning his wealth and his kingdom, his family, his new wife, and his recently born child, he set off on a pilgrimage at once Quixotic and obstinate in its pursuit of solution: nothing would satisfy him but "escape from the sad ocean of birth and death." For three years, he wandered among the gurus and seekers of his day, exploring yoga, silence, introspection, and the philosophical dialogues and religious practices of the ashrams. He learned a great deal but remained dissatisfied. Ideas did not persuade him, philosophy seemed nothing more than reiteration of the questions that plagued him, and the ritual and faith embraced by many of his companions struck him as deluded and theatrical. Finally, joined by five fellow seekers, he embarked on a sort of kamikaze asceticism, turning to fasting, abstinence and self-mortification in the hope that purification of the body would open his mind to spiritual insight. Typically, his zeal far exceeded that of his companions. For six years, he practiced austerities so extreme that they brought him to the brink of death. Finally, while bathing in the river one day, he fainted and nearly drowned. He was saved by a young woman named Sujata, who lifted his head and gave him water, stroked his brow and forced tiny morsels of rice down his throat. This simple act of compassion transformed him. All the wisdom he had gained on his pilgrimage, he said, was dwarfed by Sujata's kindness.

His disciples were dismayed. In their view, he was betraying the vows they had taken by acquiescing to the needs of his body. Indifferent to their anger, accusing them of trying, by means of their asceticism, to "tie the air into knots," Shakyamuni continued to reflect on what he had learned from Sujata. Early in his quest, he had understood the dangers of self-indulgence, the extent to which the need for comfort and sensual gratification obstructed the spiritual path. Now, edging toward the famous "Middle Way" which would become the cornerstone of his theology, he saw that self-punishment, which then as now was more or less the rule among those devoted to spiritual practice, was no less dangerous than its opposite. It was obvious to him that the body and mind could not be separated. To punish one was to punish the other. How could one hope to defeat ignorance by strategies which were based in ignorance themselves?

Taking leave of his disciples, he wandered alone for many days until, despairing and exhausted, he sat beneath a Mucalinda tree in the manner he had first discovered seven years before—erect, alert, stationary, attending to thought but not pursuing it. "So long as I have not done what I set out to do," he vowed, "I shall not change my position." Neither eating nor drinking, he remained thus for forty-nine days. You don't have to be a Buddhist or a practitioner of meditation to know what torment and temptation he must have suffered during this time, but defiant as he'd always been, he refused to be intimidated. Gradually, he came to understand that his quest, until now, had been misguided, an effort to escape the world of suffering, subdue the anger, greed and ignorance that poisoned his mind—in other words, an attempt to deny the reality to which all human beings are born. What he saw now was that such escape was impossible; the only hope was to accept things as they are. If reality was groundless and impermanent, one must not deny it with illusions of continuity. The state of mind that followed this realization was unlike any he had known before. When the morning star appeared on the forty-ninth day, he knew that he had found at last what he had sought since leaving his father's palace. His great realization, variously interpreted throughout the centuries by different Buddhist sects, is distilled by Zen masters into two related statements.

1. All beings, as they are, have the Buddha-nature.

2. Above the heavens and below the earth, I alone am.

The religion known as Buddhism, followed today by more than 500 million people, began with these realizations—the perception, first, that enlightenment is not a singular, ecstatic experience but an unavoidable fact of human existence, and second, that it consists at its root in a dissolution of personal boundaries. In other words, the discrete, particularized self in which suffering congeals—the realm of thought and memory, the physical body, the whole spectrum of psychological conditioning—is a dream that dissolves in the light of wakefulness. In effect, the basic equation of Buddhism is tautological—self equals ignorance; ignorance equals suffering; suffering equals self. The great realization, no less available to all human beings than it was to Shakyamuni, is nothing more than dissolution of what has never actually existed.

.   .   .

My father is short, just a shade over five-six, but he seems large and expansive, as if the space he occupies is insufficient, squeezing him like a pair of tight shoes. When he walks through the house, he lands so hard on his heels that a thunderous sound echoes through the rooms. On the street, he walks ahead of me and, when I race to catch up, increases his speed so that I always remain a step behind. During dinner he taps his foot beneath the table and drums his fingertips on its surface. In restaurants, he often gets up to pay the check while the rest of us are having dessert. He has broad, sloping shoulders, thick ears and a large, hooked nose that for some reason looks remarkably handsome on his face. It is as if he's earned his nose, won it in contest, wears it like a cowboy wears his hat. Years later, when he is in his seventies, I will realize that his blue eyes are childlike and frightened, slightly bewildered, but at this point in his life, avoiding his eyes whenever I can, I don't even know that they are blue. He never says "thank you" or "please." When he shakes your hand, he squeezes it hard and, in a display that I know for a fact he considers friendly, jerks you toward him, pulling you off balance and slapping you on the shoulder. Sometimes, when feeling affectionate toward me, he squeezes my wrist with two fingers in a sort of vise-grip until I drop to my knees in pain. When he writes, his mouth contorts as if in agony, and he presses so hard on his pencil or pen that he makes holes in the paper and his letters take on the appearance of Braille. At night, after dinner, he goes to his easy chair and usually, reading or listening to music, remains there until it is time for bed. We are not permitted to speak to him. Hardly moving, he sits with his brow furrowed, his free hand stretched across his forehead so that his thumb and middle finger grip his temples, breathing through his mouth with a convulsive sound that borders on a gasp. He wears the same clothes he wore to work. I don't recall him changing his shoes or even loosening his tie.

Though he runs a large business, he is helpless around the house. It is as if he and my mother have a contract that prohibits his participation in housecleaning, cooking or other domestic chores. Racing behind him, she picks up his clothes, closes the refrigerator door he's left ajar, turns off the water he's left running in the bathroom, sponges the milk or coffee he's spilled on the dining table. I have never seen him mow the lawn, sweep the floor or change a light bulb. Not long ago, when mother was ill with laryngitis, running a fever of 102 degrees, she whispered to him while he lay reading beside her in bed, "You know what would taste good now? Some hot chocolate!" "That's a great idea," he said. "Make some for me too."

To my knowledge, the only times his mood climbs higher than mild depression is when he wins at cards or golf or lectures us at the dining table. He has golf partners, gin rummy partners and of course business associates, but no personal friends. Conversation rarely engages him until it becomes an argument. He almost always disagrees with my brother and me, even if we are repeating something he has said himself. "That doesn't hold water," he replies or, more often, "You're exaggerating." Perhaps it is because he has so few preferences himself that he is irritated by displays of preference in us. He doesn't like to admit, when talking with us, that one thing is better than another. When I buy oranges and squeeze juice for breakfast, he can be counted on to say it tastes the same as frozen. All breakfast cereals taste the same, there is no difference between butter and margarine, and, even if we are talking about a Chevy and a Cadillac, one car is as good as another. My brother once asked him why he wasn't using a beautiful ceramic cup my mother had given him for his birthday. "What's the difference?" he said. "A cup's a cup."

In argument, he takes on the Great Subjects without a trace of reticence. Basic Anxiety. Religion Throughout the Ages. The Limitations of Language. The Fundamental Problem of Human Existence. He is drawn to vertiginous levels of self-reflection, thoughts about thinking, words about language and silence, ideas about the dangers of abstraction. "What do we hope to gain," he'll ask in the middle of an argument that he himself has started, "by answering these questions?" Sometimes it seems that no subject interests him except those that are beyond him. When he senses that a subject is over his head, he raises his voice, becoming more adamant and insistent and even less inclined to listen, but even if he loses his train of thought, he will never back down or admit that he is wrong.

When he quit high school, he went to work for his father in the family business, a small wholesale operation located in a poor section of Memphis. He was sixteen years old, and it was 1924. For the next two years, he sold piece goods on the road in Mississippi, Arkansas and Tennessee. Then he married my mother, settled down in Memphis and convinced his father to open a retail store. It was called—not, as some suspected, to indicate the color of its customers, but because its façade was actually this color—the "Black and White Store." Within a year another store was opened, and by 1940 there were eleven. By 1951, when he brought *The Wisdom of Insecurity* to the dinner table, there were thirty-seven Black and White Stores— three in Memphis, and the others in such towns as Dyersburg, Tennessee; Jonesboro, Arkansas; and Kosciusko, Mississippi. They were cut-rate stores with fluorescent lighting, Formica display tables and separate drinking fountains and restrooms marked WHITE and COLORED, and they sold work clothes and cotton dresses and cheap cosmetics and shoes and boots and notions. Since the clientele at all the stores was 70 to 80 percent black, the name Black and White Store became a liability when the *Brown* decision was handed down by the Supreme Court. Mounting an advertising campaign, they changed the name to Shainberg's when I was in high school, blanketing radio and TV with a jingle—"We're changing our name to Shainberg's!"—which for me became a constant and excruciating announcement of the wealth I had tried to hide from my friends. "Aw, come on," said Dad, when I mentioned my discomfort to him. "You're exaggerating!" But he was no less anxious to hide his wealth than I was. "Not exactly," he always said, when I asked if we were rich. " 'Well off' is how I'd put it."

But the stores are visible and their ownership no secret. Wherever we go in Memphis, we are treated with that odd combination of resentment and respect that creates a kind of impermeable membrane between the rich and everyone else. However crowded the pediatrician's waiting room, we are ushered in at once. We get special treatment from dry cleaners, plumbers, electricians, auto mechanics, even schoolteachers, and at home we are waited on by a cook, a maid and a "yard man." My brother and I have grown up embarrassed, but not unequivocally. Like our parents, we expect special treatment but crave anonymity, all the deference accorded to wealth without the consequences. In a world where whites are elevated above blacks and middle-class whites above rednecks and Jews above non-Jews and rich Jews above poor Jews, how can we escape illusions of superiority or the arrogance it engenders?

Dad is said to be a "genius" at what he does, but "What's the point in it?" he says. "It's shallow, boring work, an exercise in greed requiring no intelligence at all." Though he cannot be entirely free of desire to keep the business in the family, he makes it clear to my brother and me that he does not want us following in his footsteps. He will do everything in his power to see that we do not stay in Memphis or become businessmen. "Why make the mistake I made? Find something you love. Something that challenges you." What makes his advice all the more impressive is that he burns with envy at any sign that we have taken it to heart. He wants us to have everything he has denied himself but it so happens that among the things that he has denied himself are pride and vicarious pleasure related to his children. Indications that we are happy, it seems to me, only remind him that he isn't. Isn't it inevitable that a man addicted to disappointment will have mixed feelings when his children show signs of turning against such addiction in themselves?

Honest to a fault, he is anything but unaware of his pas-

sion for self-denigration. "I'm the sort of person who always
wants to be somewhere else. Anyplace but where I am. All my
life I've been frustrated. Restless, anxious, out of touch with my
surroundings. Sometimes, I don't even know where I am." Frequent though they are, however, such observations seem to
have no effect on him. The fact that he is always dissatisfied is
just another thing that he is dissatisfied with. His mind is bipo-
lar, a perfect symmetry of desire and disappointment, idealism
and cynicism, and in his view, no different from anyone else's.
"Human beings live in a state of constant desire. All they want
is escape. But what is it they want to escape from? I'll tell you
what—desire itself! I don't care what name you give it, the object of desire is always the same. Call it 'happiness,' call it 'enlightenment,' call it 'God'—all we really want is the freedom to
accept ourselves the way we are."

·   ·   ·

The coffee shop where Roshi and I are having breakfast is only
two blocks from our zendo. It's called Elephant and Castle but
he calls it "Elephant." When he wants to go out for breakfast
after morning sitting, he sidles up to me soon after we stand up
from our cushions. "Go Elephant?" Chronically blocked on
names, he often shortens them like this or, in the case of students, replaces them with labels. One fellow is "Washington"
because that is where he lives; another, who meditates on two
thick cushions, straddling them like a horse, is known by no
other name than "Horse Riding."

When the waitress comes, he asks me to order for him.
His appetite is robust, especially in restaurants, but he often
defers to me like this. Is it because he has trouble reading the
menu or because the Buddhist prejudice against discrimination

("One instant of discrimination," says the Sutra, "and heaven and earth are set apart forever") is more than a concept for him? Is taste simply a function of ego, another thing that must be sacrificed?

He asks the waitress for a coffee refill. Before we leave the restaurant, he will drain four cups, each with two heaping teaspoons of sugar and plenty of milk. On his return to the zendo, he will make himself a cup of green tea, which packs such a wallop that in Japan they give it to racehorses before sending them out to the starting gate. Despite the fact that it makes him manic and giggly as a child, he claims that caffeine, like alcohol and cigarettes, has no effect on him.

It wasn't he who suggested breakfast this morning. I have asked to meet with him because I am having problems and want his advice. Now I can't remember any problems and there is nothing I want to ask him. As often in his presence, I am feeling lucid and carefree, slightly reckless, high as if on amphetamine. Either that or my brain is dysfunctional. My memory isn't working and, like his, my mind has gone maniacally concrete. When we first sat down, I mentioned that for dinner last night I prepared the miso soup he taught me to make, and he's been talking miso ever since—where to buy it, how it is manufactured, why Japanese miso is better than American or Korean miso, miso's medicinal properties, a technique by which miso, placed in a circle around a woman's navel, can improve her chances of becoming "president," and, of course, how to handle miso in half-a-dozen recipes he's dictated, while I write them down on my napkin. My voice is too loud and pitched about an octave higher than usual, and I am no less giggly than he is, and my language has more and more come to resemble his. "I go sleep last night eleven o'clock, Roshi, but I no sleep well." Is this liberation or regression? If you were watching us from an adjoining table, you'd think both of us were looped or stoned, but what's our drug? Zen? The endless expanse and compassion of the Buddhist vision? Or simply the energy released when past and future are jettisoned and one lives, as Roshi always seems to do, entirely in the present?

But when I am with him, all my moods are volatile. A single wave of passing thought can take me from joy to sorrow, love to anger, clarity to confusion. Now I am suddenly claustrophobic. His incessant talk and compulsive laughter are grating on my nerves. There is too much energy at this table. We have exceeded not only my tolerance for discontinuity but my capacity to treat it as a teaching. A few minutes ago his face was an inspiring mix of ferocity and compassion, but now his honey-colored skin looks jaundiced, his narrow eyes cold and manipulative. Why must everything he says be punctuated with a giggle? Not for the first time, this habit strikes me as weak and a bit hysterical, a leak of energy through a hole in his self-containment, absolutely antithetical to everything I believe a Zen master should be. The happiness I feel (yes, even now) seems dangerous, unhealthy, like the pleasure one takes, while calling the habit suicidal, from alcohol or cocaine.

But a few minutes later, as we leave the restaurant, I remember what I wanted to speak to him about—a feeling of disorientation, bewilderment verging on panic, which has lately come upon me whenever I sit in meditation. Nothing makes sense anymore, I tell him, and Zen makes less sense than anything. "Yes! Yes!" he cries. "Very nice! You making progress, Larry-san!"

·   ·   ·

After Dad closes Watts's book, we eat for a few minutes in silence. Then Mother says, "I have such a headache." She taps her forehead. "It starts here, but it goes right to the back!"

She is a small, stout woman with short, dark hair and blue eyes that alternate between sadness and fear and a rare, bright, childlike innocence that never fails to make me wonder if the fear and sadness are my imagination. Even now, in her mid-forties, she is often described as "cute." She walks as if on short stilts or very sore feet, wobbling at the ankles. I cannot watch her cross a room without an urge to go to her assistance. A chronic tremor causes her hand to shake as it lifts the fork to her mouth. She is afraid of water, cats, dogs, and strenuous exercise, and she is accident- and illness-prone. In the past five years, she has had two major operations on her feet and one to remove her gallbladder, and in the next ten, she will have back surgery, cataract surgery on both eyes, and a number of major bouts with dentists, periodontists, podiatrists and dermatologists. A vinegar addict, she is mopping the salad bowl with a piece of white bread. She is the only person in the family who actually enjoys her food. She loves ice cream and Hydrox cookies and Raisinets at the movies, and she makes special trips to a diner on the other side of town because they make fried-egg sandwiches just the way she likes—two eggs, well done, lettuce and tomato and mayonnaise on seeded hamburger rolls.

Her days revolve around her aging, senile parents who seem to resent her more the more she does for them. In fact, they never stop accusing her of being indifferent to their needs, and for this reason, they are often, as tonight, the principal subject she brings to the dinner table.

"You know what Daddy says this morning? I don't care about anyone but myself. Can you imagine? I'm cooking their

meals, doing their laundry and schlepping them back and forth
to the doctor, all the time thinking of no one but myself. You
know what he said to Mother when I came in this morning?
'It's only Dorothy!' Only! Three times a day I'm there, waiting on them like a *shvartze,* but who gives a damn? It's only
Dorothy!"

"Well, maybe he's right," Dad says.

"Who?"

"Your father. Who do you think? Maybe you don't care
for him as much as you think you do."

Mother cocks her head and shakes it slightly, like a swim-
mer with water in her ear. "I beg your pardon?"

"I've said it before, honey, but I'll say it again. You're
blaming others for problems you create yourself. Night after
night you tell the same stories. Everyone takes advantage of
you! Isn't it time you asked yourself why you invite such mis-
treatment? I'll tell you why! Because you mistreat yourself! Because you have no self-respect! You think you're being
generous, but what you're really doing is bribing people to
love you. You need them to love you because you don't love
yourself."

Mother flinches as if he's struck her. "So then, if I understand you correctly, it was my fault all along. Is that right? Correct me if I'm wrong! I bring this on myself. It's my fault they
insult me. My fault you leave the refrigerator door open. My
fault Larry can't get up five minutes earlier and feed his own
dog before he goes to school. Did I get it right this time?" Crying now, she puts her fork down and covers her face with her
napkin. "I cook their meals and wash their clothes and clean
their house and do their shopping! What do they want from
me? What do you want from me?"

Dad sighs. "You're just proving my point. Only someone who hates herself would interpret what I said as criticism. Don't you see I'm trying to help you? No, of course not! Why should you? You don't want to be helped! All you want is to go on being the victim!"

Mother stands and throws her napkin to the floor. "I don't have to take this! If no one wants me here, I'll pack my bags and get out!" This is not an uncommon threat, but it seems more vehement than usual. She takes a step backward, then sinks to the floor. Crouching beside her, Dad dips his napkin into a water glass and mops her face with it, but she doesn't move for nearly a minute. Opening her eyes at last, she says, "Huh? Where am I?" And then: "Get away! Leave me alone! I've tried my best! I've tried to do what's right! Why am I being tortured?"

Dad's voice is high-pitched, almost a whine. "Not just your best! More than your best! Not just with Mom and Dad but us too. Where would we be without you? Lost! Lost!"

As often during these fights, my mind is somewhere else. They might as well be neighbors fighting on the other side of the wall. While he helps her to the bedroom, I am thinking about the Backwards Law, trying in vain to recover the happiness I felt, the space and ventilation that Alan Watts engendered in my brain.

Returning to the table, Dad shakes his head in disgust when he sees I haven't moved. "So your mother's lying on the floor and you don't move. In my whole life, I've never known anyone so egocentric." He pours himself a coffee, lights a cigarette and blows smoke toward the center of the table. "Selfishness!" he cries. "The worst of all diseases! And what is it? Nothing but self-hatred! Instead of turning it on yourself, you

turn it on others! If you don't care about yourself, how can you
care about others? Think about it, Larry! Think about self-
hate! Think about your mother faints and you don't even try to
help her. Think about how empty your life will be if you don't
get ahold of this problem now!"

                              .   .   .

It was two years before he brought Watts to our dinner table
that my father entered psychoanalysis. In the months after his
forty-second birthday, he had become so depressed that, as he
told me later, he seriously considered suicide. What got him
out of it was a book he discovered on a business trip to New
York. It was a collection of essays by Karen Horney and analysts associated with her: *Are You Considering Psychoanalysis?*
The one that impressed him most was by Horney's principal
colleague, a man named Harold Kelman. Immediately after
reading it, Dad looked up Kelman in the New York telephone
directory, and on hearing my father's voice, Kelman acted as if
he had expected the call. On the following day, Dad became
Kelman's patient and, arranging his business trips to New York
so that he could have a week to ten days of double sessions
every couple of months, he will remain, as they say, "in therapy" for the next twenty-five years.

      Never one to doubt that what is good for him is good for
us, Dad takes it for granted that my mother, my brother and I
will commence our own therapies as soon as possible. Mother
has already begun with one of Kelman's colleagues, but for
David and me, only Kelman himself will do. In fact, Kelman is
the primary reason David is now attending Columbia College,
and he will be the reason I enroll at Columbia three years
hence.

It is Kelman who introduced my father to the books of Alan Watts. Several years ago (along with Erich Fromm, Karen Horney and a number of other New York psychoanalysts) he audited the course on Zen that D. T. Suzuki was giving at Columbia. Suzuki is something of a culture hero these days. He is almost single-handedly responsible for the growing popularity of Zen in America. A great scholar with excellent command of English, he had Zen monastic training. Now, in his classes and books, he is offering Western intellectuals an authentic but extremely limited version of the practice. Zazen is rarely mentioned in his books, the word "meditation" only in reference to rooms designed for this purpose in Japanese houses. Later, it will be postulated that Suzuki's reticence to speak of zazen derives from the fact that he believes it antithetical to Western culture. Instead, he presents Zen ideas and stories, exploring their connections, on the one hand, with art, the tea ceremony, flower arrangement and other aspects of Japanese culture, and on the other, with Western psychology and philosophy. He is open and eclectic, an avid student of American art and culture, drawn especially to psychoanalysis. Stressing affinities and downplaying differences between it and Zen—the fact, for example, that Zen is suspicious of ego while psychoanalysis aims to strengthen it—he will unwittingly reinforce the inclination among analysts like Kelman to think of themselves as gurus rather than physicians. Later on, when Zen masters arrive in the United States, a similar misunderstanding will lead students to expect psychological guidance from them, and only the most mature teachers will be able to resist the temptation to offer it.

Kelman tells Dad that Zen and psychoanalysis are "mirror images of each other." In fact, he says, psychoanalysis can be seen as a Western version of Zen. A true psychoanalyst has

to be a sort of Zen master, and his patients have to understand
that they are involved not just in a medical treatment but in a
kind of meditation which, like all spiritual practice, continues
throughout one's life. This is only one of the reasons why Kelman does not believe in short-term therapy. Despite his hefty
fees, many of his patients have been seeing him for decades.
Self-examination, he says, is an endless process. The belief that
it has a time limit or a goal is itself a symptom of neurosis.
"What you're doing here," he tells Dad, "is discovering yourself. How can you ever get to the end of that?"

.   .   .

After his tirade against my egocentricity, Dad retires to the
study, or what we call the "Sun Room," and puts Beethoven's
Violin Concerto on the phonograph. Fortunately, he has left
The Wisdom of Insecurity on the dinner table. I take it to my
room and climb into bed with it. It seems to me that if Watts
were a basketball coach his book could not be more explicit in
its relevance to my game. Everywhere I read in it I see my shortcomings as a player—too much thought, too much self-consciousness, too much fear of making mistakes—but far from
making me despair, each discovery generates hope and excitement. It's as if Zen is a kind of medical treatment in which diagnosis equals cure, its logic a sort of reversed telescope through
which my problems look small and insignificant. When I wake
up the next morning, I feel as if reborn, a resolution and a confidence I've never known before. Naturally, I cannot wait to get
on the court again.

     After school, a group of us meet, as we always do, in the
school gymnasium. It is a friendly but competitive game, very
intense because formal practice will begin in a couple of weeks,

tryouts for the varsity. My confidence lasts maybe five minutes into the game. Watts is in my head like static on a radio. I can't stop reminding myself of qualities he stresses—"flexibility," for example, or "letting go"—and every time I do so I get the feeling I've taken myself out of the game. I feel slow and clumsy, no touch, the ball heavy in my hands. Naturally my shot is off, my defense and passing as well. It's been a long time since I've played so badly or felt so uncomfortable on the court. By the time the game is over, I feel as if Watts has put a curse on me. The things that he reminds me of are precisely those I need to forget.

.   .   .

Soon after Kyudo Roshi and I go up to Yankee Stadium, I have what I take to be an enlightenment experience. His remarks about sacrifice have been almost constantly in my mind, but suddenly, while sitting in meditation, it seems to me that I am living them out instead of merely understanding them. My mind is unmarked space. Memories, fears, expectations—everything falls away. There is no self. I've sacrificed everything. For the next half-hour I live in a blissful state of immediacy, each instant a self-contained unit, untainted by past or future. So great is my exhilaration that when I stand up from my cushion I phone Roshi at once. I have never done this sort of thing before, but then again, I have never *felt* this sort of thing before. Isn't it his job to confirm, as masters have since Zen began, the enlightenment of his student? He listens patiently while I describe my experience, and then, as I ought to have known he would, takes it all away from me. "Larry-san, listen to me, OK? In the word 'Buddha,' even the letter *B* is nothing but dust."

Dust is his word for all that's ephemeral, all that, if one becomes attached to it, gets one into trouble. In other words, all that, at Yankee Stadium, he admonished me to sacrifice, everything the Buddha relinquished when he sat beneath the Mucalinda tree. The logic is always the same: the source of fear is attachment to the impermanent. Conversely, if you befriend impermanence instead of denying it, you won't be afraid of anything. What complicates the issue is that ideas like this are dust as well. Since Buddhists become attached to Buddhist theory more than anything else, there is no greater source of dust, as he's just pointed out to me, than Buddhism itself. Once I asked him if monks "improved" as a result of their training, which is to say the training he had himself received, and he said: "No. Usually become more worse. Develop fixed ideas. Develop pride." It isn't Zen practice or meditation he questions. It is Zen concepts, Zen excitement. Zen ego. He views the mind in general as a dust factory and meditation as a means of wiping dust away. He likens our formal meditation— zazen—to taking a shower, advises us to think of our breath as a windshield wiper which, sweeping back and forth with inhalations and exhalations, cleans dust from the mind as wipers clean a windshield.

Between internal and external dust he makes no distinction whatever. To wash this dish perfectly or clean this mirror till it shines or handle a vacuum cleaner with authority is no different from sitting with one-pointed concentration—washing away your mental dust with the vacuum cleaner of awareness—on your cushion. Ask him about his plans for the weekend, and without a trace of irony, he'll answer, "Clean zendo," or "I washing my undershirts." Such chores, far from being onerous, are in his view therapeutic, purifying. A student who complains of depression is advised to clean his toilet, a woman contemplating suicide to wash her car. He cleans the zendo three or four times a week and resists all offers of help. It is not just that he believes we don't know how to clean properly but that, as he admits, he is selfish and doesn't want to share his pleasure. There is no cleaning chore—dish-washing, window-cleaning, snow-shoveling, etc.—about which he is unknowledgeable or unenthusiastic. He mops with his hands, at high speed, bending from the waist and sweeping a rag across the floor, cleans the brush attachment of the vacuum cleaner with a pair of tweezers. If he catches you vacuuming perpendicular to the seams of the floor so that you are not picking up the dust that collects between the boards, he concludes that you are a child and, even though he knows he is supposed to teach rather than penalize, will do his best to see that you are not assigned this job again.

An immaculate shoe rack, cleaned every day, stands just inside the door of the loft that contains our zendo. A rag, freshly dampened twice a day, is placed at the door of the zendo itself so that we can clean our feet of this, if not the deeper, dust we bring from the outside world. You don't step inside the loft and then remove your shoes. You wipe them on the doormat—also cleaned every day, of course—and remove them before you enter. In the dressing room, you hang your clothes on one hanger, preferably the one from which you've just removed your robe. He does not like to be explicit about it, but he views the use of more than one hanger as taking up more space than you need. In other words, an egoism, an act of selfishness, inattention. The way in which you wear your robe is crucial. More than once, he has told us that he can look at a Zen student, especially a monk, and discern from his robe how long he's been practicing. All of this seems compulsive until it strikes you, as it does with greater and greater frequency the more you hang around him, that your wrinkled robe or your sloppy habits with the vacuum cleaner are symptoms of inattention and distraction, the mindless fog in which most of your life is spent. During retreats, when you go to the kitchen for food and bring it back to your cushion, you walk behind rather than in front of others because if you don't, "dust come out" in the direction of their food. The vacuum cleaner is stored with the hose folded on top just so on this particular shelf with the orange extension cord wound like a rope with its plugs connected to each other. For loan when the weather surprises us, six umbrellas on which he's painted SOHO ZENDO hang from the shoe rack. We have two floor brushes for the vacuum cleaner, one labeled ZENDO, which is not to be used anywhere else in the loft. In the bathroom, hand towels hang from labels he's cut in half so that they fit neatly around the hook. Replacement facial and toilet tissue are as carefully centered on the toilet tank as the Buddha, the water bowl and the incense burner are centered on the altar. On a recent Saturday, he tells me, he went out early in the morning and did not return until late at night. In his mail, he found a telephone bill. He climbed to the zendo on the fourth floor, removed his shoes, went to his desk, wrote out a check, placed it in an envelope, put on his shoes again, went downstairs and walked to the corner mailbox in order to send it on its way. It was mid-December, very cold, almost midnight, and he was fifty-five years old. "Why the hurry?" I asked. "Why not wait until you went out again?" "No!" he cried. "I want to clean it up!"

On the other hand, one of his favorite expressions is "Fish not grow in pure water." Though he is orthodox and reverent and attentive to the precepts, nothing arouses his revulsion like piety. "You in jungle, tiger attacking you, you raise your rifle and think, 'Oh, no, cannot shoot! I Buddhist!' Such a one not Buddhist! Such a one attachment to Buddhism! Not understand at all!" He proudly describes how he killed cockroaches while living in the monastery. "I help cockroach! Cockroach help me!" If Buddhist excitement is dust, Buddhist orthodoxy is mud. Any suggestion that he is "religious" strikes him as insulting. Most spiritual seekers are "like drunk." Though his reverence is obvious when he speaks of the Buddha, he never tires of reminding us that, just before his death, after teaching for sixty years, Shakyamuni said, "I have taught nothing at all!"

. . .

After his realization, the Buddha remains in meditation for a period of seven weeks. Rising at last, he heads for Isipatana (modern Samath, near Benares), 250 kilometers to the north, in search of his former companions in asceticism. Crucial though his realization is, this walk will be equally important in Buddhist history because it is now that he processes and assimilates what he has learned, and prepares himself to teach. First, of course, he must deal with the paradox inherent in this impulse. On the one hand, he knows that his enlightenment is meaningless unless it is shared, but on the other, he is well aware that what he has to share is nothing more than the birthright of all human beings. How does one teach what is already known? By his own definition, there is no one alive who does not have the Buddha-nature. It is like bringing water to the river. Still, water does not appease one's thirst until one drinks it. Though all possess what he possesses, most remain no less oblivious to it than he himself a few days before. Insulated by ignorance and egoism from their true nature, identified with the limited, impermanent self of body and mind, they live in constant fear of suffering and death. River or not, they are dying of thirst. What choice has he but to share his water with them?

His former companions have gathered at the Deer Park in Isipatana. Despite the fact that they remain angry at him for his rejection of the ascetic path, his radiance and conviction are such that they cannot help but listen to him. He tells them that he has found—by direct experience, not by thought—the truth that they were seeking, the holiest of laws. It begins with the understanding that there are two extremes that all true seekers must avoid. "One is to plunge oneself into sensual pleasures, and the other is to practice austerities which deprive the body of its needs. Both of these extremes lead to failure. The path I have discovered is the Middle Way, which avoids both extremes and has the capacity to lead one to understanding, liberation, and peace. . . . It is a path which does not avoid or deny suffering but allows for a direct confrontation with suffering as the means to overcome it."

Thus, his teachings begin with what may be the most difficult of all the paradoxes he will offer: a task that involves, in the dissolution of self and ego, the most threatening of all prospects, can only be achieved through moderation. Both effort and its absence, the two great poles of ego desire, are challenged. Problems recognized by the ego can only be solved by its dissolution. What makes his message really threatening, however, is not its content but its explicitness. After all, as he so often acknowledges, there is nothing he says that they do not know already. Who among them is unaware that, as far as spiritual undertakings are concerned, self-indulgence is a cul-de-sac, and all but the most subtle effort is sure to be self-defeating? But why, if they know this, have they continued to deny it? What the Buddha's Middle Way attacks is the need within the rational mind to make the obvious inaccessible and mysterious. Mystery fuels desire, and desire fuels ego. It is not insignificant that these ardent seekers need to believe that the truth is outside of and beyond them, a goal accessible only by means of effort and self-denial. The basic equation of desire requires that it be directed toward what is not, and it is precisely this equation that the Buddha challenges. Mild though it seems, his first teaching is fierce and uncompromising. The target toward which he directs their consciousness is the one which, above all others, consciousness abhors.

· · ·

"Why are you crying?" says Dad, joining me at the breakfast table. Since he was in the grandstand last night, I can't believe he has to ask. In a crucial game, I committed several blunders that led directly to our defeat and, in all probability, loss of the state championship. More than an isolated failure, it is a bottom-line catastrophe, the end, I am convinced, of my basketball career.

I mean to remain detached, offer the coolest summary of my feelings, but soon I am sobbing like a baby.

"Hey!" he says. "It's only a game. You're being too hard on yourself." He dips a spoon into a jar of instant coffee, drops it into his cup, and pours hot water over it. "You did your best! What more can you ask?"

I try to describe what I felt on the court, the helplessness, the hysteria, the sense that my head was about to explode when the pressure of the game and the sound of the crowd converged. "My thoughts were racing. My legs felt heavy and I couldn't catch my breath. Even before I went on the court, I knew I couldn't do anything right."

This is no easier for him than for me. Both of us would choose almost anything in the world over intimate conversation with each other. He shifts in his chair, lights a cigarette, picks up his coffee cup and puts it down without drinking. "The book you should read," he says, "is *Zen in the Art of Archery*. Wait, I'll read you something now." He goes to his study and returns a moment later with the famous book by Eugen Herrigel that has only recently been published. "You remember this book, don't you? It's the one I was reading the other night at dinner. Don't think it's just about archery. Herrigel's coach was a Zen master! He makes him perfect his skills, but he never lets him forget that it is not just skill he's after. 'The goal,' he tells him, 'is not the target . . . it's yourself!' "

He reads a few paragraphs, then fixes his eyes on me. "Isn't that beautiful? I've read this twice before, but it's like I just got it! Believe me, Larry, if you saw basketball from this point of view, you wouldn't be crying now. You and me both— we're too involved in success. We lose sight of what's important! What really matters! We try to hit the target rather than ourselves! When you missed that shot last night, that easy one you took in the third quarter, the sort of shot you make ninety-nine out of a hundred times in the driveway, why did you miss it? I'll tell you why! Because you put too much pressure on yourself. Like you'll kill yourself if you miss. The sun won't come up tomorrow morning. But back up. Why the pressure? Doesn't pressure come from fixing on the goal? Aiming at the basket rather than yourself? You know what Herrigel's master tells him? 'It isn't me who shoots the arrows. The arrows shoot themselves!' Ask yourself, who took that shot last night? Did the ball shoot itself? Hell, no. The ball knows where the basket is!"

. . .

Confused about a decision I must make, I go to Roshi for advice. My girlfriend and I are having problems, and I know it's because we've both got one foot out the door: should we break it off or take the leap into commitment? Never mind that this is a man who went to all-male schools before he entered the monastery, who's never had the sort of relationship I'm talking about and, by his own testimony, never had sex in his life. On the day he graduated high school, sitting around with a group of classmates, he suddenly announced, "I never marry!" When I ask him why he made this decision, he says, "I don't know. Just come out!" But a moment later he makes a stab at it. "You know, Larry-san, marriage very beautiful. Two people live together, do each other laundry, cook each other. Slowly two people become one. But me—I one already!" It is seventeen years since he left the monastery, and he still finds it difficult to look at a woman. Only recently, he tells me, has he overcome the impulse to turn his head away when he sees a man and woman kissing on television. Now fifty-six, he likes to brag about his diminishing potency. "Until I fifty, my sausage much stand up! Now, almost never! Very good for practice! All my energy for zazen!"

We're having tea at the zendo before evening zazen begins. While he stands at the sink preparing the Japanese brew he serves (along with a bowl of Pepperidge Farm cookies), the telephone rings, and we hear a voice on the answering machine. It's a prospective student, seeking our zendo schedule, leaving his name and address so that we can send him information. "Larry-san," Roshi begins, pointing to the notepad next to the phone, "please you take down name." But then he pauses for a moment, listening hard to the man who's speaking. "No, don't bother—insincere voice."

Not too long ago, another man found our number in the phone book, and this time Roshi answered.

"Are you a Zen master?"

"Yes, I am."

"I need to talk to you. I want to commit suicide."

"Good idea!" Roshi said. "Right away! Don't hesitate!"

In contrast to our usual, informal meetings, when we discuss business matters (taxes, membership dues, etc.) relevant to my role of vice president or make small talk, Roshi has donned his robes and assumed a serious demeanor, as if to remind us both that my request for advice this afternoon requires him to be my teacher rather than my friend. We sit at the table in his kitchen which serves as his living and dining room. The only social area in this loft, it is adjacent to his tiny, windowless bedroom, the interior of which is hidden behind a sliding glass door and a set of venetian blinds. The zendo is down the hall, a large, sunlit room with an immaculate altar, tropical plants, scrolls on the walls and of course the cushions on which we sit in meditation. Looming above us, covered with a yellow brocade altar cloth embroidered with Japanese calligraphy, is his favorite possession, the television set and VCR the membership gave him for his birthday last year. His favorite show is professional wrestling—especially when Hulk Hogan fights—but he also fancies reruns of "Kojak" and "Dallas" and beauty contests like those to select Miss Universe and Miss America.

When I've finished describing my quandary, he remains

silent for several minutes. Erect in his chair, eyes half closed, it's as if he's doing zazen in order to give me full attention. Finally, he says, "Larry-san, must make great decision." He makes a fist and extends it slowly, like a piston, into the air between us. "Even if terrorist gun to your head, you not change your mind!"

"Well, sure, Roshi, I know that. But it's not so easy. Something tells me we won't be able to make it, but I can't bear the thought of hurting her."

"Always, you too kind! Want to please everybody! Irresponsible, Larry-san! In the end, cause more pain."

"But isn't Dharma about compassion? Aren't we supposed to think of others before we think of ourselves?"

"The Dharma," he says, "is only going in one direction. You make great decision, you make great Dharma. You wandering, you wasting your life. Forty-seven years old, Larry-san! You wandering now, you wandering under cemetery."

This is not, of course, the first time I've heard such advice from him. Such is his belief in willpower and self-motivation that no aspect of behavior seems beyond their influence. Even one's own neurochemistry can be mastered with the proper mix of faith and courage. Depressed? "I give you advice," he said to one woman, "must cheerful!" And to another, despondent about the failure of her marriage, "You make decision, Sarah-san: forget it!"

What else should one expect from a man who believes that any problem can be dissolved by keeping one's back straight and watching the mind in which confusion percolates? He likes to quote the Buddha's famous parable about the wounded warrior on the battlefield. Though dying from an arrow in his back, he resists when someone offers to remove it, insisting that he must first know who shot it, what direction it came from, what mistake he made that caused him to be hit, etc. The belief that growth proceeds from understanding and description, unraveling the chain of cause and effect, is a recipe for paralysis. The first arrow is the analytic mind. How can you hope to heal your wound with more analysis?

There are days when I am amenable to this point of view, but today, as it happens, is not one of them. I feel as if he's dismissing my pain, offering bromides. What's the good of advising a man who can't sleep and has no appetite and, most important, is suffering from a paralyzing case of indecision, to "make a great decision"? It's as if I've got a broken leg and he's telling me to run the marathon.

"Listen, Roshi, I've come to you with a problem. I don't know what to do, OK? In America we call this 'indecision.' Are you familiar with the word?"

" 'Indecision?' " He pronounces it "indeeseeshun" with accent on the last syllable. "Yes, I understood, Larry-san. Cannot decide. Wandering mind. Indeeseeshun. Very good word!"

"And yet you're telling me that the cure for it is to make a decision?"

"Yes, yes. Great decision! Never shaking! Never turn back!"

"But Roshi . . . I've just been telling you. A decision is just what I can't make. Have you never had that problem?"

He puts out his cigarette and reaches for another. Again and again, like other students here, I've complained about his smoking, arguing that he owes it to us, if not himself, to care for his body so that he can remain healthy and be our teacher as long as possible. "Why I want that?" he says. "I live too long, everybody die, then I lonely!"

"Of course I have that problem," he says. "Twice."

"Twice!"

"Yes, after high school, when I cannot decide what to do. And again before I go to monastery."

"Before the monastery! That was thirty years ago! C'mon, Roshi, admit it. You don't know anything about indecision! I'm a fool to ask you for advice. It's like I'm crawling up a mountain and you fly past me in a helicopter."

"Hellicopper?" He squints at me, puzzled. "What you mean 'hellicopper?' "

Thinking he's trying to evade the issue, I snap, "It's a kind of airplane."

He hands me a piece of paper. "You write for me, OK?"

I print out "helicopter" while he fetches his dictionary from the bedroom. Still annoyed, I watch his lips shape the word while he searches out the definition. At last, pronouncing the Japanese word, he cries: "Yes! Yes! Hellicopper! I hellicopper! You crawling on mounting! I flying! You crawling! Ha! Ha! Ha!" He takes a long drag on his cigarette, stubs it out in the ashtray, then suddenly turns serious again. "Listen, Larry-san. I fly over you, I see what you not see."

"What's that?"

He presses his thumb against his forefinger and holds them poised together above his teacup. "You and mounting-top—only this far apart."

.   .   .

In late summer, between my junior and senior years of high school, Dad takes me to New York. He's in a fever these days,

having recently discovered the Indian philosopher J. Krishnamurti. He claims that Krishnamurti has broken through his
need for answers by making him "examine the mind that asks
the questions." When he looks at me, his eyes have the mad,
all-too-familiar gleam they get when he wants to make me over
entirely. What I want to do in New York is see the Yankees
play, but it turns out that won't be possible because almost all
our time is scheduled. Arriving late on Friday evening, we are
off the next morning to a seminar given by Alan Watts and a
woman named Charlotte Selver, who teaches something called
"sensory awareness." Of course, I have no idea what that is,
and neither, I think, does Dad, but on the plane he shows me a
brochure that speaks of "opening and balancing the body."
How on earth can I doubt, he says, that this will make me a
better basketball player?

There are four two-hour sessions, Saturday and Sunday,
morning and afternoon, and Watts gives a talk before each of
them. He is a slender, dark-haired man of medium height with
an asymmetrical face and a walleye that seems to fix on your left
ear when he addresses you directly. It is hard to know which of
his eyes to look at when you talk to him. A relaxed, polished
speaker, he presses for understanding even as he denigrates it.
"Let's understand at the outset that words can only point us
vaguely in the direction of Zen. Nothing contradicts Zen like
trying to articulate it." When an elderly woman confesses that
she hasn't understood a word he's said, he replies with a grin,
"Well, then I must be doing something right!"

Introducing Selver, he says that her work is "Zen in action—an exploration of the unity of body and mind." It is from
him I hear, for the first time, the Zen story about the hundred-
foot pole. "A Zen master will assign his monks the question

'What do you do if you find yourself on top of a hundred-foot pole?' You can't stay where you are and you can't move. All your options are unworkable. What do you do? It's a question you can't answer rationally, but Charlotte Selver can show you how to answer it because the only answer is to let go and that's what she is teaching." Explaining that Zen is about "this, just this, and nothing more," he pauses and grins mischievously. "Sounds simple, doesn't it? But that's just the trouble. Human beings can't tolerate simplicity. You can't know 'this' until you don't know anything else!"

Selver is a small woman with an angelic smile and elegant posture. When sitting, she keeps both feet firmly on the floor and does not use the back of her chair. She seems kind and intelligent, but something about her frightens me. Like Dad, she speaks a lot about "self-acceptance" while pointing out things in me that need to be improved. My body is "constricted," she says, "misaligned." Such imbalance affects the way I walk, breathe and think. Even so, the worst thing I can do is try to change it. Nothing's worse than being "goal-oriented." The most important thing to remember, she says, is that I'm fine the way I am.

We are about thirty people in a cavernous high-ceilinged room at a midtown Manhattan hotel. The majority are women in their fifties and sixties, but there are half-a-dozen middle-aged men and a couple of women in their late twenties or early thirties. By ten years at least, I am the youngest, and for this reason, both Watts and Selver pay me special attention. "Oh what I'd give," says Watts, "to have been introduced to this path when I was your age."

In the first session, Selver gives each of us a bowling pin. Sitting cross-legged on red plastic-covered exercise mats, we are directed to grip the pins with our eyes closed, "feel their weight," and explore the difference between holding them and allowing them to hang from our hands. The idea, Selver says, is to "get in touch with gravity." After this, we experiment with different ways of lying on the floor. Reminding us that dogs and cats can relax anywhere, she asks us why human beings should be any different. We try to feel the difference between "a rigid body with pockets of tension" and one that's "fluid" and "open." Isn't there a world of difference between "giving your body to the floor" and holding yourself apart from it? Exploring flexibility, we crawl through wooden arches and, lying on the floor, try to "get in touch with" the length and the width of our bodies. In the midst of this exercise, I suddenly feel as if I weigh a thousand pounds. It's as if at the same time I've grown denser and acquired a kind of volume that makes my body vast. When I describe this sensation, Selver says it's "just the sort of breakthrough we're after here—the body opening to its inner space." Sitting beside her at the front of the room, Watts says that in his view I've had "a direct experience of Zen mind, total awareness, breaking through the limited, relative sense of one's body, dissolving its ordinary boundaries."

After the last session, on Sunday afternoon, Dad and I and Watts go out for Chinese food. Dad has arranged for Watts to speak in Memphis—two lectures at a local college and several small discussion groups at our home, where Watts will stay. Watts seems pleased by Dad's invitation but also a bit uneasy. While they talk, he keeps glancing at me with a quizzical, almost boyish expression. I avoid his eyes. The weekend has weakened my resistance to him, but I've not forgotten what he did to my basketball game. How can I not be wary of him and his ideas?

Once the Memphis visit has been arranged, Dad turns the conversation, as he turns most every conversation these days, to his new passion, Krishnamurti, whom he calls "K." He was led to K by a reference in Watts, and since that time, some eight or nine months ago, he's read no one else. Indeed, with the exception of Kelman and Watts, no other authority has enjoyed such a long reign at our dinner table.

Though Watts himself is a great admirer of Krishnamurti, Dad insists on viewing them as adversaries. Citing Krishnamurti's negative views of organized religion, ritual, authority, teacher-student relationships, and any form of structured spiritual practice, he asserts that no one who really understands Krishnamurti can remain an adherent of Zen. "Desire is the problem," he says. "That's what K makes clear. If you go to Zen in search of liberation, it's just another desire. How can it help but make you worse?"

Watts laughs. He's on his second vodka, and ever since we sat down he's been staring at a beautiful Oriental woman at the next table who is, unbeknownst to her companion, staring back at him. "Well," he says, winking at me, "anything that makes us worse can't be all bad, right?" Before Dad can reply, he turns his attention to me. What did I think of the workshop? What courses am I taking in school? What do I plan to study in college? His interest is so sincere that my resistance falls away. When I tell him I have no plans yet for college, he congratulates me. Not-knowing is the best of all conditions! It keeps the mind open, protects you from your habits, your fear. Eyeing the woman as he speaks, raising his voice, it seems to me, so she'll be sure to hear, he tells the Zen story about a monk who answers "I don't know" in answer to his master's question. "Ah," says the master, "not-knowing is most intimate!" "Life," says Watts, "will never get the best of you if you can learn about that intimacy. Be patient with not-knowing, Larry! When the time comes, you'll know what you want to do. The important thing is to invent your own life. Don't let it invent you."

Since Dad has had a couple of drinks as well, the tension eases after a while, and conversation turns to lesser matters, like food and sports. When Watts discovers that I am a basketball player, he is interested and respectful. I find myself describing what happened after Dad introduced me to his book, confiding what I concluded at that time, that thoughts about Zen were the worst sort of thoughts a basketball player could have. Watts closes his eyes and listens intently while I speak. As it happens, he says, it is precisely this paradox, what he calls "Zen contradictions" that he's trying to get at in his new book. On the one hand, Zen gives you a vision of being natural and spontaneous, but if you remember the vision and try to act on it, it makes you tense and self-conscious the way it made me on the basketball court. "It's what psychoanalysts call a 'double bind,'" he says. "As soon as you try to let go, the desire itself makes letting go impossible."

Pausing for a sip of vodka, he quotes the master who said that clinging to yourself is like having a thorn in the skin and that Buddhism is a second thorn to get rid of the first. "When the first thorn is out, you should throw both thorns away. If Buddhism, or any other philosophy or religion, becomes another way of clinging to yourself, a way to be a better person or a better basketball player, you've got two thorns instead of one. The medicine is another disease! If you want to understand Zen, forget it! It can free you up and make you happy, but believe me, if you get attached to it, it can become a nightmare worse than any you've ever known."

. . .

Next day, the Yankees are playing the Tigers at the stadium, but I can't go. I have my first appointment with Dr. Kelman. It is Dad's idea, of course, an event for which he's prepared me for years and one to which I accede with no particular sense of choice. He gives me the address, puts me in a cab, and the next thing I know I'm sitting in Kelman's office. Getting out of here, as it turns out, will be as hard as anything I've ever done, but getting in is simply a matter of being a dutiful son. There is no way I could reject psychoanalysis without rejecting my father.

A large beefy man with eyes that never seem to blink, Kelman is completely bald. He reminds me of one of the Zen masters whose photographs I've seen in Dad's books. He didn't smile when he shook my hand and he isn't smiling now. All my life I've been drawn to men who—like Dad—do not like to smile, and Kelman is no exception. Not five minutes into our meeting, I'm already trying to win him over and certain I can't if for no other reason than that I'm trying to.

Kelman faces me in a high-backed leather chair, his ample belly pressed against the edge of his desk. While we talk, he smokes constantly, and like Dad, his brand is Pall Malls. He also has Dad's habit of holding his cigarette with his teeth rather than his lips. Occasionally, he places it in the center of his mouth, and his lips spread wide and encircle it so that his teeth are exposed and the cigarette looks like an arrow in a bull's eye. "Your dad tells me you play basketball."

"Yeah, I do."

"How's it going?"

"Not so good."

"What's the problem?"

"I don't know. I think I'm just not good enough."

"Good enough for what?"

His eyes are half-closed, poised, as I read them, between boredom and sleep. Does the thought occur that if I don't perform he'll choose the latter? Sartre once wrote that the role of a patient in psychoanalysis is simply to be neurotic in order to affirm the analyst's authority. I sense this, I think, from the moment I sit down: my neurosis is the way to his heart, and nothing will disappoint him more than signs that I am healthy.

"Good enough for what?" he says again.

I describe my disastrous failure in the championship game, tell him how my game, ever since, has gone downhill. "A year ago I thought I was a good ballplayer, maybe even very good. Now I may not make the team at all. There's too many guys better than me. Who knows why? Maybe I'm too small, too slow, maybe I don't have the right attitude or the right kind of mind. Whatever the reason, I'm not good enough."

Kelman scribbles in his notebook, using the fattest fountain pen I've ever seen. He is a friend and associate of Karen Horney, and all her books are arrayed on a shelf behind his desk. Prominent among them is the one from which Dad has often read at our dinner table: *The Neurotic Personality of Our Time.* His office is carpeted in a thick green pile and features the Guatemalan fabrics, artifacts and prints he buys on his annual Easter visit to Lake Atitlán. I know of these trips from Dad as well as from my brother, David, who has himself been Kelman's patient since enrolling at Columbia three years ago. Kelman also spends two months every summer in Lausanne and makes a Christmas trip to the Caribbean. Now and then, Mother remarks these trips and tries to joke about our financial contribution to them, but Dad is without a sense of humor on the subject. He accuses her of "cynicism" and "hostility," suggesting she's "threatened" by Kelman's influence, his "challenge to the family system."

Kelman points his fountain pen at me. "Tell me about 'not good enough.' Do you have this feeling about other things? Have you had it often in your life?"

The effect of his question is almost narcotic. It seems urgent that I answer, but my mind is absolutely blank.

"What are you feeling?" he says. "Right now!" And then: "Relax, Larry. Go easy on yourself. It's not like the outside world here. You don't have to be 'good enough' here. All you have to be is yourself."

I tell him I feel uncomfortable, agitated, unbearable pressure, and all of this has made my mind a blur.

"And this blur, this pressure, is it a new feeling or something you've known before? Would you say it's like feeling 'not good enough'?"

It seems to me my head is spinning, but the blur is so extreme I am not even sure of that. Traffic sounds on the street below are more accessible than my thoughts.

He lights another cigarette and sends his smoke across the desk in my direction. "This pressure, this feeling not good enough. Go into it! Tell me how it feels!"

Again, I cannot answer. Is the feeling, he says, limited to basketball? Have I felt it often in my life? What about when I read or study or when I'm talking to a girl? "My guess is that you've been walking around with this feeling most of your life. You're so accustomed to it that you hardly notice it anymore.

You judge yourself, Larry! Put yourself down! You always feel inadequate!"

To my surprise, I find myself agreeing with him and feeling as I do an amazing sense of relief. It's as if my brain is suddenly functioning again. I take a deep breath and sit up in my chair. And to complete the circle, Kelman smiles for the first time. It's as if, by agreeing on his description of me, we've come together, established a bond. "Are you aware," he says, "that until a moment ago, your breathing was constricted and irregular? When you smiled, it changed completely! It was as if you'd thrown off a straightjacket. Did you feel it? You let go of something! Your face relaxed and a light came into your eyes."

I agree to this as I agreed to what he said before. No particular thought is involved in such agreement. It seems automatic, Pavlovian. Whether I *actually* agree is irrelevant. It's as if we're on the tennis court and nodding yes is how I return his serve.

By the end of the session, I have achieved a kind of competence in this game. Kelman has an amazing ability to take a series of remarks, feelings, or facial expressions, and join them in sequence, a causal chain that seems to link everything I do or think or feel to something I did or thought or felt an instant before. "After you said such and such, your mouth got very tight . . . but then you sat up straight in your chair and smiled. It was right after that that you said . . ." The comfort and hope that I derive from such descriptions is almost exactly what I felt when I first read *The Way of Zen*. I cannot doubt that explanation is liberation. Problems defined are problems solved. I was not aware, when I entered this room, of any desire for psychoanalysis, but already this seems itself a problem, what Kelman calls "denial." All my life, he says, I've evaded my anxiety. But evasion, of course, causes more anxiety, so I'm "caught in a vicious circle." The only solution for such problems is "awareness," and that's what psychoanalysis is all about. He says I have seen a perfect demonstration of awareness in the way my breathing changed a few minutes ago. And that's just the beginning. Once released, the power of awareness is such that there is no limit to what it can accomplish. Relationships change. You think better and work harder and have less trouble making decisions. Such possibilities, he says, are not a romantic dream but the simple, inevitable result of the sort of dialogue that we have begun this afternoon.

. . .

For all his gentleness and compassion, the Buddha's initial teaching at the Deer Park is not by any means easy on the mind. From a certain point of view, in fact, it is a brutal attack he mounts on his old friends. The essentials of his enlightenment, he explains, can be contained in four "Noble Truths" of which the first three deal with understanding and the last the means by which to actualize it. As it happens, the first of these truths, the one on which his entire theology will be based, is the one from which his father had set out to protect him and the one that he himself, as he has gradually come to understand, set out to escape when he left his family and embarked upon his pilgrimage: "Birth is painful. Aging is painful. Sickness is painful. Death is painful. To be attached to what one dislikes is painful. Not to get what one wants is painful. Therefore, oh monks, you must begin by understanding the First Noble Truth: existence itself is painful."

Thus, the path that aims at transcending suffering begins with its acceptance. Far from alleviating pain, the Buddha views the dream of such alleviation as the means by which it is perpetuated. The First Noble Truth is a rejection, first of all, of the payoff mentality, future-oriented thought, the whole matrix of hope and expectation which, to use his words, "turns the wheel of birth and death." In effect, there is nothing more certain to make you feel worse than the dream of feeling better. Is it any wonder that, throughout its history, Buddhism will often be confused with nihilism? That its greatest teachers will never cease reminding their disciples that "Buddha and the devil are never more than a hairbreadth apart?"

"The Second Noble Truth," he continues, "is that the cause of suffering is found in desire. It is craving, accompanied by delight and greed, pleasure and lust. It is the search for pleasure and the avoidance of pain." This statement can be seen as an amplification of the one that preceded it. Once again, the target is hope, but let us remember that the Buddha is no apostle of hopelessness. From a certain point of view, in fact, we could say that his teachings stand on the subtle but absolute distinction—the Middle Way again—between freedom from hope and hopelessness. If hope is disavowed by the first two Noble Truths, it is reaffirmed by the third. "Those who accept the first two Noble Truths will arrive inevitably at the third: the end of suffering is the complete cessation of craving, the withdrawal from it, the renouncing of it, liberation from it, nonattachment to it."

How is it possible to conceive of such renunciation? If suffering is synonymous with existence and rooted in desire, how is one to be free of desire without being free of existence itself? By any ordinary logic, the Third Noble Truth is either a contradiction of the first and second or a repudiation of life itself. Are we dealing with freedom here or self-annihilation?

Unless I'm mistaken, the Buddha would say that there is no difference between the two. All along, his goal has been to find "what doesn't change," and the self, by definition, is impermanent.

But he brings them yet another Truth, yet another contradiction. Having asserted that there is nothing to achieve, he tells them now how to go about achieving it. After rejecting willfulness and purposefulness and therefore the programmatic ethics on which all religions before him have been based, he offers them, in the "Eightfold Path" that is the fourth of his Noble Truths, an ethical system which for rigor and thoroughness equals any that has preceded or succeeded it: "If you understand these three truths, oh monks, and if you practice the Noble Eightfold Path of right understanding, right thought, right speech, right action, right livelihood, right effort, right mindfulness, and right concentration, you will be liberated from your own suffering and you will liberate others from theirs. This in its barest essentials is the enlightenment which came to me."

. . .

Acting on a suggestion by Kelman, I begin a diary when I return from New York. Self-referential, centered on my "problems" and the effort to "understand" them, it is mostly a continuation of my conversation with him. I write in it only when my mood sinks, which is more and more often these days, and I feel better as soon as I pick up my pen. A typical entry begins, "Feeling totally depressed, I don't know why." No matter how much one entry resembles another, I am always excited when I begin. Often, I write in my diary as soon as I wake up in the morning, hoping to organize my thoughts or at least slow them down. Away from the house, I make notes if possible for future entries and, if I cannot write them down, make mental notes which, if I forget them, leave me bereft and obsessed to remember them. Sometimes, the thought of the diary alone can lift my spirits, and sometimes too, it seems that I derive so much pleasure from writing in it that I cultivate my problems as a writer cultivates his material. No pain, fear or confusion is so great that it cannot be alleviated by describing it in the diary. Writing at school has always been difficult for me, but in the diary I write quickly and even fluently. Just as in Kelman's office, my words seem slightly disconnected from my thoughts, and this makes it seem as if my pen is ahead of my mind, almost as if my hand is writing on its own. With the exception of masturbation, there is no other activity in which my concentration is so complete or my sense of time so absent. As often as not, I am certain that the writing is profound. Sometimes I have visions of its being posthumously published. Later, when I read it over and find it vague and muddled and embarrassing in its self-absorption, my disappointment does not discourage me but leads instead to another entry: ". . . feeling depressed that I spend so much time writing in this diary . . ."

Though the narrator and the subject of the diary are of course identical, its basic assumption is that they are two different people. I write of myself as a therapist of his patient, and it is taken for granted that the patient will be cured by means of my descriptions. In effect, since description has become a kind of medication for me, it is impossible for me to believe that there can be too much of it. And since all this description is about me, it follows that I cannot observe, understand or explain myself too much. Like Kelman, I create scenarios, chains of causality: "It's clear to me that the depression I was feeling

yesterday began the night before when . . ." Such scenarios almost always bring relief. Sometimes they make me ecstatic. It's
as if I am an archeologist unearthing an artifact that links two
moments in history.

In addition to books that Kelman has recommended—
Karen Horney's *The Neurotic Personality of Our Time* and
Erich Fromm's *Escape from Freedom*—I am reading Watts
again, and Krishnamurti too. All influence the diary and are
occasionally quoted in it. Psychological and spiritual understandings appear with equal frequency and to me seem inter-
changeable. I am beginning to be familiar with words like
"ego" and "desire" and "emptiness." Like Kelman and my father, I see Zen and Krishnamurti as extensions of psychoanalysis, a sort of Oriental pipeline that fuels the engine of my diary.

. . .

The summer after my graduation from high school, my father
and I take a trip out west. We are headed for the Krishnamurti
talks in Ojai, California, but on the way we spend three days in
Las Vegas. At dinner the first night in Vegas, before we enter
the casino, he gives me a lecture. "Bet with the house or against
it. That's the first rule of gambling. Don't switch. The best bet
in a casino, the best odds you can get, is with the house at craps.
The trouble is, it's the dullest bet in the house as well. That's
why I never do it myself. But if winning is your first priority,
that's the only way to go. Craps is the best game anyway, the
most exciting and the most complicated. When we start, I'll
show you how to bet. After that, I want you to leave me alone.
I'll give you five hundred dollars to play with, but after I show
you the ropes, I don't want you hanging around."

The secret of gambling, he explains, is money management. You have to trust your instincts. If you feel hot, go all the way. Don't be timid. If you can't trust yourself, you shouldn't be in a casino. "Winners play to win, losers to avoid losing. No place can show you quicker than a casino whether you're a winner or a loser. That's what you're gonna find out tonight."

He takes me to a table and teaches me how to bet. "You can bet with the shooter or you can bet on a particular roll of the dice. Basically, you create your own roll. The next number that comes up—that's your point. If it's a seven or an eleven, you win, even if the roller loses, and if it's craps or twelve, you lose. If you want to back the shooter, you put your chips on this line. Once you get your point, you can get odds on it by putting chips behind the line. They give you eight to five on six and eight, three to two on five and nine, two to one on four and ten. See, that fellow over there is taking odds on the six. That's called 'pressing' your bet. But no matter how you bet, the main thing is concentration. If you don't get your mind completely focused, the dice will never listen to you."

He is wearing a yellow sport coat, blue-and-white-striped pants, a red polo shirt with an alligator on the chest. A gold key chain stretches from his belt loop to his hip pocket, picking up the overhead light to form a sort of neon line that snakes across his thigh. He gives the croupier five $100 bills for a stack of chips which he then turns over to me. "From now till dinnertime," he says, "I don't know who you are." I wander around the casino for a while, but I can't muster the courage to bet. Eventually, I return to his table, taking up a position at the opposite end and making sure to avoid his eyes. By now, he has a corner to himself. He is leaning on the chip grooves that rim the table, elbows on a row of multicolored chips in $25, $50, $100 denominations. In his right fist, he grips a stack of chips like a piece of pipe, betting with one hand, sliding chips off the top with his thumb the way a bus driver slides coins from his changer. It is an impressive move, almost elegant, the sort of thing you could only learn from practice. Using the sort of backhanded motion he makes when dismissing a point I have made in an argument, he pitches chips toward the croupier and calls out his bets: "Hard six and hard eight! Four and ten!" His voice is deeper, his southern accent more pronounced, and when he stands erect to watch the dice roll across the table, he looks like a younger, stockier version of himself. When it's his turn to roll the dice, he shouts to others at the table that they had better get behind him. "I'm ready! I can feel it!" He puts four $100 chips on the "Come" line and rolls two straight sevens. When an eight comes up on his next roll, he presses it with another $500 and an extra $50 on the hard eight—a ten-to-one bet. "This eight is coming out hard! Don't say I didn't warn you—get down on the double fours!" Holding the dice between his forefinger and his thumb, he kisses them, then closes his fist and shakes them hard and pitches them down the table, crying "Forty-four!" Just as he predicted, two fours come up. Since at least half-a-dozen people, including me, have taken him at his word and bet on the hard eight, there is a cheer like you hear at football games when the home team scores a touchdown.

Stopping only to sleep and eat, we gamble almost constantly for the next two days, and at the airport, before flying on to California, we play the slot machines until our plane is called. Dad is almost unrecognizable to me. He makes more gestures when he speaks, and his eyes are glistening, slightly manic. Now and then, he slaps me on the back, and once, when we are at opposite ends of a crap table, he gives me a wink. He has never done that before, and he will never do it again. When we leave, he is ahead by $15,000. Me? At one point I was up by nearly $1,000, but I have lost all that plus the money he advanced me. He says it is because I lost my concentration. "If your mind is focused, you can feel when the dice turn against you." It is not the sort of criticism I've heard from him in the past. It seems friendly, almost affectionate, and it doesn't bother me in the least. "One thing you can bet your bottom dollar on, Larry. Win or lose, every gambler feels disappointed when he leaves a casino. If he loses, he kicks himself, and if he wins, he didn't win enough. But what the hell. You had fun, didn't you? You didn't lose more than you could afford. What else matters? Smart gamblers—nothing can disappoint them because when they walk into a casino, they know they're gonna lose. Trouble is, there's no such thing as a smart gambler. That's a contradiction in terms. A really smart guy, he wouldn't go near a place like this."

· · ·

As I'm leaving the zendo after evening sitting, Roshi asks if I've come to a decision about my girlfriend. It's a question I've been dreading. "No. I can't decide."

"Can't decide? Ah, great decision, Larry-san! My teacher, he say, 'If you confused, do confused. Do not be confused by confusion.' Understand? Be *totally confused,* Larry-san, then I guarantee: no problem at all."

· · ·

At the airport in Los Angeles, Dad and I rent a car and drive to Ojai, home of the Krishnamurti Foundation and the Oak Grove School, a twelve-grade boarding school based on Krishnamurti's theories of education. Dad is silent as we drive. Ever since we left Las Vegas, his mood has been deteriorating, the struggle to turn his mind from crapshooting to loftier matters visible on his face. Not feeling so good myself, it's not easy for me to look at him. Vegas has left me exhilarated. I want to believe that these feelings will last, but I know in my heart that they've already begun to disappear and I can see on his face the direction in which I'm headed.

In addition to the one in Ojai, there are Krishnamurti schools in England and India. Born to a poor Brahmin family in India, Krishna-ji, as he is called, was "discovered" at the age of fourteen, when C. W. Leadbeater, of the Theosophical Society, caught sight of him and—"convinced," he said, "by an aura that hasn't a single trace of selfishness"—decided he had found the "World Savior" whose appearance had been predicted by Theosophical doctrine. Leadbeater and Annie Besant, then president of the society, persuaded Krishnamurti's father to appoint them guardians of him and his brother. Eventually, both were sent to England so that Krishnamurti could be prepared to assume his messianic mantle. For many years, he played his role impeccably. Surrounded by reverence, educated and groomed according to English upper-class priorities, he gave talks at society meetings and slowly collected an idolatrous following. At the age of thirty-three, however, a great apostasy came over him. His reverence for the doctrine seemed deluded and regressive, a sort of neurotic conspiracy into which he'd entered with those who paid him homage. He told his audience that they were using him, as disciples had used teachers throughout history, to abdicate responsibility for themselves. Far from enlightening the student, guru-disciple relationships, he said, increased dependency and narrowed the

mind. "Whatever is sought by a fearful mind will only perpetu-
ate its fear. Only those who understand the roots of fear will be
free of it, and no teacher, religion or philosophical system can
assist us in that quest." Eventually, after a lengthy period of
inner turmoil, he resumed writing and lecturing, but now,
maintaining that he was no one's teacher and adhered to no
belief system, he railed against organized religion, gurus, and
formal spiritual practices like yoga and Zen. Embracing contradictions that are not at all uncommon in spiritual practice, he
wrote and talked about silence, offered a "pathless" path, attracted more and more students the more he protested that he
was not a teacher. Only love mattered, he said, a love that was
"neither personal nor impersonal, exclusive nor inclusive," and
such love was available only to one who listened to himself with
the rigorous, nonjudgmental attention that he called "choiceless awareness."

Arriving in Ojai on a Friday, Dad and I are scheduled to
stay the weekend and attend the talks on Saturday and Sunday
afternoon. When I find that our hotel contains a tennis club, I
slip into my shorts and sneakers and head out to the courts as
fast as I can. It is true that my passion for tennis has come to be
the equal of my passion for basketball, but this is not the only
reason for my haste. Dad's descent has continued with every
mile we've put between ourselves and Vegas. Silent and distant, he's resumed his foot-tapping habit, and I am beginning
to feel that nagging sensation I've known since childhood, that
his relentless self-loathing is directed no less at me than at himself. It's as if he is examining every breath either one of us takes
to see if we could have done it better.

I have been playing tennis since I was seven, and I have a
lot more talent for it than I do for basketball. Still, my psychol-

ogy is the same in both. Just as in basketball, I always expect myself to be better than I am. It always seems as if my mind beats me before my opponent does, and in this I'm not altogether wrong. I am what is known as a "rallier." That is to say, I look terrific warming up but fall apart in competition. Coaches praise my "potential," but I always lose to players I ought to beat. For three years, I have been playing in tournaments on the city and state level, but I have never gone beyond the third round. As in basketball, I sometimes feel ecstatic on the court, find a groove in which, for a time, I can do no wrong, but far more often, I follow good shots with a rash of bad ones, curse myself and throw my racquet, feel devastated when I'm done. Failure makes me more tenacious on the one hand, less disciplined on the other. Though I head for the court as soon as basketball season ends, I rarely practice for more than a couple of hours. Only years later will I realize that the really good players work out for five or six hours a day, sometimes more, and that the failures I blame on mind and psychology are more likely a matter of conditioning and skill. But what's the difference, finally? Isn't mind and psychology the reason I do not practice enough?

I can't find a game this afternoon, but hanging around the office, I meet the hotel's resident pro, and he offers me a discount price for half an hour's workout with him. He is a tall, left-handed player whose name—Tom McGriff—is vaguely familiar from the sports pages. Like most good teaching pros, he returns everything I hit with the pace and steadiness of a machine. Such teachers always make you look better than you are, but this alone cannot explain the startling improvement in my game. What is it? California air? The energy I picked up in Vegas? Every shot feels effortless and instinctive, free of psy-

chology, the ball exploding off my racquet and placed so well
that I feel an almost magical connection to it. I'm hitting top-
spins, slices, perfect lobs and overheads, moving with a quick-
ness I've never known before. It's as if I have broken with all
my limitations, become at last the player I am meant to be.

As we walk off the court, Tom invites me to return—"no
charge, of course"—for a couple of sets in the morning. He
asks me what tournaments I have played, and he wants to know
if I am "ranked" in my age group. When I tell him I have no
ranking, he seems shocked. He is certain, he says, that this is
because I have not devoted enough time to my game. He urges
me to take it more seriously. Give it a try for at least a year.
"You owe it to yourself to find out how good you are." Finally,
as we're toweling off, he asks a favor of me. The hotel has a
team that competes with those from other hotels in the area. A
match is scheduled here for Sunday morning, and his number-
one player is out of town. Would I be willing to take his place?
It's a friendly competition, no trophies involved, but it draws a
crowd and iced tea and cookies are served, and the proceeds go
to charity. "It's true that the guy you'll play won't be on your
level, but I don't think he'll bore you. At the very least, you'll
get a workout."

On the following afternoon, Dad and I attend the first of
Krishnamurti's talks. Having played as well this morning as I
did the day before, my exhilaration is such that even Dad's depression cannot diminish it. The talk is held on the grounds of
the school, a new-mown lawn encircled by towering oaks at the
height of summer foliage. The audience is mostly elderly or
middle-aged, but I see at least a half-a-dozen boys and girls my
age or younger. About a hundred folding chairs are arranged in
rows before a small platform where Krishnamurti already sits

on a simple wooden chair. Occasionally, he smiles and waves to someone he recognizes, but for the most part, he is perfectly still, hands beneath his thighs, face ingenuous and watchful, eyes searching the audience as if he wants to know each one of us. A small man, slightly built, more than a little androgynous, with smooth copper-colored skin, white hair, and the alertness of a cat stalking its prey, his posture is so erect and stable that it looks as if one could remove his chair without disturbing him in the least.

Once the crowd is in place, he continues to gaze at us, allowing the silence long after we're uncomfortable with it. When he finally begins, it is clear that he is not speaking from memory. His effort is visible as he searches his mind. There are long silences between and within sentences, and almost everything he says seems speculative and exploratory. More than anything, it is this that I will remember about his talk—the improvisation, the suspense it generates, his alertness and the alertness it creates in me. So naked and exposed does he seem that at times I am almost pained to look at him. Though I understand him very little, I trust him absolutely, and when the talk is over, I feel an excitement that's almost scary. It's as if the lecture is of a piece with the transformation I felt in Vegas and on the tennis court this morning, one more bridge I've crossed between what I used to be and what I've become, and pleased though I am with my changes, I feel as if I'm heading out into uncharted waters.

"Well, I don't know about you," says Dad, as we head back to the hotel, "but the main thing I got from this is a deep silence in my mind. It's more than quiet. It's as if all the words have been washed away. All our attempts at self-knowledge and understanding! What do they amount to? Useless, stupid,

a waste of time! Seeking, seeking, seeking—we're always looking for answers. Like K says, the man who seeks truth will
never find it. The truth is right here! Right now! Why can't we
get this through our thick heads?"

We are walking alone on a narrow, unpaved road. Banks
of trees on each side have formed an arch that makes it feel as if
we're in a sort of tunnel. Always a fast walker, Dad for some
reason has increased his speed, and as usual, he seems to accel-
erate in order to keep ahead of me. He speaks to me without
looking back. "But for once I really got it! All these years I've
been reading this stuff, but this time it got through! Consciousness itself is the problem! It's the nature of consciousness to
locate truth outside itself! It's a vicious circle! And the words
I'm using now are part of it!"

Turning onto a wider, more traveled road, I see the entrance to the hotel about a quarter-mile ahead. A tourist bus is
parked at the gate, and an American flag, limp in the windless
sky, dangles from a pole above it. There is no sidewalk, so we
walk single file on a narrow dirt path a couple of feet from the
curb. To our left, partially shielded by a stand of bushes, is the
chain-link fence that encircles the hotel. Behind it, a tennis
player all in white appears and disappears sporadically, as if il-
luminated by a strobe. I hear the hollow rhythmic thump of
balls rebounding off the racquet strings. Sweet as any sound I
know, it's like the pounding of a tribal drum, and hearing it
now, I remember again how I played this morning and feel the
joy I felt on the court.

Dad turns to face me. "But what about you? Did you get
it? This is not just ideas, you know. If you understood what K is
saying, it would completely change your life."

Our eyes meet for an instant, but mine drop quickly to the

ground. Reflex perhaps, or maybe I don't want my thoughts of tennis interrupted. I feel compelled to respond, and as always when I feel like this, my mind becomes a blur. "Well, you'll get it when you get it," he says. "I don't want to push you." He turns away, walks a couple of steps, then stops and turns to me again. "But for God's sake, Larry, if you remember anything, remember 'choiceless awareness.' That's all you need! And don't confuse it with self-consciousness! It's not the same at all! When we're self-conscious, we're judging and criticizing ourselves, but in choiceless awareness there is no judgment, just listening. Like K says, self-consciousness is violent. It cannot lead to change. But choiceless awareness is different. No judgment, no criticism. Not the means to solution, but solution itself!"

. . .

One evening, during meditation, one of my fellow students has an attack of flatulence while sitting. Farting is not all that rare in zendos, but this is a bout of unusual volume and quantity which goes on so long that it disrupts the atmosphere. Later, one of our senior members, an elderly woman of aristocratic background, complains to Roshi. She wants him to see that such "foulness" doesn't happen again. Roshi, however, could not be less inclined in that direction. "Honest fart OK," he says. "What I not like is little poop, but honest—boom, boom, boom—that's bravery gas!"

. . .

Next morning, Dad's spirits are even higher than they were in Vegas. He doesn't say much, but he downs a massive breakfast—pancakes, two fried eggs and several strips of bacon—

with a kind of enthusiasm I've rarely seen him show for food. Accompanying me to the courts, he says he awoke in the middle of the night with an understanding that shook him to the core. "Everything I said to you on the way back from the talk . . . forget it . . . it was all memory and ideas! Awareness is not memory. It's now, the present, just this moment. Not ideas— it's reality!" After this realization, he says, he could not get back to sleep. All night he paced the floor in a state of confusion and despair. "Everything seemed false. Watts, Zen, even Krishnamurti. 'It's all nonsense,' I thought. All these people do is make you more unhappy. You can't get away from consciousness and if you can't get away from consciousness, you can't get away from ideas and memory, and if you can't get away from ideas and memories, you can't get away from lies. But then, all of a sudden, I saw my mistake. The real problem is trying to get away. Period. All the rest is a lot of who-shot-John. What are we trying to get away from? Ourselves! The real problem is self-improvement! Trying to get better, happier, smarter, more secure, doesn't matter what, anything but what I am. When K says 'Accept yourself,' I'm thinking, 'That's the ticket! If I accept myself, I'll be happy!' When he says 'Be aware,' I think awareness is the answer. That's the trap, understand? We turn acceptance into nonacceptance! But last night I understood: to accept yourself means to accept everything. Everything! Even unhappiness. Even failures, even your shortcomings! The good and the bad! That's choiceless awareness! That's what K is after! When he talks about love, that's what he means!"

The weather—warm, windless, dry and slightly cloudy— is perfect for tennis, and these brown clay courts are the kind on which I play my best. I am trying to feign indifference to it, but this match has become dangerously important for me. My two outings with McGriff have left my mind swollen with excitement. I'm having fantasies of taking his advice, finding a coach, devoting a year to training and tournaments. Meanwhile, I keep thinking of Krishnamurti: his concentration and alertness, his honesty, the way he trusts himself and thinks aloud in public. It's as if everything has come together—the breakthrough on the court, the insights of Krishnamurti and the excitement I felt in Vegas—and all my limitations have been cast aside.

Beside the court, there is iced tea and cookies and sliced oranges and lemons on a table shaded by an umbrella that says PERNOD. On another table are stacks of white towels and a number of unopened cans of Pennsylvania balls. Since another match is in progress on the court where mine is scheduled, Dad and I take seats in the grandstand. There are fifty to sixty people here and more arriving all the time. Many are wearing tennis whites, the women in short pleated skirts and half-socks with brightly colored puffs at the heel, the men in white shirts with alligators or other emblems on the chest and ribbed white socks that rise to the middle of their calves. Green plastic sunvisors, terry-cloth hats, multicolored wristbands, leather tennis bags shaped like racquets with airline tags in the handles. Everyone seems to know each other. I exchange glances with a terrific-looking girl about my age who takes a seat in front of us. She's small and thin, with tanned, broad, right-angled shoulders and a blond braided ponytail that hangs between the straps of her white tank top. Past experience ought to make me wary of this glance. I've got a dangerous tendency to use girls like this to take myself out of the game. But such is my confidence now that I feel immune to her. She's just another of the sweets which have appeared on my plate today.

As often, Dad's vision is turning global. Talking loud enough, it seems to me, to be heard throughout the grandstand, he asserts that the search for self-improvement is the cause of all the strife and violence that afflicts the human race. "Like K says, the more trouble there is in the world, the more one seeks security. But it's precisely this seeking that created trouble in the first place. How can it help but create more trouble, more violence, more anger and conflict and suffering?"

When the preliminary match is over and it is time for me to play, he stands and leaves abruptly. "OK!" he says. "I'll meet you back at the room." Until this moment, I've not been aware of any particular need for him to watch me play, but I feel like an infant he's abandoned on the street. It's as if I've had the wind knocked out of me. As I walk on the court, my knees are actually shaking. How many times have we done this little dance together? How many times has he deflated me by turning his eyes away? It's as if my brain is wired to respond like this, instant regression in response to withdrawal, a frenzy of desire released by the increase of space between us. Is it only my imagination that his departure results from the fact that he felt my confidence and found it unbearable?

My opponent is short and chubby, a balding man in his mid-sixties who commits the unforgivable sin of wearing black socks. On the court, he is what we call a "hacker." His strategy is defense. Returning every ball I hit with lazy lofting shots to the deep center of the court, he seems unconcerned with winning points, only with keeping the ball in play. As Tom predicted, his game looks so inferior to mine that an observer might conclude that I am giving him a lesson. As it happens, however, he is exactly the sort of player who brings out the worst in me. His patience exposes my impatience, his steadiness my inconsistency. No matter how hard I hit the ball, he returns it easily, unaggressively, in a spirit almost of friendship. Unlike me, he seems actually to be enjoying himself. Within minutes, I begin to feel slightly insulted by his returns. Anger makes me hit too hard and too long, and the more my balls go out, the angrier I get. It's a classic tennis situation, consistency and patience defeating erratic power and form that looks good but is mostly superficial. In fact, it's absurd to think I am better than he. He's a smart player and I'm a dumb one. In all probability, he knew he would beat me when we were warming up.

When not thinking about the girl in the grandstand, I am thinking of Krishnamurti. I take deep breaths and try to focus my mind the way he seemed to focus his while sitting on the platform. Now and then, the words "choiceless awareness" appear in my brain like a phrase from a TV commercial. Just before hitting a serve into the net, I think, "Concentrate! Empty your mind!" Knowing what I want to do almost guarantees that I'll not be able to do it. It isn't long, of course, before the mental chatter shows up in my body. My reflexes are slow, my breathing shallow. Even my eyesight seems diminished. Now and then I make a good shot, but it is invariably followed by three or four unforced errors. More than once, I hurl my racquet into the net and curse myself aloud.

When I return to the room, Dad is on the terrace, reading a book—*Krishnamurti's Notebook*—he bought at yesterday's lecture. "How'd it go?" he says.

"Fine."

"You win?"

"No."

"Are you crying?"

"No."

Returning to his reading, he seems not to have heard me. I
head for the shower. Sobbing, I hide out under the water and
review my mistakes. My errors seem like flaws in my character,
failures of intelligence or courage, sins I'll never live down. The
litany is familiar with one exception. Weaving in and out of it is
the memory of Krishnamurti. Just as with Watts a few years
ago, I cannot doubt that he is the reason my game fell apart.
Choiceless awareness! Concentration! What did I gain from
such ideas? What did they do but make me self-conscious?
How could anyone manage to play good tennis with that sort of
clamor rattling in his brain?

As I'm toweling off, Dad calls to me to hurry. The talk
begins in forty-five minutes and he wants to sit as close to the
stage as possible.

2   *Everything that man has handled has a tendency*
to secrete meaning.   —MARCEL DUCHAMP

"Everybody knows about Zen," says Francine. "You sit on a beach and look out at the water and try to focus your mind, you could say you're doing Zen. Sharpen pencils, take drugs, make love, run, pray, watch TV—whatever you do to quiet yourself has something in common with Zen."

A small dark-haired woman with thin lips and a steady, slightly tyrannical smile, she is a former roommate of my girl-friend and future wife, Andra. Her distinction for the moment is that she has just returned from two years in Taiwan, where among other things she studied with a woman Zen master. This makes Andra, for good reason, anxious about our meeting. She has made me promise to behave myself. Herself much inclined toward the Oriental solution, passionate reader of books on Zen, Sufism, Gurdjieff, etc., she has experienced firsthand my hostility to Zen and other eastern thought. Even worse, she cannot pretend that my opinions are driven by ignorance. How can she discount someone who once had dinner with Alan Watts and attended Krishnamurti's talks sixteen years ago in Ojai? Who has been "in therapy" for fifteen years with an analyst who studied with D. T. Suzuki? Who has a father—hasn't she heard him lecture when he comes to New York and takes us out to dinner?—whose fuzzy, convoluted mind is a perfect example of the dangerous side effects of the spiritual point of view?

"On the other hand," Francine continues, "there are monasteries. There are Zen masters and Zen monks and Zen koans and Zen sutras, and there is a kind of formal meditation called zazen. Zen monks practice zazen on a level that some would call fanatical. Did you ever heard of zazen? No? Of course not! You won't read about it in Alan Watts's books. Even Suzuki hardly mentions it! Zazen is not like sitting on a beach and it's not like sex and it's certainly not like watching TV. It's very hard, more a physical than a mental exercise. My teacher, for example, says that if your posture isn't good, you're wasting your time. The most important thing about it, she says, is keeping your back straight and unsupported. If you're leaning against something, you might as well be lying down."

This is October in New York, 1970, brunch on a sunny autumn afternoon in our newly renovated loft. We are on the border of the neighborhood that is just beginning to be called Soho. The art world is moving in on the factories, and every lamppost announces a poetry reading, a concert or a movie screening. At the end of the loft is a large northern window that faces Houston Street and three new buildings designed by I. M. Pei that are owned by New York University and inhabited by people who, perhaps because they are under the impression that the buildings opposite are factories, rarely draw their curtains. Their windows are my TV set, every apartment a different channel. I have an old Morris chair where I sit in the evening with my binoculars, and my involvement with this particular form of entertainment is a perfect measure of my state of mind.

For the last four months I have been so depressed that my nightly investigation of these windows is one of the few activities I anticipate with pleasure. Given my love for Andra and the fact that my first novel is coming out in the spring, I ought to be happy these days, but I seem to be immune to good fortune. If anything, it makes me feel worse. The simplest decisions are impossible, I haven't had a good night's sleep in weeks, and I'm so impatient and restless that it is almost impossible for me to read, much less write.

It doesn't help that when I am able to read the writer I turn to is Samuel Beckett. This is by no means my first attempt at him, but it is the first time I have seen beyond the morbidity and the absurdist cul-de-sac with which he is usually associated. The result has been at once a revelation and a nightmare. I see an urgency in his work that is nowhere present in my own. I was proud of my novel when I began to read him, but when I think of it now, it seems shallow and inauthentic, an idiotic waste of energy and time.

Such despair, of course, is not unusual when a young writer confronts a great one, but I have been consumed by it. I don't see any reason to write unless I can make my work as honest and authentic as Beckett's, and—with a remarkable combination of grandiosity and oversimplification—I have come to the conclusion that the only way to do so is to write in a present tense that excludes everything but what I actually feel or think at the moment of composition. In effect, I have declared off-limits any subject but the movement of my mind as I face the empty page. It's as if I want to write the way an abstract expressionist paints. A more experienced writer would understand the risk of this undertaking, the self-consciousness it generates and the self-indulgence it invites. Not me. In the past three months, my "work" has consisted, for the most part, in observing my mind obsessively, watching for thoughts and images while trying to ignore the fact that I am stifled by my self-consciousness. Watts might say that the Backwards Law has trapped me once again. Is it any wonder I look forward so to evenings with my binoculars?

It is from Francine I hear, for the first time, the alleged statement by Arnold Toynbee which Buddhists will quote so often in future years: "It may be that the most important historical occurrence of the twentieth century is the movement of Buddhism from East to West." She's trying to give us a capsule history of Zen in America but, barely concealing my condescension, I interrupt to ask if she can describe this thing she calls zazen. "Do you do anything or is it just introspection?"

"No, it's not introspection. Not if you can help it, anyway. You just sit."

"Sit?"

"Yes, like this."

Taking a cushion from the couch, she places it on the floor and sits cross-legged in a full-lotus posture, pulling her feet up onto her thighs. She places one palm on another and, thumbs touching, rests them in her lap, then rocks forward and back and side to side several times, pushing her head toward the ceiling. "This is really all there is to it. You face a wall if you can, pull the shades and disconnect the phone, and it's best to do it on an empty stomach. My teacher says it's very important to do it at the same time every day, whether you feel like it or not. If you only do it when you're in the mood, like when you're feeling down and you get this urge to meditate, that makes no sense because you're still, as she puts it, a slave to your mood. She says mood is the first tyranny and the whole idea of zazen is getting free of it. If feeling good is what you're after, she says, it's better to take drugs. You don't do this to feel better. You do it to feel however you feel. To face yourself. You don't criticize yourself, and you don't praise yourself either. While you sit, you count your breath—one on the first exhalation and two on the second, and so on, and when you get to ten, you go back to one again. Of course, if you're anything like me, you'll never get to ten, because your mind flies off in all directions. It's scary, you can't believe how distracted you get! But she says that's OK. It's the nature of the mind to wander. When you see it's wandered, just start at one again. The main thing is, don't put yourself down. Don't imagine this ideal concentration. Distraction, she says, is just the mind's way of reminding you it's there."

I am not exactly captivated by this description. "Sitting" seems the last thing in the world I'd want to try. Don't I watch my mind enough already? Why should a man who's already drowning in self-consciousness engage in a practice that encourages it?

But next morning, true to the ambivalence that permeates my life just now, I try it out. No particular will or decision is involved. Guilty and terrified about my lack of production these days, how could I resist a way to think of doing nothing as doing something? I take a cushion off a chair and place it near the wall and sit down with legs crossed and hands folded in my lap. My legs are rigid and resistant, but I force a foot up onto my thigh in a poor approximation of the posture Francine demonstrated. As best I can, I straighten my back and balance myself on the cushion. I feel awkward and stiff, but I focus on my breath and count one on the first exhalation and two on the second. As Francine predicted, my mind scatters and I lose the count before I get to three. I feel silly doing this, oddly embarrassed, as if I am watching myself from a distance and cannot believe what I see. Next time, I make it to "four" but the next I'm gone at "three" again. The impulse to get up occurs so frequently that it's like an echo of the breath I'm attempting to follow.

With my watch at my side, I resolve to sit for ten minutes. It is 8:15 when I begin, 8:17 at my first time check, 8:18 at my third. When I finish, I feel like I've sat for an hour. There is sharp pain in my right ankle that will be gone in a few minutes, a stiffness in my neck that will persist for several hours. If there is any psychological benefit from what I've done, I am unaware of it. Certainly, I am no less agitated and no less depressed at the thought of facing my work again. For the most part, when I remember myself on the cushion, I feel the same embarrassment I felt when I first sat down.

But I sit again that evening and again the following morning. As before, there is little sense of choice involved. I simply find myself returning to the cushion. Different as this is from anything I've called "sitting still" in the past, it is in many ways familiar. Just as when I sit at my desk and try to settle my mind, I find now that the search for stillness only increases my distraction. Every effort toward my breath seems to lead me away from it. Later that day, when I go out for a walk, I am nervous and irritable, as if after too much coffee. As before, thoughts of sitting embarrass me, and every now and then, embarrassment turns to fear. Why fear? Do I sense already a habit forming, a threat of seduction or entrapment?

It is a gloomy day, the skies grey and threatening. I walk quickly, with no destination and little awareness of anything around me. It is only gradually I realize that, for all my doubts about zazen, there are moments when my agitation disappears and, for no reason I can fathom, I am filled with a sense of elation. It's as if I've gained a sort of foothold on a slope which until now seemed impossibly steep and slippery. This sensation is no more durable than anything else I feel, but later, when I sit again and search for it in vain, its absence will leave me even more annoyed with zazen than I felt when I began.

Later that day, I have an appointment with Kelman. An instinct tells me not to mention zazen to him, but after all, I've been seeing him now since I entered college, and I am so addicted to describing things to him that I don't believe in their reality until I've done so. As I speak to him of sitting, he closes his eyes and nods sympathetically, as if nothing I say is news. "Fifteen years we've been working together," he says. "It's finally paying off!"

Lifting the bell that is used to begin and end meditation periods, Roshi moves it a few inches to the left. All eyes follow his hand, sixteen of us sitting cross-legged in two rows on either side of him. The bell sits for a moment, and then he moves it back. "OK, what you say now? 'The bell it used to there . . . now here . . . now there again!' Right? How you know? Memory? Thought? You thinking 'here'! You thinking 'there'! Mind making words! Ideas! Listen: bell just here. Understand? *Just* here! *Just* now! This moment this moment. Nothing else. Don't hold memory! Don't attach! Follow your breath, only this breath! Only this! And only this! What used to be is dust!"

Giggles circulate, passed along like gossip or a yawn. Is everyone thinking, as I am, that he is the only one in the room who does not understand? Does the word "bullshit" appear in no other mind but my own? Even when his remarks strike me as revelations, there is a part of my mind that withdraws from them like a finger from a scalding surface. But if I am to trust what I see on other people's faces, I am alone with my skepticism. Looking around the room, it occurs to me that there is a particular sort of grin his talks elicit. At once knowing and slightly demented, it sets the lips to trembling with self-effacement on the one hand and the dream, or, who knows, perhaps the reality, of illumination on the other. I watch with condescension until I realize that I am wearing the same expression myself.

"Must asking yourself, 'From what point of view here? From what point of view there? 'Here' and 'there' nothing but words! Ideas! Zen not words! Zen reality! If you interested in words, please, you wasting time here. Read book! Go university! Please! Don't waste this precious time! In relative world, all things different from each other. Understand? You and me, night and day, good and bad, here and there. Subject and object! Understand? You look at bell like object. You subject, bell object, right? No! No! You and bell same! In Absolute, no separation at all. No word, no idea, no picture! Listen, I give you famous Zen proverb: 'Two mirrors facing each other. There is no image in between.' "

He continues speaking for more than an hour, digressing to memories of his childhood in Japan, a recent episode of "Dallas," a Hulk Hogan story he's told at least half-a-dozen times before. He is a punctual man, always on time, particularly conscientious with regard to the zendo's schedule, but once he begins to talk, he seems to lose, or, what's more likely, abandon his temporal bearings. My head is reeling with the vertiginous mix of anger, distraction and euphoria his talks always elicit in me. I feel as if I can't remember anything he's said, but next time I'm on my cushion much of this will reappear like threads from recovered dreams.

Suddenly, deep into another digression, he turns to the woman next to him: "Uh, Mary-san . . . please you tell me, what I talking about?"

"I don't know, Roshi."

"Me neither!" he cries. "Getting old! Good night!"

. . .

Soon I'm sitting every day when I go to my studio. Ten minutes becomes fifteen, and fifteen becomes twenty. On good days, it seems to me that zazen is making me calmer and more confident, giving me a sort of leverage on my thoughts, and on bad days, when it leaves me confused or agitated, I can think of nowhere to turn for relief but zazen itself. Within a couple of months I am sitting twice a day for forty-five minutes. For the most part, the practice remains disappointing, even bewildering, but now and then I have ecstatic or even "mystical" experiences that remind me of others I've had in the past—midnight on the bow of a boat crossing the Atlantic when I was twenty-one years old; a blissful experience of death on nitrous oxide; several times when I entered what athletes call "the zone" on the basketball or tennis court. I'm not sure that it happened this early in the practice, but it may be that such experiences are already occurring with frequency. Perhaps Zen has already begun to show me that this sort of mind-expansion is much more ordinary and commonplace than I've ever imagined it to be. I know it won't be long before I begin to realize how much I've undermined myself by yearning after states of mind that are are not so different from those I inhabit normally.

Since Andra, as it happens, has also taken up sitting in the wake of our meeting with Francine, we often sit together, either first thing in the morning or in the evening, before dinner. We find a store that sells meditation supplies and buy two sets of black cushions which we install—the small round cushion, or "zafu," resting on a large square one called a "zabuton"—in a corner of our bedroom. We buy a kitchen timer and use it to time our meditation periods, keeping it under a pile of underwear in a dresser drawer so that its ticking won't disturb us. Without deciding to do so, we find ourselves removing our shoes before entering the bedroom. We buy Japanese sandalwood incense and a bowl in which to burn it and a bag of aquarium sand from a pet shop to put in the incense bowl and black, loose-fitting pants to sit in, and we start browsing in the one New York bookstore which, at this point in time, specializes in "spiritual" literature.

Zazen posture comes easy to Andra, who is innately supple and has studied yoga. For me, it is agony. All these years of knee bends, push-ups and running may have helped me in sports, but they have tightened precisely the muscles and tendons that need to be loose for meditation. Pain moves around my body—back, knee, ankle, neck—and the longer I sit, the worse it gets. I buy a book on yoga and begin exercising twice a day to stretch out my quadricep muscles and the tendons in my ankles and groin. When reading or watching TV, I fold my legs into half-lotus (dreaming of full, of course) so as to work on their flexibility. Soon I achieve a pretty good approximation of the half-lotus, one foot on my thigh and both knees touching the floor, but it is not by any stretch of the imagination comfortable or painless. In fact, my discomfort is so constant that it becomes synonymous with zazen. If I were comfortable, how could I know that I am not just sitting but *sitting*?

Meanwhile, I have become so obsessed with breath-counting that I do it when I'm out for a walk or on the subway, even at times while sitting across from a friend at dinner. Zen teachers are always reminding their students that the practice is no different from ordinary life, but I have already stumbled into the common Zen confusion that makes the practice seem extraordinary and the ordinary reductive and distracting.

A few weeks later, a fortuitous event occurs. A former girlfriend who has become a devotee of Tibetan Buddhism sends me a recently published book called *Zen Mind, Beginner's Mind*. Its author is the late Shunryu Suzuki Roshi, the founder of the San Francisco Zen Center and the Zen Mountain Center at Tassajara Springs above Carmel Valley. Suzuki was a Zen master, not a scholar. Unlike other Zen books I've read, his focuses on zazen, not Zen theory. As his title indicates, he makes no distinction between the enlightened mind and the beginner's. All students, even at the beginning of their practice, are considered to be inherently enlightened. Such ideas are anything but congenial to a linear mind like my own, which has already made Zen into a self-improvement program, enlightenment something more or less akin to an Olympic gold medal, but *Zen Mind, Beginner's Mind,* far from attempting to explain the ordinary, "nothing special" view of enlightenment, is simply its concrete embodiment. When reading it, I often remember Beckett's observation about Joyce: "He doesn't write *about* something. He writes something." Suzuki helps me understand, for the first time, the meaning of Zen as "practice." The meditation he describes has less in common with the search for insight that exemplifies, for me at least, the Zen of Watts and D. T. Suzuki than with the endless repetitions of athletes, musicians and dancers. Ends and means are inseparable. One does not sit in order to become enlightened. One sits because, as the Buddha exclaimed at the moment of his awakening, one is enlightened as one is. The practice is simply a means of realizing this fact, which the ordinary, dualistic mind obscures. "These forms," says Suzuki, "are not the means of obtaining the right state of mind. To take this posture is itself to have the right state of mind."

Separately or together, Andra and I read from Suzuki almost every day. Familiar though we are with his warnings against excitement—"Zen is not some kind of excitement, but concentration on our usual everyday routine"—our mood with respect to the practice is very near to intoxication. On Sunday mornings, sipping coffee in bed, we have long, caffeine-enhanced discussions in which Suzuki's insights and those we've gained from our own practice seem to illuminate every aspect of our lives. Our talk is so blissed out that it seems to transcend talk itself. Nothing is beyond words because everything is. Paradox begets generalization and generalization the sort of conviction that leaves no room for paradox. We talk about Zen and psychoanalysis, Zen and writing, painting, and music, Zen and tennis, Zen and power and language and sex. Never have I felt so smart or so vain about intelligence, but I ward off conceit by telling myself that my voice is separate, an almost autonomous entity, as if I'm not speaking but, like a medium (like a master giving the Dharma talk that we call "teisho"?), allowing Zen to speak through me. So long we've lived in darkness—can't we be forgiven that this faint newly discovered candle seems to light up the universe? Is it not to be expected that, in the midst of such conversations, the blanket swells with my erection? Or that, when we finally make love, sex will seem like a higher form of Zen? Who would have thought that this austere, ascetic practice is such a powerful aphrodisiac? And later, when we get up and sit together on our cushions, zazen seems as much an extension of sex as sex has been an extension of it. Sometimes we get so high on our quiet and concentration that, when the coffee wears off and our ordinary minds resume, we crash as we might after drugs or alcohol.

But for all my excitement, my writing block is getting worse. When I go to my studio, all I want to do is sit. Zen makes me impatient with language, almost condescending toward it. I don't even want to read. Beginning an argument that will never release its hold on me, I fill my diary with art-Zen dialectics, endless discussions of the differences and similarities

between the spiritual and the esthetic point-of-view. Of all
writers, only Beckett, it seems to me, expresses the wisdom one
finds in Zen masters. Is it possible that the irony and conflict on
which writing depends ("Give me an argument," said Flaubert,
"and I'll write you a novel") are symptoms that Zen attacks and
cures? Is the attachment to writing—to language and description, all the traps of dualistic mind—a means by which one per-
petuates one's suffering? Time and again, when sitting on my
cushion, I come to the conclusion that this has been the case for
me. Far from alleviating the distraction and confusion that
have gnawed at me all my life, my work has reinforced them,
given them a sort of romantic credibility.

Meanwhile, outside my studio, I am becoming evangeli-
cal. With friends, I speak of nothing but zazen. Wisdom of this
order must be shared! Is there anyone alive who doesn't need
this practice? Not realizing how much I am echoing my father
or how much violating Zen's precept against proselytizing, not
to mention how little I know of the ideas I'm espousing, I try to
convert almost everyone I know. Often, I get down on the floor
to demonstrate zazen technique as Francine once demonstrated for us. "Ten minutes a day!" I exhort. "Just try it for a
week!" When my entreaties are ignored or, as is often the case,
resented, I am sad or even angry, shocked to have friends so
attached to their suffering. Day by day, it becomes more difficult to resist the belief that those not inclined toward Zen are
somehow less than those who are.

.   .   .

The Buddha's teachings evolve and proliferate, moving north
toward Tibet, east into China, leaving a trail so sparsely recorded that its fact and myth will remain forever inseparable.

Most historians agree, however, that the first Buddhist monks arrived in China in the first century A.D. bringing with them not only sacred texts but the meditation practices that had grown from the synthesis of Buddhist ideas and the early techniques of yoga. In China, Taoist practice, the teachings of Lao Tzu and Chuang Tzu, were so consistent with the teachings of the Buddha that a quick synergy developed, creating new forms and practices. A southern Indian Brahman called Bodhidharma, who arrived during the Liu Sung period (420–479), is generally considered the man who brought "the seal of the Buddha mind" from India to China. Though his writings were not markedly different from those of traditional Indian Buddhism, he is believed to have been unique in his focus on one particular word—"pi-kuan," or "wall-gazing." Legend has it that he lived to be 150, sat for nine years without interruption before the wall of a monastery, and countered great hostility from those who equated Buddhism with the recitation of sacred texts. Despite his influence, however, the practice retained much of its Indian influence until the eighth century, and most of its arguments as well. From the time of Shakyamuni, the ranks of the faithful had been split between those who believed in the universality of enlightenment, which is to say its accessibility to "ordinary" people, and those who believed it the province of monks and nuns who'd abandoned secular life to devote themselves entirely to the teachings. An important subtext of this argument was that the latter were mostly "gradualists" who viewed the movement toward enlightenment as a long, arduous struggle against delusion, while the former insisted on the possibility of sudden breakthrough. On closer examination, the disagreement, like all such neat polemics, broke down—no Buddhist master would deny the need for practice

or what Zen teachers call "polishing," and none would deny
that enlightenment could occur for any being at any moment—
but its deeper roots had to do with the Buddha's paradoxical
view of causality, the fact that he had, on the one hand, affirmed that all human beings are subject to the laws of cause
and effect, and on the other, that the distinction between cause
and effect is not absolute, but a function of conceptual mind.

The dialectic finally turns on the question of change—
what can be changed and what cannot, what is inherent in
human existence and what can be modified. A man cannot
change the color of his eyes, but he can change the way his
mind relates to it. Or if he cannot change the way his mind relates to it, he can identify himself, not with it, but with the "Big
Mind" that sees the small one. The basic suffering that comes
with birth cannot be escaped, but the desire which rejects that
suffering can be penetrated and transcended. Buddhism turns
on these distinctions—what is relative? what is absolute? what
is karma? what exists before and after it?—and the "Middle
Way" is finally a point of view which says that they can neither
be solved nor left unsolved, or more precisely, that to recognize
their intractable mystery is to solve them once and for all.

Among other things, Buddhist thought attacks the human
instinct for metaphor, the mental process that replaces fundamental problems with limited ones. An addict believes he will
feel better if he obtains his drug, a Buddhist that his pain is his
addiction and, furthermore, that the dualistic mind is by definition an addictive one. In the relative realm, the realm of cause
and effect, I will feel better if I can locate a cause that is, in my
view, the source of my discomfort. My parents abused me. I
don't have enough money. My hands are dirty. Depressed, I go
to a therapist. Unhappy in my marriage, I sue for divorce. You

could say that Buddhism, defining pain as the realm of cause and effect or "the wheel of birth and death," rejects such limited solution. Thus, in Zen practice, one learns not to get up from one's cushion when feeling discomfort but rather to deal with the discrimination between comfort and discomfort as it evolves in the dualistic or relative mind. One presses to see the root problem—the discriminating mind; the separation of cause and effect—rather than the limited versions of it that serve as its metaphors.

But as the Buddha affirmed, the separation of cause and effect happens at birth. Even though he recognized birth as the source of suffering, he had no retrograde impulse—he was not a nihilist. Far from bemoaning the fact of human birth, he celebrated it as the means by which one is offered an opportunity for enlightenment. The realm of cause and effect cannot be denied. It is, in fact, the source and fuel of everything that happens in a human life: what else but cause and effect had brought him to the Mucalinda tree? What else brings us to our zendos and our ashrams? Why else did he, having seen through the separation of cause and effect, create the so-called "Eightfold Path," which is nothing if not an attack on the casual chains of habit?

One framework in which these arguments evolved was the distinction between the so-called "Hinayana" and "Mahayana" paths. The former, often called "the Lesser Vehicle," was generally thought to evolve from a recognition of cause and effect, its practices aimed at dealing with the effects of memory, thought and psychological habit, while the latter arose from the view that cause and effect are inseparable and that the self or ego which the Hinayana sought to heal was essentially nonexistent. While it's true that anyone who studies Buddhist thought will find such polemics dissolved—one could define the Middle Way as a union of the Hinayana and the Mahayana—they persist even in the present day. Hinayana Buddhists, practicing what is called "Vipassana meditation," are generally more tolerant of psychological insight (indeed, Vipassana is sometimes called "insight meditation"), while Mahayana practitioners, seeking to penetrate, even annihilate the ego, will often consider any sort of psychological thought a detour or a distraction.

Though it too will always wrestle with the paradox of causality, "Ch'an"—or Zen—Buddhism, which emerges in the eighth century, is believed to be a culmination of the Mahayana path. Its crystallizations begin with the teachings of Eno, the so-called Sixth Patriarch of Zen. He is a poor peasant boy with no formal knowledge of Buddhism who experiences a sudden enlightenment on hearing a group of monks chanting the Buddha's words as they were recorded in the Diamond Sutra: "No mind, no abode, and here works the mind!" Penetrated and transformed by this perfect articulation of the Middle Way, he asks the monks where they come from. Informed that they are disciples of Master Gunin, who presides over a monastery on Mount Obai, he resolves to join their ranks. Gunin recognizes Eno's realization when he arrives at Mount Obai, but since the boy is young, illiterate and unversed in Buddhism, he puts him to work in the rice hulling shed. A few years later, Eno is one of the featured players in a famous contest that illustrates the Mahayana-Hinayana dialectic. Master Gunin challenges his monks to write poems that demonstrate the level of their realization so that he can decide which of them is worthy to be his successor. His head monk, Shinshu, offers the following:

The body is the tree of bodhi,
The mind is like the stand of a bright mirror.
Moment by moment wipe the mirror carefully.
Never let dust collect on it.

Eno admires Shinshu's poem but finds it insufficiently pene-
trating. The mirror, after all, is clearly a concession to the existence of self, the act of wiping it an attempt to clear up the
confusion and suffering generated by the dualistic mind. Unable to write himself, he enlists a fellow monk to transmit his
rejoinder:

Bodhi is not originally a tree,
Nor has the bright mirror a stand.
Originally, there is nothing.
So where can any dust collect?

.   .   .

Though most of our friends are artists or writers and there
must be many among them with spiritual inclinations, Andra
and I know but one person who is "officially" involved with
Zen. She is a beautiful woman named Sara who writes poetry
and works in a bookstore and is said to attend a place called the
New York Zendo on the Upper East Side of Manhattan. Nowadays, Zen is so rare that this alone makes her reputation exotic. There are rumors that she is about to become a nun, that
she is moving to Japan, that she has taken vows of celibacy, that
she has given all her possessions away and lives in a small bare
room with a mattress on the floor. One day, on a whim, I phone
her. Yes, she says, she is indeed involved with Zen. She sits at

the New York Zendo and studies with the roshi there, a man named Eido who, as it happens, is giving a talk tonight at the zendo. Would we like to come? It is free, she says, and open to the public.

The coincidence is so remarkable that it cannot be accidental. Andra and I cancel a dinner engagement and, trying our best to hide our excitement, head off to the zendo in time to arrive forty-five minutes early. A line has already formed at the door. Seven people stand silent on the sidewalk—two young women with long hair, exotic earrings, and virtually matching Guatemalan skirts; an elderly couple in blue jeans and sandals; another couple with briefcases who look like they've come from Wall Street; a man in his mid-twenties, wearing plaid polyester pants a couple of inches too short, reading *Zen Mind, Beginner's Mind* and fingering what looks to be a rosary. Ordinary people, two of them grossly overweight. My heart sinks as I take them in. Given my romance with Zen, I had expected warriors here, steely-eyed stoics, the hippest of the hip or, at the very least, haunted beings, eyes ablaze with psychic desperation. Taking my place on line, I feel as I might if I'd finally made it to Wimbledon and discovered that all the other players looked like my obese Ojai opponent, with his black socks and baggy shorts.

This is April 1971. At present, there are several Zen centers in New York, but the New York Zendo is by far the best known. Its existence is testimony to the energy, ambition and organizational skills of Eido Roshi, who arrived in this country only six years ago. Originally, Eido had a small zazen group that met in his third-floor walk-up apartment in Greenwich Village, but when his living room became inadequate, a search for larger quarters was initiated. The group was penniless and the space it needed very expensive, but Eido was a man who somehow embodied all the images westerners brought to the idea of a Zen master, and ever since he'd left Japan, he'd been able to attract support. Soon after he began his search for a zendo, a wealthy couple showed up unannounced at his door and offered him almost unlimited funds. The present building, where Andra and I stand waiting, is the result of their munificence. It is an elegant brownstone that once served as the embassy of a Latin-American country. Six years ago the first meetings of Eido's zazen group attracted ten people on a good night. More than two hundred attended the ceremony when this building opened two years ago.

As always when about to take a further step into Zen, I am stricken with exaggerated, slightly regressive, contradictory emotions: hope and dread, excitement and timidity, romanticism that persists even when it embarrasses me. Every time I glance at the carved wooden doors and the plaque inlaid with Japanese calligraphy that hangs above the entrance, my breath quickens and I feel the sort of "butterflies" I felt as a child on the night before I left for summer camp. It's as if I'm about to take a trip instead of simply entering a building, as if I'm about be challenged or endangered, confronted with another culture.

At precisely five forty-five, the doors are opened by a tall, stocky fellow with a barrel chest and a great mop of blond hair that hangs to his shoulders. He is wearing an ankle-length, coffee-colored robe and horn-rimmed glasses on which the screw at one of the corner hinges has been replaced by a safety pin. His back is straight, his shoulders slightly arched in the manner of a soldier at attention. So austere is his presence that his languid southern accent seems anomalous, like a streak of color in a black-and-white film. "Shoes in the rack, coats in the closet.

Take any cushion in the zendo except the ones at the head of
the line."

It is an insular space we enter, a silence dense and palpable. Oiled wood floors, sandalwood incense, shoji screens at
the door of the zendo and within, two long rows of tatami mats
on either side with thirty sets of black cushions like those on
which Andra and I sit at home. In the center of the room, a
massive bronze gong, three feet high and a couple of feet in
diameter, rests on an embroidered brocade cushion which in
turn sits on an elaborately carved wooden stand. On the wall
opposite the door, the altar is a simple platform about three
feet high with a water bowl, an incense stand, a candleholder, a
vase containing half-a-dozen yellow roses, and an exquisite
black standing Buddha nearly four feet tall.

Only two cushions are occupied when we enter. Facing
the center, a black-robed, baldheaded American monk sits
nearest the door and our friend, Sara—also in a black robe—
faces the wall at the head of the line, next to the altar. To my
surprise, my legs begin to hurt as soon as I take my seat on the
cushion. How is this possible when at home I am now able to
sit for forty-five minutes, even an hour, without discomfort? If
I were a more experienced Zen student, I would know that this
sort of pain is not unusual. I may be experienced at sitting
alone but this is the first time I've sat in a formal Zen environment and the first time I've sat with others. The weight of tradition is all around me, the weight of authority. Time is kept by
someone else. I cannot move without disturbing others. Sitting
next to me, the young man in polyester pants is breathing heavily and wearing a reeking, malodorous aftershave. Each new
person who enters the zendo breaks my concentration. I hear
every footstep, every rustle of skirt or trousers, every throat

cleared, every swallow. You could say I've simply entered into a social context, but what I'm doing with these strangers is extremely intimate, solitary, internal. Soon enough, I'll come to understand that this sort of communality is integral to Zen, but my knees, like the butterflies I felt earlier, are telling me that I'm anything but comfortable with it.

One thing is clear: no one in this room is unaware of the essential rules about movement which are followed here as in every zendo in the world: move if you must, but be assured that if you do it too much you will be asked to leave. Few of us can understand that, according to Zen logic, this prohibition has more to do with freedom—from selfishness, self-indulgence, the tyranny of discomfort, etc.—than inhibition, but even though most people in this room are probably beginners like myself, and many no doubt are as uncomfortable as I am, the room remains absolutely still.

Sitting begins with the four chimes of a gentle, high-pitched brass bell, or "inkin." After forty minutes, it sounds again and a pair of wooden sticks are clapped together, signaling us to stand. The gunshot sound of the sticks is especially shocking after the gentleness of the inkin, but Zen of course specializes in such juxtaposition. In monasteries, these sticks are struck in complex rhythms to summon monks to meals or zazen. So consistently do they follow or precede the inkin that one never hears the clap of the sticks or the chime of the bell without expecting its contradiction.

Unfamiliar with all of this and fearful of calling attention to ourselves, Andra and I watch our neighbors to see what we should do now. Rising from our cushions, we face the opposite row and bow, or "gassho," with palms together at our chins, turn to our left and begin the walking meditation that is called "kinhin." It is a slow and studied walk, circling the zendo three times, eyes on the feet of the person ahead. At one point, the monitor calls, "Mind in your feet! Don't look around!" but otherwise we walk in silence. Like so much else I have encountered tonight, kinhin strikes me as rigid and slightly militaristic, but eventually I will learn that, like all Zen procedure, it is entirely practical, a means by which one can stretch the legs without interrupting one's meditation.

Sitting down for the second period, I am not only free of knee pain but off on another romantic excursion, struck with thoughts about the "power" and the "energy" of this atmosphere, leaping as I so often do on the cushion to dreams of ultimate peace and concentration. How ironic that a practice so insistently inclined toward moderation should generate such hyperbole. A minute later, the monitor stands and walks behind us with the "keisaku," or "helping stick." When he uses it, smartly striking the fleshy area between the shoulder blade and neck, it makes a smacking sound, not unlike the wooden sticks, but the knowledge that this noise is produced by flesh makes it, to say the least, arresting and intimidating. If you're dozing or dreaming or, like me, spacing out on fantasy, the sound alone can wake you like an alarm clock. This is one reason it is called the helping stick. The other, as I'll discover soon enough, is that the points of contact on the shoulders are energizing in the manner of acupuncture or shiatsu.

Facing the wall, I cannot see the man who wields the stick, but, unaware that only those are struck who ask to be (by placing palms together in gassho), I am fearful as I sense his approach and relieved when I am spared. My relief, however, is short-lived. In lieu of the stick, the monitor corrects my posture, and the readjustment is far more disconcerting than any pain he might inflict upon my shoulders.

Over the past few months, I have become more and more relaxed and confident, indeed, even a little vain about my posture. I know that I'm no paragon on the cushion, but considering how inept I was when I began to sit, my present level of stability seems almost miraculous to me. Corrected now by the monitor, I realize to my astonishment that I have been listing at an angle of fifteen or twenty degrees. Straight by his perception, I feel, by my own, like I could topple onto the person sitting next to me. How is it that my sense of myself has nothing to do with reality? Is the monitor perverse? Cross-eyed? Playing games with my mind? Perhaps the "adjustment" he offered is some sort of exotic Zen teaching meant to humble my intellect or undermine my self-perception. Whatever it means, his adjustment destroys the tranquility and alertness I had begun to feel. Such is the discomfort in which he leaves me that I can think of nothing but holding myself erect.

A few minutes later, the bell is rung, and we all turn around to find Eido Roshi before us. He wears a black robe with a brown ropelike belt and a strange black bag around his neck. In his perfect Lotus posture, with his shaved head rising from his robe, he looks like a black mountain with a snow-covered peak. He is a handsome, unblinking Japanese man with a bull neck and narrow eyes, and, as Watts and Krishnamurti once did, he sends me off on a foray into the Rorschach test that such people become when they take on the mantle of spiritual authority and invite the gaze of impressionable eyes like my own. One moment I see gentleness and compassion, the next an icy, almost cruel detachment. Masculinity, femininity.

Playfulness, anger. Paternalism, indifference. Nothing is constant except my own yearning for a durable description of him.

He arrived in New York in 1964, just a few years after
Suzuki Roshi. He is one of the disciples or what we call
"Dharma heirs" of the famous Soen Nakagawa Roshi, who in
the last ten years, making regular visits to the United States in
order to lead retreats, has attracted a number of devoted students and, at least among the cognoscenti, established a reputation that is nothing short of mythical. Soen and one or two
other teachers have laid the foundation for Zen in America,
and now Eido and Suzuki, along with several younger teachers
who have arrived in the last few years from Japan and Korea,
will begin the long, endlessly argued process of its Western ad-
aptation. All of these teachers are male, disenchanted with the
institutional Zen of their native countries, and captivated by
the innocence and enthusiasm, what Suzuki calls "the beginner's mind," of American students. They have also discovered
that at least a few of these students have the willingness and
the financial means to support almost any vision of Zen they
suggest.

Gazing around the zendo, Eido searches faces individu-
ally, waiting for us to settle down and become uncomfortable
before he begins to speak. His English is adequate, but conso-
nants defeat him, and sometimes, as when he says "crap" instead of "clap," or "horee day" for "holy day," his mistakes are
comical. They elicit, however, no laughter from his audience. If
anything, perhaps because they put us slightly on the defensive,
his errors seem to enhance his authority. Perhaps too there is
something a little mesmerizing about a man who speaks with
confidence in a language not completely mastered. He is like a
great foreign movie with inadequate subtitles. Though it is our

language he struggles with, it is we who reach out, who fail if we fail to understand. Then too we are dealing here with ideas that question language itself. Is there not, circulating in this room, an ethos according to which it is a virtue to be less than perfectly articulate?

"Let us understand one simple fact," he says. "Nothing is permanent. Some days we feel good, some days we feel terrible. Nothing endures. It is because of long years of habit that we prefer the good days and dislike the bad, but all of us know that this kind of thinking is a waste of time. In Zen practice, we are learning to be less judgmental, more single-minded, to accept what we call the 'is-ness' of reality. Things as they are. You could say that we are learning to give up our cleverness, our critical minds. In a sense, we are learning to be fools."

He shifts on his cushion and closes his eyes, pausing for nearly half a minute. He pronounces his *i*'s as *e*'s, and many of his words have extra syllables, like codas. "Ask" is "ahskah" and "as" is "asah." He also has a habit of hissing his *s,* so that a word like "sitting," for example, begins with a sound like a leaking tire. When all these habits combine in a single word, it can lengthen remarkably, stretching out like a sentence unto itself. "Sitting," for example becomes "s-s-s-seating-gah," and a long word like "con-ah-s-s-senta-rahshun" becomes spatial, architectural, like a corridor or a stairway. "What does it mean to become a fool? It means learning to live and learning to die. As Master Hakuin said, if we die once while we are still alive, we can truly live and we will never die again. To die in this sense is what it means to become a fool. It's not about giving up intelligence, but giving up resistance, giving up one's endless judgment and discrimination. It means following one's breath, practicing zazen without adding your commentaries, judgments, criticisms or doubts. This is what Hakuin calls 'dying.' It is the essence of Zen!"

After the talk, I ask Sara to point out the fellow who straightened my posture. By now I've swallowed the pride he hurt. The way I see it, we're playing basketball and he's found a flaw in my jump shot. I want to thank him and seek his guidance. How does one go about correcting a problem like this? Are there books on the subject? Exercises? Teachers who specialize in the lotus posture?

Street clothes over his arm, he stands outside the bathroom, waiting to change from his robe. He is tall and thin, with sunken cheeks and a thick mustache and small dark eyes under a bushy, undivided eyebrow. According to Sara, he is a psychiatrist named Ralph Kostenbach who's been sitting for more than fifteen years. "Yeah, I know who you are," he says when I introduce myself. "How'd you get that crooked spine? Accident or something?"

That I don't back off I can only explain as another symptom of the romanticism that surrounds all things connected with Zen for me. New as I am to the practice, I cannot believe that people who sit together are anything but brothers and sisters to each other, that a man like this, with all his years of experience, should feel anything but benevolent toward a beginner like myself. But Kostenbach shakes his head when I ask his advice. "Sorry, pal, I can't help you. But I can tell you one thing— if you want to study Zen, you better get yourself straightened out. Zen is posture and posture is Zen. With a back like that, you're wasting your time on the cushion."

·   ·   ·

"Larry-san, you make decision about your girlfriend?"

"Yes, Roshi, it looks like we're splitting up."

"OK. Now you concentrate zazen! Put sausage in the freezer."

"Well, I don't know, Roshi. I'm still suffering it. I feel a kind of terror I've made the wrong decision."

"Larry-san, please! You went to airport, buy chicket Japan. Now you on plane Pacific Ocean. Too late France! Too late China! Please you learn one direction! Don't waste time!"

. . .

A few nights after my visit to the zendo, I have dinner with my brother David at a midtown restaurant. Now thirty-eight, he is married, with two children, a psychoanalyst with a large private practice. He still sees Kelman, as he has for the past twenty years, but now their sessions fall under the rubric of "training analysis." He teaches at the institute where Kelman is dean, lectures at psychoanalytic conferences, and his monographs have begun to appear in the literature. Widely read in the literature of Zen, Tibetan Buddhism, Vedanta, etc., he is, like Kelman, considered a maverick in his field, a staunch advocate of the "alternative" psychoanalysis which is influenced by Eastern thought.

Just as with Kelman, I have admonished myself not to speak of these matters with him, but within minutes after we sit down, I am describing, just as I did in yesterday's session with Kelman, my visit to the zendo and my impressions of Eido Roshi. Everything I say is exaggerated and romantic, but I can't contain myself. Ever since I heard the roshi speak, I've been overheated with conviction, joyous with encountering a man I

take to be the realization of all the truth and energy I have
skirted on the cushion. How can I pretend to a detachment I
don't feel?

Visibly restless and impatient, David finally interrupts
me. "I know about the zendo. You're not the first person who's
been there, you know. I've got a patient who's been going there
for years and one or two others who've tried it out. The whole
scene is very troubling to me. You put a guy like this on a pedestal and surround him with a lot of needy, dependent people,
what you've got is a nightmare of transference. Add to that all
the accoutrements of institutional religion, all these rules and
rituals which originated in another culture, and the mix you
get, I'm sorry, Larry, it's almost lethal. I don't know why'd
you'd go to a place like that when you can meditate at home."

Though he doesn't meditate himself, he encourages his
patients to do so, and often, in his writing, suggests that psychoanalysts need to "increase their tolerance for silence, both
within themselves and in their dialogue with patients." Like
Dad, he's a great admirer of Krishnamurti, and now he recom-
mends one of his recent books to me. "What K points out is
that, like any other human activity, spiritual practice can be
driven by fear, and if it is, there's no chance for growth or
breakthrough. Isn't it obvious? The effort of a confused mind,
what can it lead to but more confusion? To tell you the truth,
I'm worried about you, Larry. You aren't working. You
haven't finished anything since your novel was published. All
you talk about is Zen. Isn't it time you asked yourself what's
really going on?"

A few days later, I receive a letter from my father. David
has told him about our recent conversation, and he too is ap-
prehensive about me.

You know, Larry, I have had a lifetime of dabbling—searching for that unknown thing or quality that will assuage our anxieties—and that feeling of worthlessness endemic to all of us. I keep remembering what Krishnamurti has said so many times: "You can sit like that for 10,000 years—straight back—lotus position and all—it will come to nothing."—The problem as we know is the perennial contradiction—as long as there is a meditator seeking something thru meditation—that's that. What I cannot get over—is the fact that you know all of this—yet you are still bamfoozled by this Japanese teacher—hypnotized—because deep down you are terribly afraid of missing something that would answer the riddle for you.

.   .   .

I've been sitting more since my visit to the zendo—three and sometimes four times a day—but I still feel a need to push harder. Every time I remember Eido Roshi, regal and fierce in his black robes, I accuse myself of holding back, playing it safe. I see him as a man who's broken through the morass of thought, every trace of fear and neurosis, and, now that I can envision this possibility, my own life seems pale and hollow, a hopeless alternative to what I might accomplish if I could only commit myself to Zen. On the other hand, it's clear to me that my resolution and discipline are not strong enough to go further as long as I'm living in the city. There's too much comfort, too much distraction, too many avenues of escape. Even Andra, it seems to me, undermines my zeal, if only because she offers me companionship. The only way I'll touch the heart of this practice is by putting myself in total isolation, a situation where I can't do anything else.

Fortunately, David has recently purchased a house on Cape Cod. Less than a mile from the ocean, surrounded by pine and oak forest, it is in the midst of vacation land in summer, but off-season it is cold and dismal, totally isolated, the ideal place for the sort of retreat I need just now. A few days after our dinner together, I call David to ask if I can use it.

It is late April, and he says I can have the house until the beginning of June. Within forty-eight hours, I set off with my supplies and my cushions and the only two books I read these days—*Zen Mind, Beginner's Mind* and Beckett's trilogy: *Molloy, Malone Dies* and *The Unnameable*. It's a damp day, unseasonably cold. Near New York, trees display an occasional sign of spring, but further north they are completely bare. My state of mind is split between anxiety and exhilaration until, as I cross the border between Rhode Island and Massachusetts, anxiety overwhelms me. It's as if I've only now registered what I'm doing, the lonely abyss toward which I'm headed. How is it I always get trapped in these transformation fantasies, choosing precisely the course of action that frightens me the most? For an instant, I think of turning back, but then, once more, Eido Roshi looms before me, and my familiar Zen voice lectures me on the dangers of cowardice and weakness. Long ago, from basketball and tennis, I learned that dread could be a source of motivation. Now Zen has made of such inversion something very like a principle. Like Beckett in relation to my work, it is the standard against which I measure myself, an endless source of self-motivation on the one hand, self-loathing on the other. It's as if nothing fires my conviction like recognition of its absence. But what of the "self-acceptance" that is so crucial to Zen? What of its rejection of judgment and vanity? Not the least of the ironies of the spiritual path is that every step toward deeper engagement is driven by forces that contradict it.

In addition to my cushions and my books, I have brought my diaries with me, all fifteen years of them, nearly a thousand steno pads neatly packed, in chronological order, in four green plastic garbage bags secured with yellow plastic ties. For years I've been addicted to these notebooks, using them to catalogue my thoughts, analyze my conflicts, record my pleasures and disappointments. Now I mean to destroy them. Ever since beginning zazen, I have seen these pages as the ultimate symptom of the disease that zazen aims to cure, a bridge that must be burned if one is to take this practice seriously.

I have also brought a supply of food that I believe to be consistent with my new way of life: brown rice and oatmeal and nuts and dried fruit and soy sauce and sesame oil. Since my meat habit, like my diary, seems antithetical to Buddhism, I have resolved to become a vegetarian. Andra, of course, collapsed with laughter when informed of this decision. Better than anyone, she knows what such deconditioning will cost me. Since childhood—probably because my mother cooked them down to tasteless, unrecognizable slime—I have been unable to eat cooked vegetables. Andra says I'll be the first vegetarian in history who doesn't eat vegetables. Watch and see, I tell her. I'll get by on cereals, nuts and salads, and who knows, since Zen is changing everything else about me, maybe it will teach me to eat vegetables.

. . .

The Seven Samurai, Roshi's favorite movie, is playing at a theater near the zendo, but its schedule conflicts with evening zazen. When I suggest that I or one of the other senior students can keep time and ring the bell for one evening so that he can play hooky, he is shocked. "This my job, Larry-san. Not yours. You book-writer. My job stay here, keep time, take care zendo. Only sick keep me away."

This is mid-January, the winter of 1982, four years since he arrived in New York and opened our zendo in Soho. During this time, with the exception of two trips to Japan, he hasn't missed a single sitting—six to eight each morning and six-thirty to eight-thirty every evening. Three months ago, after arriving from Japan at three in the afternoon, he was on his cushion for evening sitting, half an hour early as usual. I'm thinking how often he seems to contradict himself on matters like this. All his teachings, on the one hand, are about spontaneity, being open, the dangers of orthodoxy and ritual, but with regard to his own vows, precepts and responsibilities, he is absolutely unbending.

"Roshi, you're always telling us about the dangers of attachment. Why are you so attached to the schedule here?"

"All attachment not same, Larry-san. Buddha, he have great attachment, great desire. Save all sentient beings. How he do that without attachment, without desire? Selfish attachment very bad, but attach for others—wonderful! Understand? If you have no attachment, nothing complish at all. You want to write your book without attachment? 'Today I no feel like work! Maybe I go cinema!' Impossible! Same with zazen. Must sit with pain, conquer physically mentally. If mind tight, into tight! Never surrender! Great attachment! Not for yourself! For others! If not, you wasting time!"

A wave of anger rises in me. It's not so much his contradictions that bother me but his belief in willpower. It's as if he believes that there is a part of the mind that can recognize weakness and surmount it. Doesn't this amount to a kind of blithe indifference to psychology and conditioning, a belief that one can whisk away one's insufficiencies? Isn't this the ultimate, narcissistic fallacy? Where is such advice directed if not to the same mind in which weakness—and selfishness, cowardice, laziness, etc.—is generated? Is Zen, after all, a kind of neurological gamesmanship by which one part of the brain is enlisted to do battle against the rest?

"You see girlfriend?"

"No, we haven't seen each other for a month now."

"Your mind OK?"

"No, Roshi. Not too good. I'm pretty depressed."

"Yes, energy weak now. I can hear! When you come up stairs for morning sitting, very weak sound on step. Voice on the phone—dark, discourage. Must cheerful, Larry-san! Energy weak, soon become sick."

"What can I do about it? What do you do when your energy is weak?"

"Don't keep any mind. Don't hold onto anything. This moment, this moment. No fixed idea. No pictures. Anyway, don't worry, Larry-san. Be patient. To be born is to suffer. Remember? Now you suffer girlfriend. Next week you suffer something else."

"Yes, but why all this suffering? Buddhism is supposed to help, isn't it? I feel as if I've learned nothing from this practice."

"Of course Buddhism help! Zen man always transcend suffering!"

"Transcend? How? How does a Zen man transcend suffering?"

"He *take* it."

Years have passed since he made that statement, yet I've never heard a better summation of the contradictory, but to my mind inarguable, logic of sitting meditation—that the only durable freedom from pain lies in its absolute acceptance.

. . .

The house is musty and damp after its uninhabited winter. A lattice of cobwebs fills the doorway and sticks to my face as I enter. As my eyes scan the desolate scene in front of me, I am overwhelmed, once again, with horror at what I'm doing. Not surprisingly, I remember that I meant to buy a pint of ice cream to get me through this first evening. I turn back toward the car, but I'm halted in my tracks by the imperious Zen voice that lectured me on the highway. Now it offers up a quick, if elementary, overview of the Buddha's ideas—or my ideas of the Buddha's ideas—on pleasure, desire and self-indulgence. "The sage who overcomes everything, who knows everything, who is attached to nothing, who is completely free because he has renounced everything, who is without thirst—he is the true sage. This man I call 'one who lives alone.' " Such words can be as powerful and effective as pep talks I heard from my basketball coach in high school, but for me, just now, they sound like nothing so much as piety and self-denial. Returning to my car, I head for the grocery store. I buy a candy bar and eat it as I shop, fill my cart with hamburger rolls, potato chips, beer, and ice cream. With each item I drop into the cart, I feel as if I've struck a blow for independence and virility. Don't speak to me of koans or the Backwards Law. As far as I'm concerned, the battle lines of Zen are drawn through the middle of this grocery store.

Still defiant when I return to the house, I leave my cushions in the trunk when I unpack the car. For the next two days, I lie around the house, reading Beckett and writing in my diary. Echoing my father and my brother, the voices I hear are a jeremiad against the dangers of Zen. I think of nothing but how little writing I've managed since I developed my unfortunate meditation habit. The more Beckett I read, the more convinced I am that Zen practice has done for my work what Watts once did for my basketball and Krishnamurti for my tennis. Could anyone in his right mind imagine Beckett, or for that matter any great writer, sitting on a cushion and counting his breath until a timer in his underwear drawer gives him permission to get up?

But even in the midst of this tirade, the urge toward practice resumes, and amazingly enough, it is Beckett himself who engenders it. Suddenly, as I read him one morning, his lines are more than literature. It seems to me he generates an energy, an immediate concrete reality that permeates my body and my mind. What is it? How does he convey such urgency, such uncertainty and impermanence? His words are closer to Buddhism than the Buddha's!

I read Beckett all day and late into the evening. Next morning, my third on the Cape, I wake up in a panic. Emptiness consumes me, the looming weight of self-disgust. It's as if I've seen that there is no difference between me and Beckett's characters, no more shape or purpose to my life, no more continuity, no less self-deception. With scarcely a thought, I take my cushions from the car, clean and mop the screen porch, create a place where I can sit. It is cold and damp, and the wind off the ocean is rattling the screens. My clothes are damp when I take them from the drawer. I put on long underwear, sweat pants, two pair of socks, two T-shirts and a hooded sweatshirt, and sit down in half-lotus, facing a grainy unpainted plywood wall. As

usual when I haven't sat for a while, my back and legs are very
stiff. The panic, if anything, is worse than before. I tell myself:
ten minutes, maybe fifteen. But the light is coming up. I can
smell the ocean. My breath is going in and out, and at least part
of my mind is following. For the first four days, I sit two 45-
minute periods, morning and evening, but on the fifth day,
when the timer rings after my first sitting in the morning, I do
not want to stop. I walk outside for a few minutes to stretch my
legs, then return to my cushion again. By the end of the first
week, I am sitting four hours a day, and after another week, six.
The practice seems different from before, at once simpler and
more difficult, less prone to insight and intellectual excitement,
like distance-running when you've gone so far that you think of
nothing but the length of your stride or the placement of your
feet. The more I sit, the more I need to. At times I feel as if on a
pendulum, swinging between expansion and contraction,
surges of power followed almost at once by all-consuming feelings of despair. My mind seems discontinuous, and the gaps are
growing bigger all the time. Now and then, they fill with ec-
stasy, my mind vast and no thought lingering, but far more
often they fill with old grudges, petty thoughts, food and sex
fantasies, mind-boggling levels of self-importance, a level of
fear which, without the cushion, would be unbearable. Each
increase in sitting time evokes the familiar ache of homesick-
ness, as if any step in the direction of this practice is a step away
from safety or habit, the dream of sanctuary or stability, all
those images of refuge one accumulates and guards with a vengeance from the moment one leaves the womb. In the morning,
looking toward the empty hours that lie ahead, I always feel a
kind of terror. The idea that I will be sitting for the next three
or four hours continues to be shocking. Though any instant can

stretch and deepen, I never know whether such expansion, what feels like once-and-for-all freedom from time, will quiet or frighten me. Gradually, I become more and more disciplined, tightening my schedule like a vise, eliminating every trace of empty time. Sometimes it seems as if I've discovered discipline for the first time, the power not only to shape my time but to maintain my concentration in the face of mood, discomfort or other sensations that undermined me in in the past, the most powerful weapon I've ever had against laziness, passivity, self-indulgence. Up at five, one chapter of *Zen Mind, Beginner's Mind,* then two 45-minute periods of zazen. After sitting, a three-mile run, counting my breath all the while. Shower, have breakfast, sit three 45-minute periods, read some Beckett, sit again. After lunch, a walk, then sit again—four 45-minute periods—until dinner. After dinner, an hour of Beckett, then sit until it's time for bed. Eating nothing but rice and cereal, I am always hungry, but I am learning to think of hunger as a greater pleasure than its alleviation. Over and over, like a mantra, I repeat the words of a Zen master I recently read: "What is pain?—a matter of opinion!" The Zen voice, never satisfied, pushing me further, still accusing me of laziness and self-indulgence, is now my ally. I have no urge to resist it. While eating, I try to *attend* to each bite, each swallow, each taste. I count my breath on the toilet and in the shower and before falling asleep at night.

Needless to say, such attention is a two-edged sword. I am beginning to taste the way in which meditation can reverse it self, becoming fixed and rigid rather than a means of letting go. The more I sit, the more aware I am of the impermanence of my thoughts and emotions, and the more I'm seized by a need to control them. Often as not, in "following" my mind, I am actually trying to stop it. Which makes its movement, often as not, even more unbearable, etc. Regret, of course, is a constant. Either my effort seems insufficient or my pleasure is such that I cannot bear its dissolution. Now and then, I hear David's voice warning me that I've slipped into a sort of boot-camp masochism, a frenzy of control just this side of catatonic, but in general such opinions are no match for my exhilaration. So fierce is my conviction that, even when my Zen voice itself attacks it (for romanticism, exaggeration, pride, etc.), it doesn't waver at all.

. . .

Halfway into my third week, I open one of the garbage bags and take out an old diary. It was written fifteen years ago, but in mood and point of view it is not a whole lot different from those I've written recently. It is punishing to read, an irrefutable confirmation of Zen's argument against self-consciousness and analytic mind. After reading just a few pages, I pile all my steno pads into the car and take them to the dump. Three garbage bags, sixteen years of self-analysis and what I took to be revelation. A huge compactor closes on them like a set of teeth, crushes and grinds for a moment, then drops them into a dumpster parked behind the building. I feel a kind of giddiness. It's as if the compactor has chewed up my self-consciousness. As if the I-me separation on which self-consciousness depends has been compressed into singularity. After all, what am I doing on my cushion if not destroying my diary breath by breath, uniting that which watches with that which it presumes to watch?

It is later that day I get stuck in the lotus posture. Returning to the cushion, I am convinced that everything I seek in Zen is suddenly within my grasp. All I have to do is push a little harder, cast aside my caution and timidity. When my half-lotus, as often, begins to feel off-balance, I lean back and pull my right leg onto my left so that both feet, soles up, are high on opposite thighs. Until now, it has never occurred to me that this posture—the Zen equivalent of the four-minute mile—would ever be available to me, but such is my intoxication at this moment that my body seems infinitely supple. What are physical limitations, what indeed is the body itself, in the face of unobstructed concentration? My chest pounds. I am short of breath, so awash in sensuality that for an instant I feel—literally!—on the verge of orgasm. It's as if I have unlocked a vault within myself, released an energy that dwarfs anything I've known before. Ignoring the pain in my knees and ankles—how can I call it pain when I am feeling so much pleasure?—I sit like this until the timer sounds, at least another forty-five minutes. And then, when I try to move, I feel as if the lower half of my body has been amputated. My legs and feet are completely numb, paralyzed. It is unimaginable that I shall ever move them again. I consider screaming for help until I remember that the nearest neighbor is five miles away. I see David—shaking his head, reflecting sadly that I'd still be alive if only I had listened to him—arriving in June to find my bones in a neat little mound on my cushion. Five or six minutes will pass before I am able to take a foot in my hand and move it just a hair in the direction of my knee, nearly fifteen before I can stand erect and take a few steps, more than ten years before I attempt this posture again.

. . .

Five days later, I return to New York in a spirit I take for humility. In fact, I am feeling heroic, ecstatic, dreaming of monas-

tic life, going to Japan, a year or a decade of study with Soen
Roshi, my triumphant return as his successor—Larry Roshi!
Why not? Haven't I been through a trial by fire and come out
whole on the other side? Have I ever known such equanimity?
It does not hurt that more than one friend remarks the
change—"I've never seen you so calm!"—that he or she per-
ceives in me. How can I doubt the permanence of these
changes, how suspect that I have not finally left my old self behind? It isn't long before I'm imagining friends alert for signs
of my transformation, watching me like a war hero just back
from the front. Self-consciousness makes me mannered, pedan-
tic, and finally, pretentious. Within two or three days, it begins
to seem as if I have gained nothing from my retreat but exacer-
bation of my shortcomings. Depression sets in. For a couple of
days, I can barely get out of bed. My Zen voice lectures me on
exaggeration and romanticism: "How can you imagine that
you've learned anything from Zen when you turn a simple one-
month retreat into an exercise in vanity and self-importance?"
I am eating meat again, also ice cream and cookies and candy
bars and anything else I can lay my hands on. Within two
weeks, I've regained eight of the twelve pounds I lost at the
Cape. Of course, I am, courtesy of my Zen voice, ashamed of
myself. Furthermore, also courtesy of my Zen voice—which
loathes nothing so much as self-loathing—ashamed of being
ashamed. When I search for the insights I had on retreat—all
those epiphanies about Beckett and time, memory and impermanence—I find nothing but hollow, intellectual fragments,
like pieces of small talk overheard on the street. Not too long
ago, I could have discussed all this with Andra, but her Zen has
become so serious and guarded that she refuses to speak of it
with me. "I'm tired of talking," she says. "I want to do it on the

cushion." Spiritual dialogue, once a kind of foreplay for us, is suddenly forbidden, and our cushions, which used to bring us closer, are like caves in which we sit alone. In fact, though we are a year away from realizing it, this is the beginning of the end of our marriage.

Within a week, I have stopped sitting altogether. My mind spins with the argument between the Zen voice and its opposite. I've met with David and I've met with Kelman and, needless to say, they staunchly support the latter. Is Zen good for me or bad for me, a practice in humility or an exercise in narcissism? Finally, the argument becomes *interesting.* I go to my office and write about it: my Zen attraction, my Zen resistance, Beckett and Zen, writing and Zen, everything I remember about my retreat, everything that's happened since it ended. Fascinating! Brilliant! The best writing I've ever done! Three feverish hours at my desk, fifty-five pages in a brand-new notebook I've bought expressly for these reflections. I tell myself that this is not a "diary" but a "journal," the beginning perhaps of the book on Zen that I have been wanting to write since the first time I sat on a cushion. I am wrong, of course. It is a brand-new diary I have begun, and I have been keeping it ever since.

The problems are solved, not by giving new information, but by arranging what we have always known. Philosophy is a battle against the bewitchment of our intelligence by means of language. —LUDWIG WITTGENSTEIN

Soon after my return from the Cape, Andra and I receive the first of what, in future years, will become a nearly constant stream of Zen fund-raising letters. It is a glossy, professional job promoting a monastery called Dai Bosatsu Zendo, which is to be the country training center for Eido Roshi's zendo on the Upper East Side. On one page, in his black robes, ever so slightly resembling a gunfighter in a Western movie, Eido Roshi stands with hands folded at his chest, and on another,

ethereal in white robes, Soen Roshi, his teacher, "the monastery's founder and former abbot of the Ryutaku-ji, in Mishima,
Japan," offers an image so much in contrast that he might be a
print from Eido's negative. A drawing on the cover shows a
classic Japanese monastery with white walls and a soaring black
roof. According to the brochure, it consists of four intercon-
nected buildings, an interior space of more than 25,000 square
feet. It is located in the Catskill Mountains, some four-and-a-
half hours from New York City, 1,700 acres in the midst of the
resort area that used to be called the Borscht Belt. Clearly, Zen
has come a long way from walk-up apartments in Greenwich
Village, not to mention a patch of grass beneath a Mucalinda
tree. One day, says the brochure, Dai Bosatsu will house a
zendo, a lecture hall, a library, student rooms, kitchen, and dining room, "along with all other facilities required for traditional Zen life."

I am repulsed by the grandiosity of this project as well as
its tab—more than $5 million, according to the brochure. Can
anyone in his right mind believe that such an institution is required for a practice that consists in nothing more than sitting
on a cushion and staring at the wall? No way I'll go near such a
place, much less give money to support it.

But I ought to know by now that, where Zen is concerned, this sort of feeling is volatile. Later that evening, while
sitting on my cushion, I remember the brochure in an entirely
different light. It seems a kind of miracle that such a building
will exist for no other purpose but to offer large numbers of
people the experience of zazen. As soon as I rise from my cushion, I write a check which—though minuscule, of course, beside the mountain of money Eido needs—is by ten times at
least the largest donation I've ever made. Even more surprising

than its size is the exhilaration it engenders. I feel jubilant, complete, as if this simple act of writing a check has eliminated some fundamental resistance or hypocrisy that stood between me and Zen practice.

In future years, I will meet many spiritual seekers who have taken the road I have just discovered. Practices like Zen generate equal amounts of gratitude and resistance, and philanthropy can often seem an easy way beyond the contradiction. It can also be a subterfuge, a substitute for genuine commitment. Writing a check is a whole lot easier, and safer, than sitting on a cushion. Many students use money to seduce teachers, and many teachers are diabolical at seducing them into doing so. Is it any wonder that religious conviction is such fertile soil for every sort of exploitation and distortion or that, where these matters are concerned, it is often impossible to distinguish between generosity and pathology?

.   .   .

Roshi has invited me to a Chinese restaurant for dinner. We've taken our seats, ordered Chinese beer, and now we're studying the menus. On the table between us, he's placed a shoe box he brought with him. Tomorrow he's meeting with the "countant" who will prepare his first U.S. tax return, and the box contains the receipts and canceled checks he's asked me to help him organize.

"Larry-san?"

"What, Roshi?"

"What happen sex-book lady?"

"Sex-book lady?"

"You know, small one, dark hair, much paint on lips. We meet at Elephant."

Finally, I remember: "small one" is a friend of mine to whom I introduced him three or four months ago when we were having breakfast at the café, a writer who recently made a lot of money with a how-to sex manual. Despite the fact that he can't remember the names of most of his students and has trouble finding his way around the city, he rarely forgets this sort of incidental meeting.

"Nothing happened to her. Why do you ask?"

"You meet her?"

"No, not recently."

"But you say you dinner with her!"

"Well, you know, Roshi, that was just politeness. People always say things like that. 'Let's have dinner!' 'See you soon!' "

His eyes spread, and his cheeks, as often they do at moments of astonishment, puff out like balloons. He looks like a circus clown. "You mean . . . you not want to see her? But why you promise? Why you insincere? You losing virtue, Larry-san!"

This is the second time he's used that phrase with me tonight. A few minutes ago, I gave him another shock when we found ourselves in the bathroom together, and he saw me about to leave without washing my hands. It was a tiny bathroom—urinal, toilet and sink—hardly big enough for one person, much less two. He blocked the door and refused to let me leave. "You not wash your hands?"

I told him I'd washed before leaving the zendo, after evening sitting.

"But just you make peepee!"

"Yeah, sure. But you know, Roshi, I didn't get my hands dirty."

He rolled his eyes as if in pain. "Larry-san! Please! Every morning you do same! You think I not hear? Up the stairs, every day into bathroom, make peepee before you come zendo, never wash your hands! I hear from my cushion—flush toilet but no sound washing! And then you come zendo, bow to Buddha with dirty hands! Where's your mind, Larry-san? You losing lot of virtue!"

"Virtue" is a word he uses a lot, and I've never quite understood what he means. I've heard him say, for example, that one "loses virtue" by spitting on the street, wasting food, being dishonest, or, as in these cases, being insincere or inattentive. Any sort of laziness or selfishness will show up on your virtue-register. Indeed, despite the fact that he seems leery of morality in general, and any hint of righteousness arouses his disdain, his ethical system is almost Calvinist in its extensiveness and specificity.

"Roshi, can you tell me what you mean by 'virtue'?"

" 'Virtue'? I have no idea."

"But you're always using the word!"

"Well, maybe too much talk."

"Is 'virtue' another word for 'merit'?"

"Maybe."

"Energy?"

"Of course!"

"What about 'Buddha nature'? Is it another word for 'Buddha nature'?"

"Don't be silly, Larry-san. Buddha nature empty, formless. Virtue is phenomena. Three-dimensional world. Relative world. Buddha nature absolute. Never change! Virtue change all the time."

"But don't the sutras tell us that the absolute and the relative are one? That form is emptiness and emptiness is form?"
"Too much thinking, Larry-san. You losing virtue now."

. . .

Soon after we send our donation, Andra and I receive an invitation to participate in a one-day sitting at Dai Bosatsu. Scheduled three weeks hence, it is a special event to honor the visit from Japan of an illustrious Roshi named Yamada Mumon, the abbot of Myoshin-ji, one of the great Kyoto monasteries. Within two days, we have rearranged our schedules, reserved a rental car, obtained maps of the region, and once again plugged our minds into the potent Zen generator and its alternating currents of excitement and dread. We also escalate our sitting time and commence a desperate stretching routine in preparation for what we imagine to be the murderous schedule of the monastery.

If the specter of the monastery inspires my practice, it also leads me, out of anxiety perhaps, to ask some bottom-line questions: What is this habit to which I'm devoting so much time? How has it affected my life? Am I less depressed than I used to be? I think so. Less confused? I doubt it. The only indisputable difference I see in myself is that I begin every day by sitting down, keeping my back straight, and watching my mind for forty-five or fifty minutes. Is that enough to justify the sort of ordeal into which I'm now about to plunge? On good days, the answer to that question is an enthusiastic yes, on bad days quite the opposite, but of course, the fact that I sit on good days and bad days alike creates a sort of leverage on these fluctuations that I've never had before. I've not gone all that far along this

road but I'm actually terrified at times to realize how inconceivable it is to think of turning back.

We enter the grounds of Dai Bosatsu on a hot, muggy
evening in early June. We are fifteen miles from the nearest
town, and from the gate to the monastery, there are another
three miles of private road. This last is an old logging trail that
winds through dense hardwood forest beside a stream that is
turbulent now with spring runoff. Darkness prevents our seeing them, but leaving two days hence, we will discover that
there are stone and bronze Buddhas all along the banks of the
stream, a few perched on stones within it. We take a right-hand
turn over a short, wooden bridge that rumbles beneath us like
artillery. It's a frightening sound, like we've driven into an am-
bush, and, occurring as it does at the moment we glimpse the
monastery, the perfect sound track for the melodramatic movie
playing in my head.

We were supposed to be here in time for evening sitting,
but a flat tire has delayed us. By the time we arrive, the other
students are already preparing for bed. We are directed to a
large wood-frame house that is being used as a dormitory until
the main building is completed. Fifteen or twenty students
have already arranged their sleeping bags in the living room,
but we find a spot beneath the window and unroll our own.
Exhausted though I am, my mind is racing with so much excitement and fear that sleep is out of the question. I know that
I'll be dozing on my cushion tomorrow, but that of course only
increases my agitation. Zen and the Art of Insomnia. Sleep does
not come easily when your bed is unfamiliar, your schedule so
disarranged that you are in bed two or three hours before you
usually get there, and most important, when you know that
next day—or if you're entering retreat, for the next seven

days—you will be sitting for ten to twelve hours. I doubt you could find any longtime student who hasn't endured what I am enduring now, but you can be sure that Zen masters shed no tears about this sort of disorientation or the exhaustion to which it leads. More than one roshi has suggested that fatigue is good for zazen because it slows one's thought process.

Next morning, though I've not slept a wink, I am wide awake, my senses alert and sharpened, as we climb in darkness to the monastery. It is raining heavily, but someone loans us a small umbrella that spares us the worst of the downpour. The road we climb is steep and rocky and pungent with the scent of pine from the forest that surrounds us. At the entrance, pine gives way to sandalwood from the incense burning on the numerous altars spread throughout the building. We stow our umbrella in a beautiful copper urn, place our shoes in a wooden rack of no less elegant design, mount stairs made of bleached, random-width oak which, I'll later learn, has been imported from Tanzania. Every item in this building has been chosen by Eido Roshi, and the $5 million to which he's been staked by several wealthy donors, as well as a host of lesser ones like myself, has given free reign to his elegant taste.

The corridor outside the zendo reminds me of the locker rooms in which I dressed and sweated and hyperventilated before important high-school basketball games. In preparation for sitting, bodies are being stretched and exercised with last-chance desperation. The silence of the room, so dense and weighted that it might be underwater, is punctuated by forced inhalations and exhalations and, now and then, since it is easy to forget in this environment that one is not alone, a fart or a belch. As my eyes scan the room, they fill with tears. I am accustomed to being emotional in moments such as this, but it seems nothing short of astonishing that all these people have come here for zazen, left their jobs and families and congregated on this remote property for no other reason except to listen to their minds. Most are strangers to me, but at this moment the connection I feel with them seems infinitely deeper and more concrete than the link that joins me to my friends.

Their ages range, I'd guess, from early twenties to late seventies. I see robes and sweat clothes, exercise suits, billowing skirts, torn blue jeans. Shaved heads on men and women alike, a couple of tattoos, crew cuts, men with earrings and ponytails, women with sprayed hairdos and manes that hang to the middle of their backs. One particularly beautiful woman wears lipstick and eye shadow and a dramatic, floor-length powder-blue gown that would not be out of place at a formal ball. How long before the wake-up bell did she get up in order to put herself together like this?

The zendo here is an enormous room with more than sixty sets of cushions. Waves of terror—all the anxiety I've come to associate with the world of official Zen—strike as soon as I sit down. The zendo feels like a black hole sucking me toward its center. Within minutes my left knee is hurting, and sittings up here are fifty to seventy minutes long. Early on, Zen students develop precise hierarchies of pain, a sort of one-to-ten system that begins with the minor irritations like stiffness and soreness and ends with a close approximation of surgery without anesthesia. My knee is a two or three at first, but within fifteen or twenty minutes, I am convinced that the cap is separating from the bone. When the bell rings after the second sitting, it takes all ten minutes of walking meditation to fully unbend it. All this time, of course, with a kind of hysteria, I search my brain for the slogans I've collected on the subject of pain. "Pain is the great privilege of those who come to the zendo." "Zazen without pain is like pasta without sauce." "What is pain?—an illusion labeled 'pain' experienced by another illusion labeled 'myself!' " I cannot doubt that each of these pearls takes my pain to a higher level. I have vowed not to move, of course, have never in fact allowed myself to do so in situations such as this, but as sitting continues throughout the morning, my resolution weakens. Halfway through the third sitting, I slip my foot off my thigh so that I am sitting with one leg in front of the other. Immediately, I hear the wooden clappers strike the floor and a voice midway between a hiss and a shout. "Don't move! Don't be a slave to your body!" But it is not enough to feel the shock of such rebuke and the shame it strikes in my heart. My adjustment has released a pain that dwarfs what I felt before. How can my knees be appeased with this slight change of angle when what they really want is to stretch or walk or lie outstretched like normal legs are permitted to do?

Even more oppressive than the pain is the abyss of time that looms before me. I feel unbearable impatience, a constant threat of full-blown panic. Time seems an enemy against which I must defend myself, and of course there is nothing like zazen for demonstrating the impossibility of such defense. Though experience has shown me that such information will only increase my misery, I have memorized the printed schedule outside the zendo door. Thus, I can remind myself now that we will continue sitting until breakfast at 7:30 and resume at 9:00 until lunch, at 1:00, when Yamada Roshi is scheduled to arrive. After that, there will be a one-hour rest period, and then we will return to our cushions until dinner at 5:30, rest again for a few minutes, sit again from 6:30 to 9:00. It is now, I estimate,

6:15. What is the source of the masochism or perversity that prompts me to remind myself, not just once or twice but every two or three minutes, that I shall be sitting with folded legs for the next fifteen hours and forty-five minutes? To calculate, when the next bell rings, that fifteen hours and fifteen minutes remain? As the day proceeds, I will rage at time, bargain with it, reason with it, and of course try to forget it, speed it up or stop it altogether. In a futile attempt at interrupting my obsession, I will name last year's Yankee pitching staff, my schoolteachers from kindergarten through college, and three or four times, in situations increasingly obscene, imagine sex with the woman in the powder-blue dress. Have I ever subjected my perception of time to more fastidious research? As if for the first time, I am discovering that certain moments are longer than others, that the speed of time increases in exact proportion to one's patience, and that the surest way to make a moment vanish is to relish it completely. In other words, that time is mind-dependent and mind-altering, circular and paradoxical: the more you concentrate, the less it matters, and the less it matters, the more you concentrate. None of this, needless to say, has the slightest effect on my impatience.

·   ·   ·

Finished with our Chinese dinner, Roshi and I are having another beer. On the table between us, we've spread out and organized his tax receipts, stacking them neatly in piles tied with rubber bands. Still thinking about "virtue," I ask if he considers himself "a religious person."

"No," he says. "I'm not against religion, but it's an inconvenience."

"What do you mean, 'inconvenience'?"

A long silence ensues. I suspect he's annoyed with my question, but suddenly, he's back in Israel where, for thirteen years before coming to New York, he maintained what may have been the world's most incongruous zendo in the Arab quarter of Jerusalem.

"Listen, Larry-san, one day in Israel I diarrhea. Every fifteen minutes go toilet. But must go Haifa for my zazen group, every Monday evening. Taxi from Jerusalem, one hour fifty minutes. Want to shit but driver won't stop. Sitting there with seven other people, controlling diarrhea, one hour fifty minutes. I want to test my religious strength. I am third-generation Japanese priest. Buddha must help me, no? Again and again, I repeat sutras but diarrhea won't stop. Already down in my anus! I can't hold it anymore another forty minutes, so finally I tell driver he must stop. Near airport, I search for a house where I can shit. First, Arab house, then Israeli—both say no. I can't do anything. So I find corner near electric pole, pull my pants down. Six, seven children gather circle, shouting 'Japanese!' I not care! But no toilet paper! What can I do? Must use underpants! Children laughing and pointing. 'Japanese! Japanese!' Driver blowing horn, calling me hurry. I not care! I discover paradise then. Great paradise, it's going toilet. Even though I trust my family tradition, the fact that I am religious, that Buddha, my God, will help me. Well—nothing help! Just shitting, that's my paradise! Great discovery! Must take care myself! Understand? Buddha not take care. God not take care. Must take care myself! Belief or not belief, don't count, Larry-san! Only action help! I am stupid testing Buddha to help at hard time. Buddha, he say, 'No, you go shitting!' Temporary

faith means nothing! Trust or no trust—not enough! Only you
trust yourself! 'I can do it! I can do it! I will do it! I must do it!'
Then you know about religion!"

.   .   .

When the breakfast bell is sounded, we file into the dining
room. Almost as large as the zendo, it is furnished with low
wooden tables at which we sit on our heels in the posture the
Japanese call "seiza," or "tea posture." Naively, I had expected
breakfast to offer physical relief, but seiza, which puts tremendous pressure on the knees and insteps, is even more difficult
for me than half-lotus. From the moment I sit down, I am shifting and leaning and rising on my knees to take the pressure off
my feet.

There is also no relief from ritual. For over eight hundred
years, Zen monasteries have been evolving a form in which a
group of people can eat together in undistracted silence, and
Eido Roshi has brought this form to America. We don't look
around, we don't make noise with our utensils, and when food
is served, we eat every morsel with absolute attention. That's
the easy part. Much more complicated is the procedure that
supports it. It is called "orioki," its utensils "jihatsu." The latter includes a dish towel, a nest of five black lacquer bowls, and
a set of chopsticks in its own black pouch. A neat little package
about the size of a cantaloupe, the jihatsu is wrapped in a
brown cloth which, at a given signal, is unfolded to make a sort
of platform on which one's bowls are set out. Each of these
actions—unfolding the cloth, setting out the bowls, the precise
angle at which the chopsticks are placed on one of the bowls,
etc.—is carefully prescribed. There is *a way* to bow before you
begin, *a way* to hold your bowl when you remove it from its

nest, *a way* to fold your napkin, and so on. When food is served, you bow again, hold out your bowl, signal "enough" by lifting your hand beside your bowl, then bow again to thank the server. Properly handled, your bowls make no sound when stacked or unstacked, and your chopsticks graze but do not strike the edge of the bowl. When everyone has finished, a bowl of hot water is passed, and there is *a way* to wash your bowls and chopsticks and dry them with your cloth. Then a waste bowl is passed and, after another bow, you pour a few drops of your waste into it and drink the rest. Finally, the jihatsu is reassembled as carefully as it was disassembled, wrapped so tightly and impeccably in its cloth that it looks as if unused. When we were instructed in orioki last night, it seemed almost insanely complicated and self-conscious, but in the context of this silence, the precision and attention it re-quires, it becomes rational and elegant, a perfect solution, like so much else in Zen, to this particular logistical problem of mo-nastic life. How else could sixty people eat together without disturbing each others' meditation? Do it right and you won't call attention to yourself. Do it wrong and you'll disturb the table as much as you disturb the zendo when you move.

Orioki will eventually become second nature to me, a rit-ual which so heightens my sense of taste and texture that eating at times becomes an almost hallucinogenic experience. For now, however, like so much else I am doing here, it is a source of embarrassment and consternation. Clumsy with my bowls, I make more noise, it seems to me, than everyone else in the room combined. I have completely forgotten the elaborate methods of folding, unfolding, unstacking and stacking I learned last night. As it happens, I am sitting next to my old nemesis, Dr. Kostenbach, and—with gritted teeth and innu-

merable sighs of impatience—he is doing his best to instruct
me. The harder I try, the clumsier I get. Rational it may be, but
the ritual seems a nightmare now, one more example of Zen's
infinite capacity to complicate the ordinary.

Of all my errors, however, the most grievous is taking too
much food in my bowl. As it happens, the breakfast fare—oatmeal with raisins and peanuts and maple syrup—is delectable
to me. I am not only very hungry but in one of those states of
high anxiety that make my appetite insatiable. After all, with
the exception of climbing the road to the monastery, eating is
the only activity I have attempted today at which I feel a measure of competence. Too late do I realize that the mountain I've
packed into my bowl is too hot to eat quickly and that, even if it
were not, my chopstick technique is much too rudimentary to
handle oatmeal with dispatch. None of this would be a problem, of course, if the meal proceeded at normal speed, but why
should this alone be normal here? Up and down the table, people are stuffing themselves with a kind of hysteria. Food is
gulped in enormous chunks, one bite followed so quickly by
another that the chopsticks appear to be on springs. Within
minutes, when my bowl remains more than three-quarters full,
everyone else is finished. From the corner of my eye, I see a row
of chopsticks returned to their perch—at a perfect forty-five-
degree angle, of course—on the smallest bowl. As I continue
nibbling, littering my lap with oatmeal and burning my tongue
when I take too big a mouthful, I understand all too well why
everyone else has eaten so fast. I feel as if the whole room, the
construction of this monastery, the transmission of Zen from
East to West, is waiting for me to finish my oatmeal.

.   .   .

Yesterday, with Roshi's permission, a young American monk I know from another zendo came to sit with us in Soho. Now twenty-five, he has been practicing Zen since he was seventeen and is considered a sort of star in the Dharma world—devoted to his teacher, attending sesshin regularly, very kind and considerate in his dealings with other people, etc. I've heard more than one person say that no American student has a better chance of becoming a Zen master than he does.

"What did you think of my friend, Roshi?"

"Soon," he replies, correctly as it turns out, "he finish with Zen."

"What?"

"One year, two years at most. After that, no sitting at all."

"How come?"

"Too nice! Like drunk on religion. Zen monk must corrupt, Larry-san! Guerrilla! Vietcong monk! Better drink saki every night than too much sit on cushion!"

. . .

Andra and I often read aloud from a book called *The Mumonkan*. It is a famous group of koans collected by Master Mumon in the twelfth century, and one of our favorites is another incident featuring Eno, the Sixth Patriarch, which occurred some fifteen years after he received transmission from Master Gunin. Since the other Obai monks resent the fact that their master has anointed this young, illiterate acolyte who offers such clear rebuke to their belief in the gradual approach to enlightenment, Eno—following Gunin's advice—has spent these years in hiding. Now, aged forty, still a layman, he appears in the year 678 at a monastery called Hossho-ji to hear the teachings of another venerable master. Arriving at the monastery's gates, he

finds two monks arguing about the temple flag flapping overhead. Is it the flag that moves or the wind that moves? What is
cause, what is effect? Turning to Eno, they ask his opinion. "It
is not the flag that moves," he says, "and it is not the wind that
moves. It is the mind that moves." At this point, the two monks
experience deep enlightenment. As Master Mumon says, com-
menting on this story five centuries later, "The two monks obtained gold intending to buy iron."

. . .

When Yamada Mumon, the eminent roshi, arrived this morning from Tokyo, Eido Roshi met him and his entourage at the
airport. Now that they are on their way to Dai Bosatsu in a limousine, we've received bulletins all morning on their location,
courtesy of phone calls from Eido Roshi and announcements in
the zendo by the head monk, a man who goes by the name
Kendo. The flight arrived early. They've cleared customs.
They've stopped for gas on the parkway. They're on the turn-
pike and should be here in forty-five minutes. Now, as they
draw near, we are like soldiers awaiting review by their com-
manding officer. It's as if all the insecurity suffered by westerners with respect to Oriental religion, the sense that we are
outsiders in the practice and cannot hope to master its teachings or endure its physical demands, is soon to be assuaged or
confirmed. Kendo warns us against the absurd idea that
Yamada Roshi is an ordinary man. "Many roshis in Japan are
administrators or figureheads, but this man is revered for his
teachings, his writing and his calligraphy. He is 'Dharma father' to half-a-dozen roshis who are famous in their own right.
Don't think you can impress this man. He'll feel the atmosphere in this building as soon as he reaches the gatehouse. The

sincerity or insincerity of our practice will be absolutely clear to him."

Highway traffic delays the limousine. Since the roshi has been expected at any moment for the last half hour and Kendo is determined that he and Eido must find us sitting, as opposed to walking in kinhin, when they arrive, he does not ring the bell at the appointed time. By the time the car pulls into the circular driveway below, it is well after one o'clock. That means that this particular sitting period—the last of the series that began, after breakfast, at nine—has lasted more than an hour. Even by Dai Bosatsu standards, this is lengthy. It seems to me that pain is palpable in the room, relief no less palpable when the limousine arrives. Myself, I'm feeling slightly nauseous from an agony that has settled, like a small pneumatic drill, in the outside of my right knee. We hear car doors open and close, sandals scratching the gravel and footsteps mounting the stairs leading to the zendo. A moment later, Eido Roshi throws open the doors of the zendo and four black-robed figures sweep past him toward the center of the room. Leading the way is a very young monk, followed by two portly, middle-aged men— roshis themselves, I'll later discover—and finally, small and slight and wearing horn-rimmed spectacles, Yamada Roshi himself. Aside from Yamada, all have cameras, and now, aiming and focusing like the tourists they are, they collect us for their scrapbooks. Light meters are read, shutters adjusted. While we sit like statues, struggling to ignore pain and maintain posture, they bend and lean, approach or back off in search of better angles. Clearly, they are serious about their pictures. One of the roshis kneels at the end of the line and shoots it lengthwise, and the young monk takes a straight-on shot of Kendo and those who sit on either side of him. Meanwhile,

Eido and Yamada are standing near the altar, where Eido, like
a museum guide, appears to be conducting a sort of show-and-
tell about the various articles that adorn it. My inner calculator
tells me we've been sitting for almost ninety minutes now, but,
entertained as I am by all the commotion, I feel no pain at all.

.   .   .

Soon after we sit down for lunch, Eido Roshi announces that
we are not only free to talk but, in honor of our visitors, ex-
cused from zazen for the rest of the day. The pressure differen-
tial between this sudden, unexpected freedom and the
discipline of the zendo is enough to give one the bends. At first,
conversation seems a violation of the boundary established by
our silence, but once the gates are opened, it is almost impossible to close them. We talk too loud and laugh too much, gossip
shamelessly. This is meditation backlash, the underside of discipline. It's as if we reassert with a sort of vengeance the social
habits we've suspended in our meditation.

For lunch, we are offered a delicious spread of Japanese
noodles with a diversity of condiments and, to my astonishment, pitchers of warm saki. Within minutes, the room is rau-
cous, and nowhere is the change more evident than at the head
table, where the roshis are quickly shorn of all reserve. Toasts
are offered, tears shed, poems recited, and now and then the
table is pounded. One of the roshis sings a song in Japanese.
With regard to us, their touristic impulse has been replaced by
comradery, respect, even reverence. They're treating us like pi-
oneers, applauding our courage, our discipline, and our wisdom, and for us, needless to say, their praise is no less
intoxicating than the saki.

Andra and I sit opposite each other at the end of the

table, near a large window that overlooks the lake below. A monk named Jissan sits next to Andra, and next to me I recognize the doorkeeper from the city zendo. When we first sat down, he was as solemn and tight-lipped as in the city, but once we are introduced and he hears my southern accent, his eyes brighten and an infectious, gap-toothed smile spreads over his face. His name is Allan Jamison, but everyone calls him Jamie. His own accent comes from Athens, Georgia. He has full, fat cheeks and sunken eyes, the arms and wrists of a weightlifter. He's still in his sitting robe, but he's rolled up his sleeves and tied a red bandana around his neck. I note that he hasn't had his eyeglasses repaired. Just as before, at the city zendo, they are held together by a safety pin.

To my surprise, since I'd thought him to be a veteran, he tells me that it is only two years since he became involved with Zen. Like so many others, he was turned in this direction by D. T. Suzuki. He had never heard of Zen until, for a course in world religions in his freshman year at Georgia Tech, he read Suzuki's book on the life of a Zen monk. "I was going to be an engineer, but something about that essay changed everything for me. You hear as much crap as I've heard all my life, all these assholes trying to teach you something when they can't even get their own acts together, a guy like Suzuki sort of makes an impression. I went to the library and read all his books. Then somebody turned me on to zazen. In the beginning, my legs were so tight I couldn't manage more than ten minutes, but as time went on, I built it up. I still haven't got a full-lotus, but at least I can manage sesshin."

Spiritual groups need people like Jamie as much as they need financial support. In addition to being rugged and intense and loose enough to abandon his life in the outside world, he's

worked as a machinist, an electrician and a mechanic, and he's
a pretty fair carpenter and plumber. One can imagine Eido
Roshi's delight when, with construction just beginning, and
only six students committed to living on the property, Jamie
showed up on his doorstep. In exchange for his labor, Eido offered him room and board and all the teachings he could handle. For the last two years, he's been tired almost all the time,
cold in the winter and hot in the summer, sleeping on an air
mattress and working from dawn till dark six days a week, but
he considers his deal the bargain of his life. "Man, I can talk to
the roach whenever I want! If Soen's in town, I can hit on him
too!" He lived here until the roof went on last fall, and then—
at Eido's request—moved to the city to become the caretaker
of the zendo there.

Jissan is mournful and sardonic and a lot less garrulous
than Jamie, but in the spirit of the moment, he offers a bit of his
story too. He was part of the construction crew that Jamie
joined, but the road that brought him to Dai Bosatsu was more
circuitous and complicated. His given name is Sam Younger,
Jissan a so-called "Dharma name," given to him by Eido Roshi
when he took his monastic vows. He speaks with an English
accent and a voice as deep as the roshi's. To my surprise, like
several others I have met here and at the city zendo, he also
seems to shape his words like Eido and even, at times, to speak
with a Japanese accent. He tells me he is from the north of
England and has a doctorate in philosophy from Cambridge.
He came to the United States seven years ago in order to study
with Eido, but his interest in Zen grew out of feelings no less ambivalent than my own. Though he had taught Buddhism as part
of a course in the philosophy of religion at Cambridge, he had
no interest in Zen practice until he was introduced to it by the

woman who is now his wife. She is an American, a Buddhist nun with a shaved head whom he points out to us at the far end of the table. Her name is Claudia, and they met when she enrolled in his class at Cambridge. "She was nineteen at that time, but she'd already begun to sit. For a year before she came to Cambridge, she'd been sitting with Eido's group in New York. From the beginning, she tried to get me into it, but I pretended to be disinterested. Actually, I was scared to death, but I didn't cop to that at all. I had it intellectually worked out—you know, the skeptic's approach to 'the problem of faith.' But Claudia kept after me, and once I started, I never stopped."

Jissan has an enormous Adam's apple that vibrates when he speaks. His eyes are skittish and not, I think, without a touch of paranoia. His story comes in quick bursts punctuated by long silences that make it seem, at times, as if he's making it up as he goes along. He and Claudia have been living at Dai Bosatsu since the day it was purchased. She is the cook and the chief housekeeper, and in addition to working with the professional crew, he is the monitor, or "jiki jitsu," for the regular morning and evening sittings that have been conducted here since the day they moved in. He's thirty-seven, but with his shaved head and the puffy bags under his eyes, he looks at least ten years older. Six-three or six-four, thin enough for medical concern, he lays his condition to a macrobiotic diet that limits him mostly to seaweed and grains. "Purification," he sighs. "Like any good Zen student, I can't get enough of it."

When lunch is over, he and Claudia excuse themselves to bid farewell to the visiting roshis. Their plane departs later this evening, and Eido Roshi and Kendo are taking them on a quick tour of New York City. Where are the roshis headed? Back to Japan, Jissan says. Today? When they've only just arrived?

"They came only for this visit," he explains. "From what I hear they've brought no clothes but what they're wearing. Between the four of them, they've got a total of forty-seven dollars spending money."

Leaving the dining room, I run into Dr. Kostenbach. He's thinner than when I saw him last. Cheeks sunken and unshaven, he looks almost seedy. As before, he seems offended when I speak to him. Reason tells me to move on, but still blinded by the belief that all Zen students are my brothers, I offer my hand and thank him for his help with orioki.

"You still don't get it, do you?"

"Get what?"

"When you finish eating, your jihatsu should be tight, all of a piece. If you do it right, it should look as if you've never used it. You know what Dogen Zenji says about leaving no trace? If you pay attention to what you're doing, you'll leave no trace on your bowls. Yours, my friend—they look like something you bought at a flea market. Didn't anybody teach you orioki?"

"Sure. They gave us a demonstration last night."

"Well, maybe you ought to ask for another lesson."

.   .   .

It's a hot summer day, and most of us are lounging on the grass beside the lake. The combination of saki and zazen makes for a mood, Kostenbach notwithstanding, of almost universal affection. Andra and I get on so well with Jissan and Claudia that we invite them to stay with us six weeks hence, when, for the first time in nearly four months, they are promised a weekend free. The conversation is easy and the humor irreverent: jokes about the roshi, the monastery, especially Zen itself. If there is mention of the deeper, "spiritual" issues that bring us together here, it is usually couched in irony. The emotion I felt this morning has not only resurfaced but escalated dangerously toward the maudlin. I'm thinking there's no one here I'd not want to have as a friend. The communal feeling I sense on this lawn reminds me of the bond I felt with high-school basketball teammates. What could be better than such a bond combined with spiritual practice? Why not move here, become a monk, give up the distraction of life in the city and devote oneself to Zen? As the afternoon progresses, there are moments when I think I'd be insane to do anything else.

Claudia's Dharma name is Hoan. She is tall and green-eyed and almost as thin as her husband, with an angular, boyish face and a smile that completely illuminates it. Shaved three months ago when she was ordained as a nun, her hair is just a fuzz on her skull. Like many I'll meet in the Dharma world, her gateway to Zen, she says, was LSD, an acid trip in high school that showed her what she calls "ground zero." After that, her story is a virtual duplicate of Jamie's. "I read every book I could find on Eastern religion, and when I discovered zazen, I started to sit. I looked up Zen in the telephone book and found Eido Roshi's listing. One beginners' class was all it took to hook me."

While she's telling us this, we are joined by an Oriental fellow named Chang Wei. Short and massive, almost as wide as he is tall, he appears to be in his early forties. I have noticed him earlier, at lunch and in the zendo. Even at a distance, it was apparent that he has particular status here. Since he is leaving for the city, he remains only long enough to be introduced, but when he is gone, Jissan explains that he is a Chinese karate master who has a dojo in New York. He came to this country with the intention of studying mathematics and began sitting with Eido Roshi about the same time Claudia did, but it is Soen Roshi he considers his teacher. It is because of Soen that he gave up mathematics and opened his dojo, and now, according to Claudia, he is preparing to close the school so that he can become a monk. Claudia tells us that Chang rarely eats during sesshin and likes to sit through the night when pushing for the enlightenment that, in Rinzai Zen, is called "kensho." Such is Chang's energy that people vie to be seated next to him during sesshin. "There's a force field around him," Jissan says. "You can feel him pushing you, energizing you, driving you forward like an outboard motor." In addition to all his other skills, Chang is also, it seems, possessed of psychic powers, an ability to heal by a laying on of hands. Jissan says he has helped alleviate Soen Roshi's persistent headaches and Eido's chronic stiff neck and is reputed to have cured a range of disease from parkinsonism to arthritis. I have to admit that there is something a little disturbing to me about all this information—the extent of Chang's legend and the ease with which its more occult details are accepted—but in the spirit of the moment, such qualms are easy to ignore. Like everyone else, I think, I am not at all displeased to have a superstar here, an example of someone who seems to embody the power I feel now and then on the cushion, or more to the point, refutes the doubt and fear I feel when the power deserts me.

·   ·   ·

When it is time for us to leave, our car won't start. Claudia suggests that Jamie might be able to fix it. Searching him out at the old barn that serves as the monastery's garage, I find him wearing goggles, sharpening an ax on a pedal-driven grindstone.

"You busy?"

"Naw. Just fartin' around."

"My car won't start. They said you might be able to help me."

He piles some tools in a bag and follows me up the hill. "Man, ain't it beautiful up here? I wish to fuck I didn't have to go back to the city."

"Why do you have to go?"

"The roach," he says. "I do what he tells me to."

"Don't you have a vote?"

"Me? What do I need a vote for? I'd only vote for the easy way out. The roach knew that the moment he met me. And he knows there ain't nobody in this zendo less suited to live in New York than me. That's why he wants me there."

"I don't understand. What's so bad about being where you want to be? Everyone's got his taste."

"Taste? What's that mean? Whose taste we talking about? My ego's? The engineer from Georgia Tech? Mama's boy from Athens? A junky's taste is junk, but that don't make it good for him."

It takes him less than fifteen minutes to get the car started, even though, in order to do so, he has to fashion a tool from a piece of wire to get inside the carburetor. Before we drive off, he too has promised to visit us in the city. I feel as enamored of him as of Jissan and Hoan. Once again, the wooden bridge rumbles beneath our car, but its sound is no longer threatening. It's soothing now, the advance guard of my nostalgia. We're not yet at the gatehouse, but I am already homesick for Dai Bosatsu. The afternoon has stripped my brain of unpleasant memory—every trace of this morning's pain, the discomfort of sitting on my heels at breakfast, the oppression of the

ritual—and nothing is left in its place but the sweetness of
"Dharma friendship" and the community I've discovered here.

.   .   .

For my birthday that year, Andra gives me a Sufi tale she's copied on a beautiful Japanese card.

> *One day, a student of the great Master Nasrudin passes*
> *by his house and finds him on his knees, rummaging in*
> *the grass. "What are you doing, sir?"*
> *"I'm looking for my key."*
> *"But, sir, didn't you lose it in your house?"*
> *"Yes," says Nasrudin, "but there's more light out*
> *here."*

I am immediately in love with the parable. As I understand it,
Nasrudin is showing his student the absurdity of looking for
something before understanding where you lost it. If you mean
to solve your problem, find its roots. Like most people, his student is in the habit of grabbing for solution wherever he finds
it, and Nasrudin is demonstrating the impossibility of this approach by offering him a mirror of his own mind.

But Sufi tales, like Zen stories or, for that matter, any
other great literature, can enter the mind and take on a life of
their own. One sees what one is able to see, and the size of the
truth they offer is usually in inverse proportion to one's impatience to understand them. Several years later, it occurs to me
that my first reading was altogether wrong. Nasrudin is illus-
trating the absurdity of linear, analytic thought. Truth is absolute, a function of the present moment, not the past or future.
If you look for your key where you lost it, you are clinging to

the past, therefore rooted in time and limited to a relative point of view. Oblivious to the light that surrounds you, you burrow into the darkness of causality, seeking to explain your difficulty when all you need is to let go of causality itself. Look around! Use the light you're offered! Darkness is the only problem, light the only solution!

This reading lasts for nearly ten years, until I put the matter to Roshi. It's autumn, 1984, and we're taking a walk in Greenwich Village. "Do you know much about Sufism, Roshi?"

"Maybe just a little. Why?"

"You know the story about Nasrudin and the key?"

"Nasludeen?" he says. "Who Nasludeen?"

"A Sufi master. He appears in a lot of the stories. In this one, a student finds him on his knees in the grass. 'What are you doing, sir?' Nasrudin says, 'I'm looking for my key.' 'But sir,' says the student, 'didn't you lose it inside your house?' 'Yes,' says Nasrudin, 'but there's more light out here.' "

Roshi nudges me with his elbow. "Larry-san—that man over there. Yellow T-shirt. He gay? What you think?"

"How should I know? Gay people don't look any different from anyone else."

"Yes, but why earring? Why shirt so tight?"

"Many people wear earrings. Tight shirts too. Who cares if he's gay, anyway?"

"Gay not normal! Against nature! Why you think everything come in pairs? Night and day! Good and bad! Man and lady! Not natural, man and man, lady and lady. Look at those two over there! Holding hands! Not normal, Larry-san!"

"But, Roshi, aren't you always telling us that there are no fundamental distinctions? From the point of view of the Abso-

lute, what's the difference between homosexuality and hetero-
sexuality? How can we speak of pairs anyhow when all beings
are one?"

"Larry-san! You not understand. Relative world, everything different, everything conflict. You and me, good and evil,
life and death. Cause and effect! Point of view of Absolute,
cause and effect one. But you live in relative world, no? You
want to run marathon, must train body, master physical condition. You get up every morning, thinking 'cause and effect one
. . . I not feel like training today, I go back sleep.' You never run
marathon, no?"

Interesting as his argument is, I can't forgive his bigotry,
and this is not the first time I've seen it displayed. His homo-
phobic comments have driven several gay students out of the
zendo. I have also heard him express prejudice against blacks,
Koreans, and Frenchmen, offer blanket condemnations of
America—its manufacturing, craftsmanship and politics, the
laziness and selfishness of its citizenry, the insincerity of its Zen
students, etc. For that matter, chauvinist though he is, he has
little good to say about the Japanese either. Is it any wonder
I often feel, as now, so angry and disappointed with him?
Haven't I a right to expect from him at least a minimal level of
rectitude?

It is a fine autumn day, hot in the sun and cool in the
shade of buildings, the light so golden and precise it makes objects look artificial, like images of themselves. As usual, Roshi is
wearing his Yankee cap and his Yankee jacket, walking so close
to me that, especially because both of us have a tendency to roll
our shoulders when we walk, we often nudge or bump against
each other. I am always shocked to realize how short he is—five
feet at most, maybe a shade under. When he first came to New

York, it bothered me to look down at him, as if this conflicted somehow with the authority I'd invested in him, but it occurs to me now that I've come to enjoy this angle, not to mention the fact that he calls me almost every morning for opinions or advice. "Larry-san, you have newspaper? Tell me what station wrestling tonight. You know good plumber? What you think—we have Japanese noodle or Italian spaghetti at sesshin next week?"

Turning a corner, we find ourselves on a side street that is completely devoid of pedestrians. Thank God. For a few moments at least, I won't have to identify homosexuals for him. I've begun to think he's forgotten the Sufi tale, but he brings it up himself.

"So, Larry-san, what's Nasludeen saying?"

"I asked you, Roshi."

"Easy," he says. "Looking *is* the key."

.   .   .

A few days after we return from Dai Bosatsu, a mailing informs us that a three-day retreat, or "sesshin"—beginning at seven o'clock on Thursday evening and ending at four o'clock Sunday afternoon—will be held three weeks hence at the city zendo. Andra has no inclination toward it, but for me the decision is automatic. I cannot forget a statement made by Eido Roshi in the talk he gave at the zendo. "Anyone who sits can call himself a Zen student, but serious students are those who do sesshin. One weekend sesshin will take you further into your practice than sitting every day for a year."

It's true that I'm not totally unserious. I'm sitting at home for at least an hour a day, and I try to go to the zendo for the two-hour evening sessions at least once a week. There are even

times when I can believe that the practice is beginning to affect
the way I conduct my life. But the changes are slow and often
imperceptible. Zen heightens awareness of bad habits, but I
feel as if my own are made of granite and I am trying to cut
them away with my fingernails. For the most part, I walk
around impatient, disgusted with myself. Granite calls for dy-
namite, and that's where sesshin comes in. The terror it strikes
in my heart is all the proof I need that it's the perfect medicine
for me.

   As it happens, Eido Roshi is out of town. Arriving at the
zendo on Thursday afternoon, I learn, to my amazement, that
this sesshin will be conducted by none other than Soen Roshi,
who has only yesterday arrived from Japan. The opportunity to
sit with this man, whom many consider the greatest Zen master
of the twentieth century, has lured students from as far away as
Hawaii, California and New Mexico. Using both the zendo and
the meeting room upstairs, space has been found for eighty students, most of whom, like me, will sleep on the floor. According to Jamie, who is tending the door when I arrive, there are
eleven beginners like myself and—because of Soen—at least
fifteen people who've not been near a zendo in years.

   Unlike Eido, Soen does not involve himself in zendo business. He will sit with us and give formal talks, or "teishos," but
he delegates logistical responsibilities to Hoan, Jissan and
Kendo, who have come down from Dai Bosatsu. Jissan will
wield the keisaku and lead the chanting, Hoan will cook, and
Kendo will keep time, ring the bells and address the group, or
what we call "sangha," on matters of procedure. It is he who
lays out the rules of sesshin when we sit down at seven. Like the
orioki ritual, they have evolved primarily out of Japanese
monasticism. Basically, they are seven in number:

1. Practice zazen every moment, even when you sleep.
2. Keep the silence in all but emergency situations.
3. Keep your attention on yourself and do not look around.
4. Do not read or write.
5. Be on your cushion at least five minutes before sitting periods begin.
6. Do not wear perfumes, fragrant soaps, aftershave lotions or anything else with invasive odor.
7. Don't do anything that attracts attention to yourself or interferes with anyone else's practice.

Kendo takes particular pains to emphasize the last. "What it means is don't move on your cushion, don't walk with a heavy step and don't wear bright colors. Remember: we are all responsible for sesshin atmosphere, the energy we create together, and the best thing you can do for this atmosphere is disappear completely." In conclusion, he reminds us to give careful study to the schedule posted on the bulletin board so that we'll know where we're supposed to be at all times. I doubt I'm alone in not needing this admonition. The first thing I did on entering the zendo was check the bulletin board, and what I saw there was even more frightening than the schedule at Dai Bosatsu.

4:00 Wake-up.
4:30 Tea. Zazen.
7:30 Breakfast.
8:00 Work period.
9:30 Chanting. Teisho. Zazen.

1:00 Lunch. Rest Period.
2:00 Tea. Zazen.
5:30 Dinner.
6:30 Zazen.
9:00 Sleep.

After he speaks, Kendo stands, bows to the altar, and lights more incense. The clappers are struck, the gong rung, and a throbbing silence descends on the room. It's as if we've shifted to another orbit or entered a different time warp. Everyone in this room knows that for the next three days we won't be going anywhere or doing anything else but sitting on these cushions. Some no doubt are happy about this prospect, but I am not among them. At the sound of the gong, a full-scale panic attack explodes in me, and there is no Zen voice directing me to celebrate it. Beads of sweat appear on my forehead, a wave of nausea in my stomach, and my mind is consumed with all the familiar Zen questions, which boil down to one—what in God's name am I doing here? I feel I've been trapped by longtime habits of guilt and masochism in a game for which I have neither talent nor desire.

But on the heels of panic, stillness descends, and it is no less extreme than the agitation it replaces. My mind is distant, my thoughts muted, slowed, noninvasive. It's not so much that I've entered this state as disappeared within it. In whose body did the panic attack occur? In whose brain the memories of it which are secreted now? Oh, how happy I am to be here until the panic resumes an instant later.

Next morning, after the wake-up bell, we have thirty minutes to roll up our sleeping bags, join the long lines waiting for the bathroom, piss, wash, exercise (if we can make room for ourselves in the crowd), and get to our cushions. Green tea is served before sitting begins, and the jolt of caffeine launches me into sitting like a veteran. I haven't slept a wink, of course, but I am oddly happy, comfortable on my cushion, totally grateful to be here. Even more surprising, my equanimity persists through breakfast. Am I done with my vacillation? Hardly. During morning work period, my mood is shattered once again. I am assigned to the outdoor crew—sweeping the sidewalk, washing the wooden doors, cleaning and waxing the calligraphy plaque that hangs above the entrance. While I'm sweeping, a young couple, arm in arm, ambles by with a morning paper and a brown bag containing what I take to be their breakfast. A pretty Oriental girl with long black hair, a tall, scruffy fellow wearing a Mets cap, both of them in shorts and sandals, drifting, as I imagine it, toward Central Park and an afternoon of lounging on the grass. In other words, normal, happy, nonpuritanical people, precisely the sort you want to forget when embarking on sesshin. How is it possible that they will enjoy their weekend while mine will be spent on the rack of self-improvement?

After the work period, there is morning liturgy, chanting and recitation of sutras in English and Japanese. Then Soen Roshi takes his place on a small platform at the head of the room. Those who've been sitting upstairs file down to the zendo for the talk, packing the room shoulder-to-shoulder. Fortunately, sitting near the front of the room, I have a good view of the roshi. This is no small advantage since, without his body language, I would not get a word he says. He is reputed to be a great haiku poet, knowledgeable in English and German literature, a scholar of Goethe in particular, but his erudition is not apparent in his English. Small and slight, eyes alternately mischievous and intimidating, there are moments when I find it comforting to look at him but others when he chills me. He is said to be the most playful of all Zen teachers, a worthy heir to the famous Buddhist tradition we call "crazy wisdom." Jissan and Hoan tell me he often asks them to slap his bald head to knock some sense into it. He has been known to hide in a closet when students come in for the private meetings that we call "kansho." Once, at Halloween, he left a pumpkin in his place on his cushion. Discouraged once about his practice, Jamie asked him for advice. Soen replied, "Encourage others." It is said he rarely sleeps more than three hours a night and always in full-lotus posture, and that once, as a young monk, he jumped into an icy lake in the middle of winter in order to challenge his attachment to his body. In an accident many years ago, a sliver of bamboo became imbedded in his skull. For years, doctors have begged him to have it removed, but he has resisted their advice. When the wound festers and becomes excruciating, as it does at least a couple of times a year, he deals with the pain by solitary retreat, sometimes as long as six months.

His voice is operatic, deep as the lower registers of a cello. Looking about the room as he speaks, I am astonished at the faces I see. Everyone looks blissed-out, dazzled eyes expectant as an infant's at the breast. I am detached at first, a bemused and somewhat disapproving observer but, within minutes, no less aglow than the rest. It's as if his voice is a tuning fork, evoking waves of vibration in my body. What's going on? Hypnosis? Devotion? A contact high? Is my mind opening in the presence of a master or regressing toward infantilism and dependency? One thing for sure: I feel no pain while he speaks. Though sitting on my heels in the posture that is most difficult for me, I am utterly at ease. Later, I will understand that such response is characteristic of this sort of talk, which we call "teisho." Given only by roshis, it is meant to be concrete, not conceptual, a direct presentation of the speaker's practice and, ideally speaking, his enlightenment. It seeks to starve, not fuel, conceptualization, to induce in the listener an emptiness of mind. This explains Soen's rambling, his free association, his indifference to logic. It's as if together we are exploring Zen's belief that language can be used without succumbing to the dangers of abstraction.

Even if he were fluent in English, he would be difficult to understand because much of the time he eschews language for grunts and growls and whimpers, imitating animals, babies or inanimate objects that gurgle, whistle or explode when involved in a collision or whizzing through the air. If you listened to this talk on tape or, even worse, read it in transcription, it would sound like gibberish, a kindergarten teacher descending to the level of his students. All the meaning is in his presence, his movement on the cushion, the astonishing range of his voice and expression. Though I understand, at most, one out of five words, I feel an absolute connection to him, no doubt whatever about his meaning.

His subject is doing nothing. "How you say it? 'Do nothing?' 'Do *nothing*?' No, no! I say, *'Do* nothing!' Understand? *Do* nothing!" As often throughout the teisho, he repeats himself again and again. *"Do* nothing! *Do* nothing! *Do* nothing!" Of course, this is no word game he's playing. He is offering us the essence of Zen. Doing nothing means seeking nothing, desiring nothing. Those who do nothing are free of ambition, disappointment, and therefore, of suffering. And he is not recommending that we *do* nothing in the future but pointing out that we are *doing* it now. Speaking of Soen at Dai Bosatsu, Jissan said, "All Zen masters pay homage to the idea of contentment, but in my experience not many mean what they say. Behind their belief in contentment is a sort of puritanical agenda, a belief that equanimity is a sort of breakthrough or achievement, a virtue that must be earned. Which in effect means that we are not yet worthy of it. This turns Zen into a sort of closet Catholicism, a practice based in Original Sin rather than innate, universal enlightenment. But if you spend time around Soen, you will *actually feel* that there is nothing to earn, nothing to learn, nothing to realize. It's as if he gives you permission to accept yourself, forgive yourself for all your delusion, all your anger and duplicity. But if you think this means it's easy to be with him, think again. If you're anything like me, it fucks you up completely. Why? Because like everyone else, particularly Zen students, all your thoughts revolve around self-criticism, self-loathing, desire for self-improvement. Soen interrupts that desire, and what you discover is that, for all the pain it causes you, your ego cannot conceive of life without it."

Suddenly, in the midst of the teisho, one of the students leaps off his cushion and rushes toward the front of the room. For a moment, it looks as if he'll trample the roshi, but he stops and kneels before him. He is a short, slightly built fellow in his late twenties or early thirties. His name, I'll find out later, is Gregory Baines, and he is a biochemist on the faculty of the Rockefeller Institute. Silent for a moment, he gazes into Soen's eyes, then slaps him twice, very hard, on the jaw.

"Please!" says Soen. "Don't waste time!"

By this time, Jamie and Kendo have rushed to protect Soen, but he raises his hand to stop them. Leaning forward, he fixes his eyes on Baines and speaks in a whisper. "Understand? Don't waste precious time!"

Smiling, Baines nods, then places his palms together and bows until his forehead touches the floor. "Yes, sir! Thank you, sir!"

Rising and bowing quickly, apparently oblivious to the two men standing behind him, he returns to his cushion. For the time being, nothing more will be heard from him. Some would argue that he acted in a true Zen spirit, expressing precisely the sort of irreverence that is so often celebrated in the literature. Others would say he simply went crazy, lost his mind to the ordeal of sesshin. In this zendo at least, such arguments are moot. The rules of the practice supersede them. As Jissan says later, explaining to me why Baines has been ordered to leave sesshin at once and, in all likelihood, will never again be allowed in the zendo. "This is not a mental hospital. We don't have time for therapy here. We're on a trip together, and everyone has to do his job."

. . .

For all the inspiration I find in Soen's presence, his effect on my zazen is negative. When I return to my cushion, my pain is worse, and I am more obsessed with it. I study it like a naturalist observing an animal in the wild. No ache, tremor or tension, no surge of fear or anger escapes my attention or goes uncharted in relation to those that have preceded it. I know that this is basic Zen recoil, the mind gripping harder as it is urged—in this case perhaps by Soen's example—in the direction of release, but of course the knowledge doesn't help at all. During a break I go to the bathroom. A line has formed outside, and Jamie stands at the end of it. When our eyes meet, he jerks his head away as if my glance is poisonous. I am well aware of the prohibition against speech (during work period, I saw Kendo grab a student who was talking and throw him against the wall), but in my current state of mind I couldn't care less. "Jamie!" I whisper. "What do you do about knee pain?"

Though he hasn't looked at me, he jerks his head again. "See a doctor."

Two years ago, in his first sesshin at Dai Bosatsu, his first sesshin *ever,* he sat all night on the sixth and seventh nights. That is to say, after sitting eleven hours during the day, he continued while others slept, sitting from nine in the evening till the others rose again at four-thirty. When I first heard this story at the monastery, I saw him as a warrior, a samurai, but at the moment, he seems pathetic, a caricature of machismo and a grotesque distortion of the vision that has brought us here today. Returning to my cushion, I remember that I myself have been tempted in this direction, and I am determined to avoid it.

Pain escalates. There are moments of dizziness and nausea. Now and then, I become convinced that I am doing permanent damage to my knees. Worst of all, I am losing the will to fight. Searching them out as an image of sanity, I keep imagining the young couple I saw this morning, eating ice cream on the grass in the park. My Zen voice urges me on, but another voice argues that what we're practicing here has nothing to do with Zen. After dinner, I ask Jissan to step outside with me.

"I'm leaving."

Like Jamie, he won't look at me. "What do you mean?"

"Going home. I've had enough."

"You serious?"

"Absolutely."

"I think you'll regret it."

"Why?"

"I don't know. I'm just guessing."

"I'm not meditating. All I'm doing is dealing with pain. What's to be gained from this?"

"I can't answer that question. You have to answer it for yourself."

Packing my gear and sleeping bag, heading for the subway, I repeat to myself one of the loveliest mantras I've ever heard: "Free of Zen, free of Zen, free of Zen." I feel giddy and rebellious, like a kid sneaking out of school, proud of myself for trusting my instinct rather than bowing to group pressure, the fanaticism and perversity of spiritual ambition. Tomorrow afternoon, while Jamie and Jissan are suffering on their cushions, I'll be lounging on the grass in Central Park. It is less than a block to the subway, but my happiness is gone before I get there. As I descend the steps, the regret Jissan predicted is suddenly full-blown. No longer a rebel, I am the coward I've always been, a spoiled child who retreats at the first sign of danger or adversity. All my life, I have been tyrannized by fear, and now—when for once I had a chance to stare it down—I have succumbed to it again. The pain I felt in sesshin—what is it beside the pain of this tyranny, the pain I'll feel the rest of my life unless I defeat it?

. . .

During sesshins at the Soho Zendo, those who wish can meet with Roshi almost every evening. After the first sitting, he gives the bell and clock and the wooden clappers to one of the senior

students, retreats to the small dressing room adjacent to the
zendo, arranges his cushion facing another, lights another stick
of incense, strikes a gong three times, and waits to see which of
us will come. This is "kansho" (literally: the bell we ring when
we enter the room), or what some zendos or monasteries call
"dokusan" or "daisan"—not an interview but a confrontation:
one offers up one's practice for his witness. Kneeling outside the
kansho room, we ring the bell twice with all the attention we can
muster while trying not to be self-conscious because we know
that self-consciousness will make us strike the bell too hard or
too soft or, even worse, once hard and once soft so that we
sound like two different people, and because we know that, behind the door, he is listening closely and, even if he hasn't said as
much, hears our minds in the sound of the bell. Maybe Zen is
nothing more than a means by which self-consciousness is ex-
acerbated until, finally unbearable, it obliterates itself.

I've been going to kansho—with Roshi or other teachers—for more than ten years now, but I am no less intimidated
than ever. It's as if he is my ultimate father, and all the infantilism that lurks in me is coming to the surface. Our knees touch
when I sit down. Lifting his hand above his head, he waits a
moment, then lowers it slowly, as if pulling down a window
shade between us, and offers me once again the question that
has driven me crazy for the past six months. "So, Larry-san:
what is this?"

The question is called a "koan." You can't think about it
and, once it's been assigned to you, you can't not think about it
either. Zen masters and their students have been working with
koans for something like seven hundred years, each master
spicing the brew with his own idioms and inspirations. The
canon is now believed to contain more than seventeen hundred

in all. There are "primary koans"—"What is this?" "What is
the sound of one hand?"—which aim to cut through all de-
fenses and take one to the central truth of emptiness, and there
are "polishing koans"—"How do you stop a sailboat on the
other side of the river?" "How do you escape from a steel cof-
fin that is locked from the outside?"—which hone and clarify
illuminations already achieved. Koans are meant to intimidate
and tantalize the rational mind. They intimidate because they
tantalize, tantalize because they intimidate. You could say that
they tease us with the dream of going beyond ourselves as they
show us that dream's absurdity. Not because we cannot go
beyond ourselves but because there is no self to go beyond.
And because nothing excites that dream so much as this
understanding.

Once again, Roshi lifts his hand and lowers it, repeating
his question. "What is this? Answer, Larry-san!"

During the past six months, I have offered him maybe
fifty answers to this question. Being a longtime Zen student, I
know of course what he is after. This is kindergarten Zen. All I
have to do is show him "this." Not "that," but "this." Not an
object or an idea but, to use the words that appear in his teishos
more frequently than any others, "reality itself." Thoughts of
"this" are not "this." The word "this" is not "this." The "this"
you think about is always "that." Consciousness separates subject and object, and it is precisely that separation we're addressing here. Just as the self I observe when I am self-conscious has
nothing to do with my essential nature, the question of which I
am conscious now has nothing to do with my koan. My koan is
myself. How do I see myself without making myself an object?
How can I show him "this" without turning it into "that"? Attempting to answer, I have remained silent, breathed loudly,

turned my back on him, and explained the matter as I have just explained it here. Every answer has led him to dismiss me with the tiny bell he keeps at his side. Now I have no answer and I'm thinking this is the answer. The answer that isn't! How many times has he told us that the *real* answer to any koan is self-confidence? "Trust yourself," he says, "and you answer any koan." It is true that searching for such trust is like searching for your sense of humor or for sleep when you've got insomnia, but my effort continues no matter how often I remark on its futility. Roshi loves to tell us the story of a fellow monk whose teacher told him, after he had struggled with the same koan for three years, that his very first answer had been correct.

Illumination strikes. "This," I cry, "is the moment! You lift your arm and drop it! That's this!"

Shaking his head, he looks at me as if I am mentally defective, then quickly rings his bell. "More zazen, Larry-san! Zen not intellectual. Must concrete! Must sincere!"

· · ·

Kelman has put on weight. His belt squeaks when he moves in his chair, and his shirt goes taut every time he breathes. The odor of cigarettes permeates his office. He's lighting up when I come in, and a steady plume rises from a butt he's just put out in the ashtray. Were it not for the fact that he always seems bored and drowsy in my presence, I'd say that he seems exhausted, perhaps even ill today.

I have vowed that this is the last time I will come here. Several times I've stopped in the past, but for one reason or another, I have always come back. Now the shame I feel for leaving sesshin has focused my resolve. I don't doubt that he helped me a lot the first few years I saw him, but at this point

he's pure addiction as far as I'm concerned, an indulgent by-
product of the bizarre financial privilege my father bestowed
on me. If I mean to strike a blow against my cowardice, I can't
imagine a better place to aim it than at the habit that's kept me
coming here.

This morning, not for the first time, I've promised myself
to explain all this to him. I want him to understand the contradiction I see between the spiritual and the psychological points
of view, the way in which the Buddhist view of suffering has
helped me appreciate the insignificance of my personal com-
plaints and scenarios, all the ego melodramas that are our principal subject matter here. Facing him across the desk, I am
clear at first, but moment by moment my clarity blurs until I'm
speaking as if by rote, my voice so hollow it seems to be someone else's.

His eyes are closed when I begin, and they do not open
while I speak. If he weren't smoking, I'd think him fast asleep.
Finally, he says, "Well, I'll tell you what I hear. Basically, you're
asking my permission to leave. Am I wrong? All this stuff about
Zen and Buddhism—what is it but self-justification? Why do
you need my permission? Ask yourself that! You can walk out
of here anytime you want!"

He grinds his cigarette into the ashtray, then fixes me with
a stare. I can't look him in the eye, but I'm studying his posture—how he slouches in his chair, how his neck is bent so that
his chin is virtually resting on his chest—and remembering
how often, when sitting in zazen, I've broken through depression by straightening my back. There are times when simply
holding my head up straight can lift my spirits like a cup of
coffee. "But ask yourself this," he says. "What is it you really
want to leave? What do you mean by psychoanalysis? I'll tell

you what you mean. Self-consciousness! Self-criticism! Dependency! Yes, dependency most of all! Isn't that what you really want to give up? Aren't you at last coming to terms with your lifelong fear of autonomy and independence? Aren't you expressing that fear by asking my permission? Look at the circle, Larry. You're asking my permission to stop asking my permission! Have we ever seen it so clearly? It's the same thing you did with your father! You're always seeking permission to stand on your own two feet! Permission to grow up! You blame it on analysis, but did your dependency begin when you entered this office? It's the story of your life! Your life, understand? Not mine! When will you stop blaming it on others? Is that Zen? Doesn't Zen teach you to accept responsibility for yourself?"

He spins in his chair, takes a book from the shelf behind him and hands it across the desk to me. It's a collection of essays by D. T. Suzuki, Erich Fromm and Richard de Martino— *Zen Buddhism and Psychoanalysis.* "Have you read this? Well, you should. Especially Suzuki's essay. For Suzuki, there's no difference between Zen and psychoanalysis. They're two sides of the same coin! Maybe they differ in technique, but they're both after autonomy, and you know what that means. No goal but wholeness! Awareness! You've got me pegged as the enemy of Zen, but that's resistance talking. Face that resistance, Larry! *Feel into it!* That's what Zen is all about! Once you take responsibility for your dependency, you'll see that what we're doing here can only help you in the zendo. Instead of turning against me, you'd let me be your guide."

"My guide? To what?"

"To everything you're trying to accomplish by sitting on the cushion."

"But you've never sat! You've never been in a zendo!"

His face contorts with irritation and impatience. "What do you think—meditation is only on the cushion? Only if your legs are crossed and you're staring at the wall? Watts, Suzuki, Kapleau, Krishnamurti—read them, Larry! Every one of them says the same thing. *Meditation is all the time and everywhere!* Everything I do—writing, teaching, seeing patients—it's all meditation! And everything we do here is meditation! Give up those narrow definitions! Cut out the nonsense and get down to work!"

My hand is resting on the bronze Guatemalen ashtray that sits on his desk. I flash an image of myself picking it up and smashing it into his face. He lurches backward in his chair, and blood trickles from a gash at the corner of his eye. The disparity between this gesture and the weakness and timidity I feel is almost exactly what I felt on waking up at home, the morning after leaving sesshin, when I remembered the zendo and my empty cushion there. It's as if a gap as big as the Grand Canyon separates what I am from what I want to be. Far from throwing ashtrays, I can barely hold my head up, and when I speak, my voice is almost inaudible. "No, I've got to leave. Got to get out of here. I don't know what happens to me here, but I've had enough of it."

Kelman writes in his notebook. The scratching of his fountain pen infuriates me. Without looking up, he cries: "Of course you have to leave! That's what I'm trying to tell you! On your own! Without my permission! What is this work about if not letting go? Letting go of yourself, your self-consciousness, your self-criticism, your dependency on me. Only then will you open the path to awareness. And only then will we be able to work together."

A silence follows. It occurs to me as if for the first time that I am dealing with a fanatic. One step down or—who knows?—up, and he'd be preaching from an orange crate in Times Square. I know from David that Kelman has never lived with anyone. Finally, this is his life, what we're doing here. Without my consent to needing his help, he has no function, no validity or purpose. But of course, we are co-conspirators. We've built this prison together. We both believe that I can be explained, that everything can be articulated, even silence, even the understanding that we talk too much and kill ourselves with description. That any problem we understand is by definition cured, and any problem that remains is proof of insufficient understanding. Most of all, both of us believe that he knows something I don't.

Sighing loudly, he lights another cigarette, then speaks to me in a confidential voice, as if I'm suddenly more his colleague than his patient. There is something he has to tell me, he says, even though it violates his professional ethics. In addition to me, he has three other patients involved in spiritual practice. He also has two supervisees with such patients. What's becoming clear is that all of us are following similar patterns. "You began by thinking you could escape neurosis on the cushion, but you quickly discovered that meditation, if anything, makes things worse. Dependent personalities become more dependent. There's more anxiety, not less. You can't escape these issues, Larry. You've got to address them at the source!"

I stand and put out my hand to him. "Well, I'll say good-bye now."

He doesn't rise or take my hand. A rare smile crosses his face. "Ever since you came to this office," he says, "I've been waiting for this moment. The real letting go. The strength I hear in your voice now, the light I see in your eyes. Look, even your posture is different!"

. . .

When Jissan and Hoan come to visit, on their weekend break from Dai Bosatsu, we plan a special dinner on Saturday night. The friends we invite have no particular interest in Zen, but they are clearly impressed when we tell them "two Zen monks" will be present. Call it spiritual chic. God knows that the prospect of hosting such dignitaries has us very impressed with ourselves.

But as it turns out, our visitors are not exactly the people we invited. When I open the door for them, they look less like the monks I knew at Dai Bosatsu than their older brother and sister. Their hair is growing in, they wear street clothes instead of the formidable black robes they wore at the monastery, and there's an air of embarrassment about them that makes it hard for them to look me in the eye. To my surprise, since they're only here for the weekend, they're toting two enormous suitcases. As we ascend in the elevator, Jissan explains: they've left Dai Bosatsu, rescinded their monastic vows, rejected Eido Roshi as a teacher.

Andra has baked cookies and made a pot of tea, but as we take our seats around the table, Jissan asks for vodka. Aware that he has had a drinking problem in the past, I glance at Hoan, but she shrugs her shoulders. Sipping the shot I've poured him, he informs us that we are henceforth to call them by their given names, Claudia and Sam. It seems to me his English accent is more pronounced than at Dai Bosatsu. He has certainly lost the accent he copied from Eido Roshi. "Jissan is dead," he announces. "Hoan is dead. You're looking at two people who've awakened from a bloody nightmare."

At first, they don't want to explain their departure— "You two are just beginning this practice," Claudia says, "you don't need to hear this"—but their restraint is short-lived. Within minutes after sitting down, they've told us everything. Several women have accused Eido Roshi of sexual misconduct, and one of them, a reporter for the *Village Voice,* claims to have proof of his advances on a tape made with a hidden microphone. Now she is threatening to expose him in print. "But none of this is new!" says Sam. "He's been doing this for years! He doesn't care what age they are or what their condition is. I've seen him come on with middle-aged women and eighteen-year-olds, borderline psychotics and spaced-out acid heads. The whole parade of hopeless, frightened creatures who come to a zendo—they're all fair game for him. He does it at sesshin! Even in dokusan!"

More than sixty students, about 50 percent of the membership, have resigned from the sangha. A petition is circulating that demands the roshi's dismissal by the Board of Directors. In response to the uproar, Eido has firmly denied all allegations. The women who've charged him, he claims, are acting out their own fantasies, and those circulating the petition are expressing disappointment not with him but with themselves, their lack of sincerity and courage, their lack of commitment. Finally, seizing the initiative, he has dissolved the membership and closed the zendo and the monastery for thirty days. When this period ends, he says, those he wants back will be invited to return, and the rest can go somewhere else.

During the next three weeks, Sam eats almost constantly,

drinks coffee throughout the day, and though he rarely gets drunk, drinks every night. Suffering again from a fear of crowds and public transportation that afflicted him before he discovered Zen, he spends most of his time indoors. Reading and listening to music, he says he is rediscovering the appetite for culture that was stifled at the monastery. "What is this but food?" he says, holding a book aloft. "Why should spiritual practice require us to deny this part of ourselves?" Whenever I am available, he engages me in discussions about Eido Roshi, Zen and Buddhism. In a weird echo of my father and brother, he is reading Krishnamurti and quoting his criticisms of orga- nized spiritual practice and teacher-student relationships. Krishnamurti, he says, has had it right all along. Surrendering to a teacher encourages fascism and sadism in the teacher, self- effacement and masochism in the student. For the most part, spiritual students are acting out of dependency rather than any authentic search for truth. Jissan is especially disgusted with himself for getting caught up in what he calls "the Japanese trip." "Why have we allowed the Japs to define Zen for us? They've taken a practice that is essentially joyous and spontane- ous and turned it into something dark and repressive and puritanical. How can they liberate us when they're so uptight themselves?"

Claudia's anger is equal to Sam's, but it is directed less at Eido Roshi than at spiritual practice in general. This sort of cri- sis, she says, is inevitable. "Why? Because practices like these create hope which cannot fail to be disappointed. Everything we do in Zen is based on the belief that we can free ourselves of desire. Isn't that the greatest desire of all? Spiritual teachers talk about that contradiction, but in my view they're disin- genuous. When you sit on a cushion, you're looking for happi-

ness. Forget the First Noble Truth. You're hoping that if you
sit with pain, you'll escape it. Even if you tell yourself that
there's no such thing as perfection, and no worse delusion than
looking for it, you're still looking for it and hoping for it, and
when you find it isn't coming, you go into a rage."

Every morning at six, the four of us sit together for two
hours in a small zendo that Andra and I have set up with cushions, an altar, and two tatami mats. Occasionally, we are joined
by Kendo, who has also rescinded his vows and is supporting
himself by working as a typist. Often, these sittings feel unusu-
ally quiet and powerful. Sam says we're creating a "new Zen, a
practice free of Japs, a Zen for adults rather than children."
And Kendo: "It's like we're finally sitting for ourselves instead
of our parents."

Claudia and Sam stay with us for six weeks. Though both
are working as office temps, they have to borrow money from
us and Claudia's father in order to get by. In the beginning,
they were conscientious about our morning sittings, but as time
goes on, their interest wanes. By the time they find an apartment, they've stopped sitting altogether, and a chill has crept
into our friendship. We are resentful of their cynicism toward
the practice and impatient for them to leave. They've killed our
dream, and we can't forgive them. Neither of us goes to the
zendo anymore. Though we'd barely begun the practice when
we met them, we speak of it now as seasoned travelers of a
country they used to love as tourists. Do we admit that we are
not totally displeased with our disenchantment, that at least a
part of our minds is delighted to have an excuse for avoiding
sesshin, the pain and risk of spiritual practice in general? I
don't think so.

. . .

Two weeks after they move out, Claudia phones one morning with an amazing suggestion: "What would you say to our bringing Soen Roshi to dinner this evening?" The occasion is the full moon. Soen wants to perform a ceremony in its honor, but he needs a roof with an unobstructed view of the sky, and our building suits his requirements perfectly.

We spend the day cleaning and cooking, burning incense to keep us in a proper frame of mind. The floors are mopped and the table waxed, flowers bought for the altar, in our bedroom and our zendo. We arrange our schedule so that we can sit for an hour to calm our minds before Soen's arrival. I don't know about Andra, but I can say for sure that such calm eludes me. By the time the doorbell rings, I am exhausted and depressed—not from the work I've done but from anticipating Soen's observation of our life. Seeing it through his eyes, our loft looks decadent and indulgent, a shameful concession to material comfort. How can I be pleased at the prospect of his visit? It seems to me that the insincerity of my practice will be visible to him the moment he steps through the door.

I go down to pick them up in the old freight elevator that remains from the days when this building was a doll factory. When I open the doors, Soen places his palms together and offers me a deliberate bow, then extends his hand and shakes mine vigorously. "Thanking you so much. You so kind invite me here. Ah, thank you, thank you." His voice is even deeper than in the zendo. Very slight and quick in his movement, not more than five feet tall, he seems to be treating me like an old friend. Fixed on me, his eyes are mischievous and confidential, as if the two of us share a private joke. The thought crosses my mind that he has me confused with someone else, that having known so many students over the years, he thinks we've met before. He wears sandals with thick wooden soles, a grey ankle-length robe over a thin white one, a matching grey pillbox hat of the sort that Zen monks wear for travel. Draped over his neck is the embroidered cloth, or "rakusu," worn by all Zen monks. He carries a large shopping bag bearing the logo of a well-known supermarket chain. As the elevator rises, his eyes are spread with wonder. "Such wonderful elevator! Such beautiful factory house! I so happy to be here!"

His effusion continues at dinner. "Wonderful soup! Wonderful saki! Ah, such beautiful flowers!" One might expect such happiness to be contagious, but nothing could be further from the truth. The four of us are stiff as children at a gathering of adults. My grin is so fixed it hurts my jaw. For all our Zen ideas about ordinariness, equality and the absurdity of rank, we are fans in the presence of a star. Pitched about an octave above normal, our speech, as the evening progresses, bears more and more resemblance to his. "You happy New York, Roshi? When you go back Japan?" Every move he makes—his posture, his concentration when he eats, the way his head, when he laughs, seems to bounce on his shoulders—seems significant and instructive. Meanwhile, he is himself utterly at ease, giggling like a child, making great sweeping gestures with his hands, telling long stories embellished with skillful mimicry at which I laugh in a fake exaggerated manner even when I find them funny. When he tastes his soup and closes his eyes and probably just enjoys it, I see him meditating fiercely on its taste. Pouring water, he holds the pitcher over the glass until the last drop glistens at the end of the spout and finally descends, while I remember all the great Zen teachings I have read about waste, appreciation and mindfulness. Thus does Zen, when you can't let go of it, take you out of the moment it is meant to take you into. Now and again, he reaches into his shopping bag and digs out surprises—a cucumber, a large Japanese radish, or "daikon," a container of black sesame seeds, a small plastic bag full of Japanese pickles. It seems not impossible to me that all his worldly goods are contained in this sack. Finally, he offers us ginkgo nuts and a nutcracker with which to open them. Handing me one, he fixes his eyes on me and growls: "We say in Japan: Man who eat ginkgo nut can eat his own shit. With your face, you have no problem." Everyone laughs uproariously, including me, but even now, years later, I have no idea whether this was an insult, a compliment, an enigmatic "Zen" remark, or a communication from another culture that I did not grasp at all.

After dinner, we climb the fire escape to the roof. Despite the fact that buildings surround us and we are visible and audible to those who live in them, we stand in a circle and, hands lifted in gassho, offer the moon the two-word mantra he composed—"Namu! Daibosa!" (Hail to the Enlightened One!)—which is chanted at the zendo and the monastery. While he clasps his hands like a drum, we chant it again and again, louder and louder, shouting at the moon. I've no idea how many times we do it. Certain we're watched from the surrounding windows, I am uneasy when we begin and, for all my chanting, no less uneasy when we're done. It doesn't help, of course, that I feel ashamed of my discomfort. Nor does it help to see my opposite before me, a man for whom self-consciousness and vanity have seemingly never been invented. I want him to strip me of inhibition like a doctor removing a bandage from a wound, but if anything, his presence seems to be a bandage in itself.

Now he has another idea. "I and moon one!" he cries. "You and moon one! Look! I swallow moon!" He opens his mouth and takes a bite of air and gulps and swallows as if the moon just slid down his throat like an oyster. "You too!" he cries. "Try! Try!" And for several minutes, gulping and swallowing with all the conviction we can muster, we follow his example. In the building across the street, I see faces in the window. How is it possible that, in the midst of living out the nonduality principle from which the whole of Mahayana Buddhism is derived, I am worrying that one of those faces belongs to someone who has recognized me? How is it that, even as I remark that the man before me actually embodies this principle, a voice within me calls him a lunatic? Can I doubt his sincerity? Pretend that when he speaks of oneness with the moon he is merely honoring a concept? Why am I denied such faith? Such happiness? Why do I watch this moment, making *notes,* for God's sake, storing up irony and detail for the Zen book I am forever planning to write, while the mind he shows me is precisely one that doesn't watch and has no taste for irony? Why is my mind in two pieces while his is so clearly in one?

It is late when we return to the loft. Soen says, "Too late go anywhere now. OK I stay here?" On the floor of my office, we roll out a futon for him. Since Sam and Claudia can't bear to leave if Soen doesn't, we give them sheets and blankets for the bed they slept in before. When the four of us return to my office, we find Soen sitting on his heels, surrounded by his toiletries: a black toothbrush and a tube of Japanese toothpaste, a yellow plastic soap dish, a plastic cup with a childlike design, a black, threadbare washcloth decorated with Japanese calligraphy. Investigating the bathroom, he asks permission to take a bath. No, he won't need a towel. He's got one in his shopping bag. Maybe he can listen to music? He's noticed a collection of Bach cello suites on a shelf next to the phonograph. Not knowing the word for earphones, he points to his ears and draws a line across his scalp to ask if we own a pair so that he will not disturb us. Before we go to bed, he bows to us again. "You so kind man and lady! So kind house. Great Dharma house! From now on, this house name Dai Bosatsu Hotel. Friends of mine come from Japan, I tell them, you go Dai Bosatsu Hotel in Soho, New York! Kind man, kind lady there. Dharma friends! They take care of you!" As we fall asleep, I hear him running a bath for himself.

Next morning, he says he did not bother to sleep. "Too much beautiful here. Read, music, bath. Like paradise! Too much beautiful!" In addition to Bach, he's listened to Beethoven and Kodaly. He has also found a copy of my novel on the shelf and read enough to ply me with questions about it.

Searching his shopping bag again, he locates a bamboo strainer and a can of green tea that he insists on preparing and serving to us while we await him kneeling on the rug. After boiling water, warming a teapot and pouring the water slowly through the strainer, he serves each of us with a ceremonial bow. While he drinks, I watch him as I did last night. It is true he has remarkable attention, a way of holding a cup and concentrating on a taste that makes the act seem urgent, sacred, so exclusive of all other time and space that this might be the last moment of his life. Even so, I am a bit saner, somewhat less enraptured than last night. I notice wrinkles in his cheeks, minute bristles of hair poking through his scalp, his hands so tiny they might be a child's. With each such observation, I feel a bit

more comfortable with him. It's as if I regain my footing by
objectifying him, dilute the power I've invested in him by arranging him in my descriptions. Isn't this precisely the sort of
espionage from which I imagine him to be liberated?

When we're done with our tea, he says, "Where you sit?
Please you show me your cushions!"

We lead him to the room we have made into a zendo. It
has one window, bare brick walls, a small altar with a wooden
Buddha, a bronze water bowl, a vase which at present contains
a single yellow lily. For my birthday last year, Andra bought me
a miniature inkin, and it sits now on a tiny red cushion next to
my black cushion near the door. There are three sets of cushions along each wall, but we quickly remove one and rearrange
the rest so that there are two sets along each wall and a set for
the roshi, with the bell of course beside it, at the front of the
room. Before taking his place, he digs into his shopping bag
again. Extracting two calligraphies he's made, he presents them
to us as gifts. Each is about twelve inches square, signed with
his name and a red stamp on the left side. One is a collection of
fragments that look like human bones and means, he explains,
"One mind," the other a swirling character that looks something like the Aramaic letter *L*. The latter, he announces, means
"Light," and that will be the official name of our zendo. "I
name this great holy place Light Zendo! Give all beings absolute guarantee: whenever you come here, you find light! Guaranteed! OK? No matter how dark your mind, you come here,
you have completely light!"

After a brief period of chanting, he rings the bell, and we
settle into a period of zazen that is as quiet and powerful as any
I've ever known. Perhaps it's the occasion, the legendary "energy" and "vibration" that is said to emanate from Soen. Per-

haps it's simply relief from all the tension I've been feeling, the great leveling effect of zazen, which mocks teacher-student inequality by putting both on the floor together. Whatever the reason, I am free not only of my romanticism but of the largest part of my consciousness. Freedom from thought is not entirely new to me, but I have rarely known such freedom from thought about it. When the roshi rings the bell again, I have no idea how much time has passed. His growl is deeper now, almost leonine. It seems to fill the room and press against the walls. "This official zendo now. Light Zendo! First official Soho zendo! Look at the light! Look at the Buddhas! Five Buddhas, completely enlightened, sitting Dai Bosatsu Hotel! Please you appreciate your perfect beautiful nature! No need look outside for truth, put a head on top of the one you already have. Confused Buddhas! Wisdom Buddhas! All the world sitting together Light Zendo!" He rings the bell ten times in succession, allowing each ring to reverberate until it disappears. Then, after a silence, he has yet another idea for us. "OK! Every zendo have special practice. What your practice? Great secret practice! Mysterious! Different from any zendo in the world! Tongue zazen! Look, I show you!" Spreading his mouth as he did when he swallowed the moon, he sticks out his tongue and then, with his lips wide apart and his teeth completely bared, presses it against the roof of his mouth and, after achieving the proper suction, snaps it away with a popping sound. It's the sound we used to make as children to imitate the sound of a baseball meeting a bat. "Tongue zazen!" he cries. "Try! Try!"

At first, we are timid and not so good at it, the sounds we make not nearly as resonant as his. But after a moment we get the hang of it, and soon, teeth bared and mouth agape, we're getting the pop every time, snapping our tongues again and again in unison. The sound we make has a distinct and slightly military rhythm, filling the room like a drum corps. At first, I feel ridiculous to make it but, unlike last night, my embarrassment diminishes with each repetition. Soon I notice that when my pop is especially loud I feel a sense of accomplishment. Indeed, I am not only snapping my tongue with abandon but feeling a surge of energy, a sensation almost of happiness, every time I do so.

Disciples, there is a realm in which there is neither earth nor water, fire nor air; not endless space, infinite consciousness, nor nothingness; not perceptions nor nonperceptions. In it there is neither this world nor another, neither sun nor moon. I call it neither a coming nor a going nor a standing still; not death, nor birth; it is without basis, change, or stability. Disciples, it is the end of sorrow.

For that which clings to another, there is retrogression, but where there is no clinging there is no retrogression. Where no retrogression exists, and where there is calm there is no obsessive desire. Where obsessive desire is absent, there is neither coming nor going, and where coming and going have ended there is no death, no birth; and where death and birth do not exist there is neither this life nor an afterlife, nor any in between—it is, disciples, the end of suffering.

Yet there is an Unoriginated, Unborn, Uncreated, Unformed. If this Unoriginated, Unborn, Uncreated, Unformed did not exist, there would be no liberation for whatever is originated, born, created, and formed. But since there is an Unoriginated, Unborn, Uncreated, Unformed, liberation is possible for whatever is originated, born, created, and formed.
—BUDDHA

"A in't but two things I care about," Jamie says. "Zazen and fucking."

Over coffee at the loft, he's entertaining us with stories of the sex that comes his way at the zendo. As caretaker—a sort of head honcho who wields the stick and keeps the quiet and gives beginners' instruction—he works long hours for almost no pay, but among his perks is the fact that zendos attract surprisingly large numbers of interesting women, no small number of whom are turned on by monk's robes and other signs of Zen authority. It wasn't all that long ago that he considered his desire for sex—or pleasure of any sort—inconsistent with his practice, but now, encouraged no doubt by Eido Roshi's example, his understanding of such matters is more subtle. Deprivation, he says, can also be an ego trip. "Given the size of my spiritual ego, it is a helluva lot easier for me to be celibate than it is for me to get laid."

At present, he has two girlfriends, one his age and another twenty years his senior. He is also not averse to the occasional one-night stand. In his view, of course, all such encounters are opportunities for practice. Like any serious Zen student, but with a lot more passion than most, he tries to view everything he does—sex, eating, shitting, drinking beer, sweeping the floor—as zazen. He makes it a point, for example, to work on his koan when walking the streets. Among his other "practices" is a twice-a-week visit to the lingerie department at Bloomingdale's, where he posts himself in the midst of the bras and the panty hose and stands motionless for a carefully measured forty-five minutes, immersing himself in his embarrassment, practicing indifference to the stares of the salesladies who, for some odd reason, have never called the store police. No fetishism is involved. The lingerie department is simply a place where he is guaranteed maximum discomfort and therefore, by his reasoning, maximum insult to ego. A similar logic led Eido Roshi to refuse Novocaine last year when he went to his dentist for root-canal work because he viewed the pain as "a chance to get rid of bad karma."

It is seven-thirty and the three of us have just finished morning zazen. Jamie, who as usual refused our futon and slept on the floor, has been up since four. First he sat for an hour on his own, then he cleaned our loft. For the past few months, he has been staying with us on his day off, and though he has to know how glad we are to have him here, he acts as if we've taken him in off the street. "I'm disturbing you guys, I know it. Don't be afraid to throw me out, OK?" Searching out chores to repay us, he's fixed the toilet, the dripping faucet in the kitchen, the vacuum cleaner and, last week, an old coffee grinder that hadn't worked in years.

He wears the same jeans and flannel shirt he wore at the monastery, and his eyeglasses are still held together with a safety pin. Following an exotic diet that permits him to eat neither meat nor wheat nor dairy products, he's lost, I'd guess, some fifteen or twenty pounds since we met him at Dai Bosatsu. He is part of the contingent which, loyal to Eido Roshi, has been invited back to the zendo after its month-long closing. Most of the dissidents, of course, are angry at him for accepting the invitation, but he is indifferent to their opinions and, for that matter, the scandal that has them so exercised. "If the roach thinks with his dick, that's his problem. He ain't no different from anybody else. The reason people get mad at him, they put him on a pedestal. Want him to save them. Nobody

can save you on the cushion. Nobody can help you. Once I saw
that, I didn't give a fuck what he did."

. . .

Since I cannot give up the idea that I will someday write a book
on Zen, I am always pressing Roshi for details about his past. In
answer to my questions, he likes to quote the Zen master who
said, "With every inhalation, I create the universe. With every
exhalation, I destroy it." In his view, biographical information
is a kind of gossip, its elaboration more or less akin to investigating the waste one deposits in a toilet or, in one of his favorite
analogies, saving toilet paper after you've used it. Still, he is
nothing if not inconsistent, and despite the fact that he often
seems to idealize amnesia above all other conditions, he does
not aspire to absolute rejection of memory. Furthermore, truth
be told, he has a certain enthusiasm for talking about himself.
When I tell him I want to write about Zen, he says, "OK, if you
stick to your own experience." "But this means I have to interview you!" To which he replies, "OK, ask me question."
    So it is that over time, with the help of saki and green tea,
I have learned, among other things, that he was born Kyudo
Nakagawa in a Zen temple called Horaku-ji, in 1926, in the
small town of Eichijima-cho, outside Kyoto. He became a
monk at the age of six, but he is careful to point out that this
was a matter of formality, more like a Sunday School confirmation than a spiritual commitment. Though his father, his uncle
and his grandfather were all Zen priests (the last a samurai who
turned to Zen at the age of thirty-four), theirs was an institutional Zen—less the paradoxical wisdom of D. T. Suzuki than
the structure and ceremony, the social matrix, of national religion. His father's temple was less a meditation center than a

sort of church where parishioners came for funerals and ritual observance. It was also, more or less, the family business, and it was taken for granted that the son would one day assume control of it. But when Kyudo was twelve his father died, and Rinzai headquarters sent another priest to replace him. Though the family continued to live on temple grounds, the temple offered them no future. Two years later, when his mother died, Kyudo and his sister, three years older, were sent to live with their grandparents. One day, he would consider these developments fortuitous because, as he would explain, they released him from responsibility and offered "lesson in impermanence," but at this young age such detachment was not yet available to him. He was bereft without his mother, frightened about his future. Availing himself, for the first time but certainly not the last, of a strategy he would later commend to students—when confusion overwhelms you, seek the advice of a person you trust and follow it *unequivocally*—he turned for guidance to his grandmother. When she suggested he continue as a monk because the profession offered "stability," he made his life decision. He was fourteen years old. Characteristically, he did not look back, and he did not second-guess himself. It was a moment which illustrated much that would later fall under the rubric of Zen for him—volition, commitment, respect for one's teachers, disdain for hindsight and indecision.

After high school, he enlisted in the navy. He was eighteen years old and bivouacked forty kilometers away when the bomb was dropped on Hiroshima by the nation in which he would someday reside and teach. A bunkmate woke him to see the mushroom cloud, but after a single, yawning glance, he went back to sleep. Later, when he became a teacher, disaffected students would use this event, and the war itself, to explain what they took to be his bias against westerners in general and Americans in particular. He himself would use it as an introduction to the maddening lectures on politics in which he called nuclear war "the big barbecue" and democracy "great excuse for selfish." Several students would actually leave our zendo because they could not tolerate such views, but their departures, if anything, inspired him to greater heights of irreverence. Toward catastrophe of any sort, he would always be as insouciant as he was about the Hiroshima bomb.

After the navy, he enrolled at Komazawa, a Buddhist university in Osaka, studied philosophy and religion (focusing on the Upanishads) and graduated six years later. Though his degree qualified him to be a high school teacher, he had no interest in this career. His understanding of Buddhism was minimal, but, remaining true to his grandmother's advice, he spent three years at the preeminent Soto monastery, Eihei-ji, then accepted a position as resident monk at a small temple on the outskirts of Osaka. It seemed to him he had found the stability she promised. Since the head priest and his wife had no son, the temple would one day be his. Alas, he was in for another disappointment, another stroke of luck masquerading as its opposite. There was a daughter who went with the temple. Marriage with her, it seemed, was among the duties he was expected to fulfill. Furthermore, until he became a member of the family, he would be more or less its indentured servant. He worked seven-day weeks, twelve-hour days, and his rice-miso-seaweed diet rarely totaled more than eight hundred calories a day. Once or twice a week, a trap was set by the priest or his wife—a smidgen of dust behind a bedpost, a dime-sized stain on the back side of a water faucet—to test his diligence. Despite these conditions, he remained at the temple for one-and-a-half years and left only because the priest, angry about his disinterest in marriage, suggested he'd be better off at another temple or even perhaps in another profession.

Adrift again, he turned for advice to another elder—a Zen teacher in Kyoto to whom he was introduced by a former classmate. If you mean to be serious about Zen, he was told, go back to the monastery. Which monastery? Only two, said the teacher, were worth considering. Myoshin-ji, famous for its brutal discipline, was the place to go for Buddhist studies and ascetic training, but if one wanted zazen, one should head for a small monastery north of Tokyo called Ryutaku-ji. It was founded in the fifteenth century, abandoned in the sixteenth, revived—by the great Master Hakuin—in the seventeenth. Its abbot now was the same Soen Roshi who would one day pave the way for teachers like Eido, Suzuki and eventually Kyudo himself in the United States.

Kyudo had never heard of Soen Roshi, nor was he altogether sure that he wanted zazen, but within a week, he had moved the two suitcases that contained his worldly belongings to a small unheated room on the second floor of Ryutaku-ji. He was twenty-eight years old and less than happy to discover that the diet here was, if anything, less generous than the temple's. Since the sitting schedule was difficult—four hours on ordinary days, ten to fourteen during sesshin—and he was not used to any sort of extended practice, there were problems with his neck and shoulders and, more seriously, a knee hurt twelve years before in a motorcycle accident. Pain or not, however, he welcomed sesshin for the food, for it was only then that monks were allowed second helpings. Soen criticized him for eating too much, not least because it made him fall asleep during teishos, but not for years had he known such freedom from hunger.

One of Soen's first actions was to change the name of his new monk. The habit at the monastery was to call everyone by the last syllable of their first name with the suffix "san." Thus, in ordinary circumstances, Kyudo would have been "Do-san." There was already a Do-san there, however, so Soen decided that "Kyudo" must be reversed. From then on he'd be "Dokyu," his name around the monastery "Kyu-san." In later years, when he became a roshi, he'd be called "Dokyu Roshi" by some people, "Kyudo Roshi" by others. To complicate the matter further, Soen Roshi, deciding that his disciple was more a Taoist than a Zen master, would adopt the Chinese name for him and call him "Doshi." There were less than two dozen Rinzai Zen masters in the world when Soen formally anointed him a successor, but surely he was the only one who had three different names.

Most of the monks at Ryutaku-ji had friends and supporters in the outside world who brought them food or took them to restaurants, but Kyudo's friends were in Tokyo and he had no money to treat himself. His loneliness was eased by two monks, Sochu and Kozen, who were a bit older than he and from similar backgrounds. One day, all three would become Zen masters, but now, since Sochu and Kozen had been at Ryutaku-ji for five and four years respectively, he was their inferior and, not infrequently, the butt of their jokes. Like Soen, they found it difficult to understand why this short, giggly fellow so little drawn to Zen should willingly submit to the deprivations of monastic life. Zen life was easy if, as they said, your hair was on fire for realization, but to what rationale did he resort when the windows were opened on a snowy day in January so that, sitting in their unheated zendo, teeth chattering, feet and hands gone numb with the cold, one might learn to transcend the body?

One of his jobs was nursing Soen's teacher, Gempo Roshi, the former abbot of the monastery. Ninety-five years old and suffering from arthritis and arteriosclerosis, Gempo was if anything even more revered than his disciple. Though he needed help to stand and walk and sometimes even to eat, he continued to sit in zazen, either alone in his room or in the zendo. Indeed, soon after Kyudo became his attendant, Gempo embarked on a solitary weeklong sesshin, sitting twelve hours a day, taking all his meals on the cushion and sleeping in full-lotus. Kyudo would never forget Gempo's face twisted with pain as he took his seat on the cushion and, pulling his arthritic, skeletal legs onto his thighs, growled at them as if at disobedient children, "Son must listen to father!" It might be true that he knew nothing of Zen, but he knew he wanted what Gempo wanted and, more than that, wanted to want it equally.

Three years would pass, however, before such wanting was released in him. There was no particular revelation, no event from which the shift in his mind could be traced, nothing but years of practice so unrewarding that they had whittled away all hope and expectation. Taking his seat on the cushion one evening, he simply realized who he was. No aspect of his life would be unaffected by this change, and no one who knew him would be unaware of it. Thirty years later, he would describe it to me over saki one evening in a Japanese restaurant in Greenwich Village. "Many years I see branches of tree. Now I see root. What doesn't change." All his efforts as a Zen master would be devoted to helping others see this root. Only ignorance and fixed ideas, he'd tell us, made it invisible. All ideas, all images, all thoughts, all sensations are branches on the tree. They change, but the root does not. The root existed before them and will exist when they are gone. "Suddenly, I see I very lucky man. Have no knowledge of Zen, no picture. Not like you, Larry-san. Not intelligent. No Zen-book-reader. But listen! Maybe you not so intelligent after all! Maybe one day you give up your pictures! Become stupid like me! Just for one second! Then, I give you guarantee, you see root too! Just like me, you see what never change! You see yourself!"

Excited by his story, a forbidden question looms in my mind. I know that, as far as Zen is concerned, it is extremely bad form to ask it, but I cannot restrain myself. "Would you call that—what happened to you that night at Ryutaku-ji—an enlightenment experience?"

" 'Enlightenment'?" he says. "All I know about enlightenment—when I sit, my knees hurt."

. . .

In addition to Bloomingdale's, another regular stop for Jamie on his perambulations through the city is Chang Wei's dojo, which happens to be just a fifteen-minute walk from our Soho loft. One afternoon, as he prepares to leave, he asks if Andra and I would like to join him. A tai chi class is about to begin, but if we leave right away, we'll get there in time for the karate sparring session that precedes it. The dojo, he says, is "an energy pool." He likes to arrange his schedule so that he can visit it just before returning to the zendo for evening zazen. Such is the hit it provides that when he gets to his cushion later he often feels as if he's in the third day of sesshin.

I've not seen Chang Wei since we met at the monastery, but his name has often come up in conversations with Sam and

Claudia and, of course, with Jamie. When they speak of the regular zazen sessions he holds at his dojo, they are almost as reverent as when speaking of Soen Roshi. In light of the scandal at the zendo, Chang's dojo and other places like it, offering as they do a less formal zazen situation with no ties to Japan, have assumed a new importance for us all. Like so many others, Andra and I—disinclined to study with Eido Roshi—have no place to sit, and since the dojo is located conveniently near our home, we have often wondered whether Chang might allow us to sit there, even if we are not to be students of the karate or tai chi. I am drawn to him too for another reason. The posture problems pointed out to me on my first visit to the zendo seem to be getting worse. Lately, in fact, they have become so distracting that they ruin my concentration while I sit. Jamie assures me that no one deals with such problems better than Chang Wei. "I guarantee you," he says, "if you put yourself in Chang's hands, trust him absolutely, you'll be straight and comfortable in no time."

It is cool and drizzling on this late-autumn evening as we leave our building and head downtown. Jamie walks so fast that we must hurry to keep up with him. The dojo is located between an art gallery and an all-night pharmacy on the fourth floor of a loft building in lower Manhattan. The entry corridor is dark and somewhat dingy, but halfway up the steep wooden stairs, we see a clean, well-lit landing and a red door on which a wooden yin-yang plaque is mounted. Removing our shoes, we push through the door and, following Jamie's example, bow once to the center of the room and once to Chang himself, who sits on his heels some twenty feet to our left. There are twenty to thirty people in the room, each dressed in the white workout suit, called a "gi," of the martial arts. The gis are tied with belts of various colors—white, brown, green or black—that signify rank in karate. Fluorescent lights hang overhead, and the floor is red linoleum. Lining the walls are mirrors in which a number of students study themselves, working on various punches or kicks or the fluid dancelike movements of tai chi, repeating gestures again and again to polish or shape or strengthen them. Some use sets of old-fashioned weight pulleys that are bolted to the wall at various heights. Others punch and kick against the air or stretch like yogis or dancers.

Chang kneels on the floor beside a young woman lying on a wooden bench. His hands—wrists arched, fingers splayed, one below the shoulder blades, the other just above the hips— are poised on her as if on a piano. Later, I'll learn that he is engaged in a "healing" or "energizing" session, transmitting to his student the powers of which he is allegedly possessed. In addition to the range of diseases he is said to have cured by means of these treatments—diabetes, arthritis, migraine, etc.— he also treats more diffuse conditions such as depression, indecision, anger, apathy or impotence. Word has it that even brain tumors and leukemia have succumbed to the sort of treatment I am presently observing.

Before I can ask Jamie anything about it, the session ends, and the mood of the dojo shifts dramatically. Striking a bell like the one that's used in the zendo, Chang calls "Spar!" in a sort of drill sergeant's voice, and while we and the tai chi students stand or sit along the walls, eight pairs of karate students face off in the center of the room. They fight until another bell sounds, then switch partners and begin again. Each fight lasts about three minutes. For the most part, they are too fast for my untrained eye to follow, but I can see that punches and kicks are usually pulled or blocked before they reach their targets. Still, the sparring is plenty violent. People get tripped and thrown to the floor and now and then a blow connects. One fight is interrupted for several minutes because the woman who just got energized lands a kick to the groin of another black belt, a man who towers over her and looks about twice her weight.

There is a ten-minute break between sparring and tai chi, and Chang comes over to say hello. He is wearing black loose-fitting pants and a maroon tunic tied with a black belt. So short is his hair that I can't tell if he cuts it this way or shaves his head and is overdue for a trim. A round-shouldered man of medium height, he has a huge, incongruous belly that makes him look a bit like a kangaroo, toting his offspring in a pouch. His round face is surprisingly gentle, almost cherubic, but his narrow, dark, unblinking eyes are confrontational and not a little intimidating. I do not expect him to remember us, but as he puts out his hand, he says, "I was wondering when you'd get here. I heard you lived in the neighborhood."

It never fails to amaze me how much authority I find—or invest—in people like Chang. He seems a man who's never known self-doubt or indecision, who watches the world with perfect incognizance of the world watching him. Most of all, he seems accustomed to being surrounded with people who, like me at this moment, use his eyes as a conduit through which to observe—and evaluate—themselves. "What do you think of my shop?" he says.

Andra asks if this is in fact a zendo—"in the official sense." Chang points to a wooden plaque, inlaid with Japanese calligraphy, mounted on the wall behind us. "Eido Roshi made

this calligraphy and had it carved for me. We had a consecra-
tion ceremony here last year." A smile spreads over his face.
"You are standing in the Manhattan Zendo!"

"Is it private?" she says. "Can anyone sit here or only
your students?"

"All zendos are public. You know the two rules of Zen.
'Don't turn anyone away, and don't chase after anyone who
leaves.' Where are you two sitting these days?"

"At home," I say.

"At home?" He laughs disparagingly. "Come on! You
two just started to sit, didn't you? No way you can manage serious practice on your own."

I start to explain that we're uncomfortable about going
to the New York Zendo, but Chang cuts me off. "I know about
that. Everybody's saying the same thing. But all that matters is
the practice, you know? Your own mind. Your own body. People always find reasons not to do it, but meanwhile, your life
is going down the drain. Why don't you come here and sit
with us?"

.   .   .

With the exception of one two-week period of fear and uncertainty that occurs in his seventh year (as it does at this time, he
says, for many monks), Kyudo gives no thought to leaving
Ryutaku-ji until 1962, his twelfth year, and then only because
Soen himself suggests it. The route by which the suggestion
reaches him says much about the mysterious travels of Zen in
the 1960s. For some years, Soen has been making biannual
trips to the United States, conducting regular sesshins with
groups of students in the New York area, and recently he has
been teaching at the New York Zendo. As it happens, the

zendo is in the same neighborhood as the Rockefeller Institute, and a number of its researchers and professors have been drawn to practice zazen there. One of these researchers is an Israeli biochemist named Tamar Blum, who is now returning to Israel. She tells Soen that she knows half-a-dozen Israelis who sit regularly in zazen, and she is certain more would turn up if a zendo existed to encourage them. Doesn't he know someone he could send to help them out?

Soen turns to Kyudo because he is the only one of his monks who speaks a little English. When the possibility of Israel is suggested to him, he has never heard of any country by this name, and when he arrives in Israel in 1967, two days before the Six Day War begins, the only Hebrew word he knows (he learned it from an Israeli boy on the plane) is *shalom.* He is forty-two years old. When the Jerusalem Zendo opens in the Arab quarter, six students will attend its first sitting. One year later, it will have a membership of 10, three years later, 2. Eventually, attendance will climb again, but in the thirteen years that Kyudo will remain here, it will never get much beyond 30.

. . .

Under any conditions, Andra and I would be grateful for the dojo, but it has assumed an urgent importance now because our marriage is in trouble, and though we don't like to admit it, we are counting on zazen to keep us together.

I think both of us knew these problems were inevitable. She was too young when we married, and despite the fact that I'm ten years older, I was no more mature than she was. Whatever the reason, the marriage has become claustrophobic for us both. She says she feels "constricted" by it, but even though I feel the same, and in fact am grateful to her for bringing it out in the open, I feel wounded, rejected, consumed with anger and self-pity. Maybe we aren't a whole lot different from other couples who married too young and have to break up in order to grow up, but we can't believe that our five years of Zen practice haven't protected us from the grief and confusion that traps so many others. In fact, it may well be that our practice, creating the sort of muddle-headed piety that one Tibetan teacher calls "holy style," has had no effect except to top off our misery with spiritual guilt. In the midst of a jealous rage, I get a lecture on "compassion" from my Zen voice, images of my face radiant, beatific with detachment while my rage intensifies the way knee pain does when I try to reason it away on my cushion. What's more hypocritical than using Buddhist ideas in the service of repression?

Maybe I'm caught somewhere between the Hinayana and the Mahayana or falling into the trap that makes me think the latter can exclude the former. I like to think that Zen can liberate me from my psychology, but more often than not, it simply makes me imagine such liberation as a sort of idealized Zen state and feel guilty when I don't achieve it. When Andra and I practice zazen at home, I can feel as if I'm on top of a mountain, watching our problems scuttling back and forth like traffic in the valley below. From this point of view, the twenty-twenty vision of my "Dharma eye," anger is thought and thought nothing more than electrical flashes in my brain. What on earth could prompt me to create from such transient impulses an equally transient entity called "myself"? Believing that she has found a similar equanimity, how can I doubt that, when the bell rings and we get up from our cushions, we'll find ourselves in love again? The problem is that my equanimity, no

less transient than any other state of mind, disappears as soon
as I leave my cushion. Not five minutes after my blissful
luminosity, I find myself as irritable and distracted as after
drinking too much coffee. It's as if a sort of recoil occurs, confusion and small-mindedness erupting with even greater intensity than before, as if anger, pride and righteousness, like an
army temporarily outflanked, are fighting to recover positions
they have lost. You don't have to be a Buddhist to know that
ego does not take kindly to states of mind that tend to expose
its insubstantiality. And since Andra is subject to similar rever-
sals, some of our worst fights occur after particularly intimate
periods of shared zazen. This is when the Zen voice turns vin-
dictive: How can you be sincere in your practice if you can't
make it work with the woman you love? You're nothing but a
dilettante, a fake, using Zen to hide your selfishness and arrogance. But sometimes it's Zen I blame instead of myself:
What's the use of this practice if it doesn't help my marriage?
What sort of brainwashed, simplistic mentality is it encouraging in me? For all I know, the real cause of our problems is all
this piety and self-consciousness we've learned from the roshis!
But then too there are days when I think our separation is necessary, inevitable, that Zen—precisely because it cuts so deep
and leads to such fundamental change—isn't meant to help a
marriage but tear it apart. Who is to say that this is unfortunate? We're both of us children, aren't we? Why sit if it doesn't
help us grow up? If we were really serious about this practice,
we'd be celebrating now!

Despite the fact that we are the only students here who
are not involved in the martial arts, Chang and his students are
extremely hospitable to us. It is true that if a black belt sees me
leaning against a wall, he or she will reprimand me or even slip

a hand behind my back and push me forward, but given the
context, I take that as a compliment. Perhaps, because we're
here for zazen alone, we give the place a kind of credibility as a
zendo. For our part, in addition to the benefits we are deriving
from zazen, we are more and more fascinated by the workouts
and the sparring. Like Jamie, we like to come early and feed off
the energy. Between the karate and the tai chi, the former violent, discontinuous, blindingly fast, the latter a sort of slow-
motion ballet, it seems as if the entire spectrum of physical activity is unfolding before our eyes. And when zazen is added to
the mix, when the spectrum expands to include the spiritual,
the dojo seems a kind of laboratory in which the outside limits
of human potential are being explored.

   Almost every day, when we arrive, Chang is engaged in
"energizing." Sometimes he kneels beside one person on the
bench and sometimes, since he treats couples as well as in-
dividuals, two people lie side by side on the floor while he
kneels between them with a hand on each one's back. Often,
during zazen, he places his cushion near the telephone, dials a
number and puts the receiver on his low belly—the so-called
"hara," or energy center—so that, as Jamie explains, he can en-
ergize the person on the other end of the line. Many black belts
are among his clients, and now Jamie himself has joined the
ranks, making his way here for two or three treatments a week.
Broke as he is, he can't pay what Chang ordinarily charges—
$1,000 for twenty-five sessions—but Chang owns an old sports
car, and he is allowing Jamie to pay for his treatments by re-
building its rear end. This means that almost all of Jamie's free
time is spent at the dojo or the garage, but as far as he's concerned, he's stumbled into an even greater bargain than he was
offered by Eido Roshi, when he was allowed to pay with labor

to live at Dai Bosatsu. Two or three days a week, we see him
either alone on the bench or on the floor, holding hands with
his new girlfriend, a handsome blonde named Bonnie, whom
he met when she came to the zendo for beginners' instruction.
Among other things, Jamie swears that Chang's treatments
have resolved the sexual problems he and Bonnie had when
they first got together. "I don't know why," he confesses, "but
at first I couldn't get it up with her at all. Never wanted a
woman so bad, but couldn't do nothing about it. Three sessions with Chang was all it took to set me right. Now I can
hardly get it down!"

Since Jamie is one of the few people who knows that
Andra and I are having problems, he pleads with us to get energized. There is no doubt in his mind that Chang can save our
marriage. "I know this stuff looks weird, Larry, but I guarantee
you it works. I've tried it all—Zen, yoga, est, Scientology, you
name it—and I've never seen energy like Chang's. Trust him,
OK? Just put yourself in his hands, and in two or three sessions, your problems will be gone. Don't think about it.
Thought ain't nothin' but ego and resistance, and that's just
what you've got to give up."

It's true that energizing looks weird, or more precisely,
absurd, to us, but we are not entirely averse to Jamie's reasoning. Chang's treatments, after all, are an exercise in surrender,
and no one who has studied Zen or any other spiritual practice
would doubt the benefit of that. The problem is that surrender
as an abstraction is a whole lot different from surrender to one
person, someone you know. When I think of lying on the floor
with Chang's hand on my back, a sort of nausea wells in me. I
don't know anyone I respect more than Jamie, but the route he
is taking is inconceivable to me.

. . .

Roshi arrives in New York in September 1981. Using the whole
of his life savings, he purchases thirty sets of brown cushions
and pays the first month's rent on a loft in Soho. Assisted by
several students, including myself, he refinishes the floors and
paints the walls in the sand color he considers best for zazen.
He installs his Buddha, his water bowl and his incense burner
on an altar fashioned from a table purchased from a used-furni-
ture shop in the neighborhood, hangs scrolls by Soen Roshi
and his brother monk, Sochu-san, who, a roshi himself now,
has replaced Soen as abbot at Ryutaku-ji. When the zendo is
ready, he closes the doors and turns off the phone and does
three days of retreat, cleaning and chanting and sitting zazen,
to purify it. The zendo opens in October, at six o'clock in the
morning, with four students in attendance, and from that time
on, he conducts three 30-minute sittings morning and evening,
five days a week, a seven-day sesshin once a month.

I am present at the first sitting. For the first four months, I
sit every morning and most evenings. I have little life outside
the zendo, and I want none. Living alone in a small apartment
twenty minutes away, I walk here at dawn through empty
streets. Every morning, after sitting, Roshi serves green tea. By
the time I head for my office, it is eight-thirty or a little after. I
feel younger and healthier, more sanguine, relaxed and confident than ever in my life, convinced that I have found the optimum state of mind for my work. The only problem is that I am
unable to work at all. An old affliction has returned—I'm paralyzed when I get to my desk. It's as if my mind is too clean, too
calm, as if my work in the past has been fueled by the sort of
last-gasp desperation of a diver with a failing air hose, and

zazen has stifled me with endless quantities of oxygen. The act of putting words on paper seems like an insult to the bliss I achieved, just an hour ago, when sitting on my cushion.

After several weeks of this futility, I decide to put the matter to Roshi. Am I misusing Zen or misusing my work? Is it possible that Zen attacks the very source of language, that sitting on a cushion and staring at the wall, however much it does for one's soul or mind, is death to imagination? More and more, I tell him, I fear that writing and sitting are incompatible and that someday I'll have to choose between them.

Typically, he laughs at me before he gets serious. "You know your problem, Larry-san? You attached to emptiness. You go zendo, feel happy, hold on to happiness, happy become sad! No wonder you not write! You not at your desk! You still in zendo! Don't holding anything! When sitting, just sit. When writing, just write. If you think Buddha on toilet, you become hemorrhoid!"

. . .

A few months after we begin sitting at the dojo, Chang invites Jamie and me to dinner at a Japanese restaurant. The occasion is Jamie's departure, two days from now, for another sesshin at Dai Bosatsu. Chang wants to give him a proper send-off, he says, because Jamie is primed for kensho, and this is to be his breakthrough sesshin. As we take our seats in the restaurant, he exhorts Jamie as he has for the last few weeks. "You've never had a shot like this! You've had, what, thirty energizing sessions? Put them together with all the sesshins you've done, there's only one reason you'll miss. Fear! What's the American expression? 'Shit or get off the pot'? If you don't make it this time, you never will!" And then, to give his point, as he always does, its proper physical dimension, he leans and slaps Jamie on the small of his back. "Come on, sit up straight. You'll never get there if you slouch like that."

If Chang has a belief system, it is centered here, in the lower back. He has designed a series of exercises, many of them difficult and painful, to strengthen this area. While sitting, he says, one should "push hard with the lower back while pushing down on the kidneys" and, of course, breathing through the low belly. Since all concentration is located in the lower back and the low belly, it follows that, if these muscles are properly strengthened, your chances for enlightenment will be maximized. It also follows that your body condition—"all your organs"—will function at an optimum level. It is his view that one should *never relax* while on the cushion. After sitting, one should feel totally exhausted, and those who don't can be sure they've wasted their time. On the other hand, such exertion is the key to spiritual power. Only those who hold nothing back will discover their true, inexhaustible reservoirs of energy and courage.

Though convinced by his reasoning, I have never been able to put his words into practice. I've done my exercises and followed his advice, but I don't understand what it means to "push down" with one's kidneys. It's as if I am lacking in some essential muscle or muscle control that this sort of effort requires. If anything, my posture problems are worse now than when I started coming to the dojo.

It is Chang's view that one should drink beer before and saki during Japanese meals, so this is the course we take. Before the saki arrives, we each have two bottles of beer, and by the time we're halfway through the sushi-sashimi platter he's ordered after consultation with the sushi chef, we've had three pitchers of saki between us. Jamie and I are reeling, but Chang is completely sober. Talking about his work, he is rating the practices he teaches with regard to physical demand. To my surprise, he says that zazen is the most difficult. Correctly done, it is the most arduous and demanding of all physical practices. Next comes tai chi and last karate. "People look at karate and think it's really hard, but that's because they're only looking at the surface. The real work is inside, and nothing comes near zazen for that."

He grips a piece of sushi with his chopsticks and places it on my plate. "Hey, Larry, you OK? You don't look too good."

"I'll be all right."

"Better keep eating," he says, "or you'll pass out. How's it going with you and Andra?"

"Not too good."

"Both of you need to work on your energy. You're down and dragging, I can feel it when you come in the dojo. It's not like you bring the whole room down, like some people do, but I get a pain in my chest as soon as I catch sight of you. That's serious business, Larry. You don't want to mess with it. Once your energy goes bad, everything else will follow. Energy is why you can't handle your drinks right now. And why I can. Still, your vibes are OK. Be thankful for that. It shouldn't take too many sessions to get you back on track."

"Vibes" is the dojo's word for one's intangible energy vibrations, in effect, one's level of spiritual attainment. Everyone who comes to the dojo, student or visitor, is rated in terms of vibes, and it is taken for granted that a serious student of zazen and the martial arts will not only have "good vibes" himself but be able to read another's vibes like a book. Chang says a sensitive person can feel your vibes when he enters your house, hears your voice on the telephone, picks up a book you've been reading, or sees your coat on a hook. If he knows you well, he'll feel your vibes whenever he thinks of you. Obviously, he'll feel them if he sits zazen next to you or, since posture is a manifestation of vibes, sees you on your cushion. Vibes have nothing to do with appearance or circumstance. The other day, during a lecture, Chang said that a demented fellow who lives on the streets around the dojo and often threatens passersby has "great vibes, some of the best I've come across." Low energy is not quite the same as bad vibes, but the two conditions are obviously related. Zazen or karate will improve your vibes, but if your energy is bad, your only hope, says Chang, is the sort of treatments he provides.

People are not alone in having vibes. Last week, one of the black belts paid Chang $250 to check out the vibes of an apartment she wanted to rent. Another student, about to enter graduate school, asked him to energize her schoolbooks. Chang seems to feel that all of us, as a group, are possessed of energizing power. A few months from now, when a book of mine is published, he will place it on a table in the middle of the dojo during one of our all-day sittings so that, by means of the energy we impart to it with our zazen, we can assure its success. He makes it clear to me that if the book does well I will be expected to express my gratitude with a contribution to the dojo. A former monk at Dai Bosatsu told me that Chang became angry at him when he did not make such a contribution. Months before, when he was unable to find a job or an apartment, Chang had given him a small crystal and guaranteed it would bring him luck. The monk put the crystal in his drawer and forgot about it, but eight months later, when he told Chang that he'd recently found a good job, Chang, believing that he owed his good fortune to the crystal, was furious that he'd not expressed his gratitude.

Chang has never tried to sell me on his treatments, but now, taking another sip of saki, lowering his eyes and smiling at me with an odd, almost seductive expression, he says, "How come you don't get energized?"

"He's a rationalist," Jamie says. "An intellectual."

Chang taps the side of his head. "That's what blocks his energy. You're top-heavy, Larry. Too much thinking. I felt it when I met you. You doing any other practice beside zazen? Anything physical?"

"I'm running."

"How much?"

"Five miles, sometimes six."

"Every day?"

"Just about."

"What's that mean, 'Just about'?"

"Four days on, one off."

"What speed?"

"Eight-minute miles, maybe a little slower. Depending on how I feel, it takes me forty or forty-five minutes."

Chang repeats my words sarcastically. " 'Depending on how I feel.' That's where the problem is. When you're listening to your mood, you don't have a chance." He dips a piece of sashimi in soy sauce, taps it gently against a mound of horseradish, then deposits it in his mouth. "Running's a good workout, but it won't help your energy."

"Why's that?"

"Because you're not running with me."

Suddenly, I realize that Jamie's eyes are fixed on me. "Listen, Larry, you're not gonna like this, but I'm drunk and it's the

honest-to-God truth and I love you, and if I don't tell you now,
I never will. It came to me the other day that you've got to give
up writing. I'm mopping the floor at the zendo and it hits me,
bang, just like that: 'If Larry doesn't give up writing, he'll never
get outside his head.' Don't be mad at me, OK? It just came
over me. All the zazen in the world won't help you as long as
you're in your head. Writing's what's wrong with your marriage, and writing's why you're afraid to get energized. If you
give it up, I give you my word, everything will turn around."

A long silence ensues. We stare at each other until Chang
leans and straightens Jamie's back again. Using two hands this
time, he pushes him in the lower back and pulls back on his
shoulders. "What's with the lecture?" he says. "Worry about
yourself, OK? Once you get your kensho you can worry about
somebody else."

·   ·   ·

During kansho, I ask Roshi to explain "Buddha nature" to me.
This is the crucial concept in our practice, the essential ground
from which all being emerges, the universal truth the Buddha
realized when he said, "All beings, as they are, have the Buddha nature," but it occurred to me during sitting this afternoon
that I haven't the slightest idea what it means.

"Formless cannot be explained," he snaps. He picks up
the bell to dismiss me, but then he adds, "Larry-san, your TV
have Channel Two, Channel Four, Channel Five, no?"

"Yes, Roshi."

"What Channel Zen?"

"I have no idea."

"Channel Zero! Can any channel! Channel Two can only
Channel Two, but Channel Zero can any! Understand? Listen,

mathematics you have, how you say, numenator, nominator. Nominator can any number, numenator always zero! Nominator, one, eight, fifteen thousand, doesn't matter—into zero, answer always zero. Formless, understand? Anger, delusion, insincere, even selfish, all nominator. Into zero equal zero! Your life always zero! Thoughts always zero! Memory always zero! You completely free!"

This exchange occurs on the third day of sesshin. On the following day, for reasons I can't discern, my mind turns dark, heading into the gap. Suddenly, I get a whiff of death so strong it brings me to the edge of panic. I've known this before, of course, especially on my cushion, but never with such intensity. During my next kansho, I describe all this to him.

"Die now, Larry-san! Then you not have to worry anymore!"

.   .   .

A week later, the day after Jamie's sesshin ends, there is an early-morning call from Bonnie. "Bad news. Jamie freaked out at sesshin. He's in a locked ward at a mental hospital near the monastery. He wants us to come and see him."

The three of us rent a car and drive up to the hospital. It's a modern, four-story, red-brick building that overlooks a golf course. Jamie is in a single room on the third floor. There are mattresses on the walls, a fluorescent light on a pair of chains hanging from the ceiling, one small window with a grid of iron bars. Wearing a slate-blue hospital gown, Jamie sits in full-lotus on his bunk bed, massaging the bottom of his foot with a closed fist and examining it as if it contains the answer to his problems. His face is stunned and dulled, but now and then, it seems to me, slightly triumphant, like someone who's seen what he set out to see and can't make up his mind between gratitude and terror. Bonnie sits on the bed beside him, Andra and I on the floor. After a silence, he fixes a stare on each of us in turn. His voice is hoarse, as if from laryngitis. "Cause and effect are one," he says. "If you don't believe me, check it out."

"What do you mean?" I say.

"Check it out," he says again.

"Jamie," says Andra, "what happened?"

"I told them to put me here."

"Why?"

"Because I'm dangerous."

"You?"

"Yeah, me."

"Why?" says Bonnie.

He ignores her question. "I was ready when sesshin began. Oh, man, was I ready! But after two or three days, I lost interest. Then I got hot again, and all hell broke loose." He pauses a second, then turns to me. "Take it from me, Larry. Stay away from the Japs. They don't know shit about Zen. All they do is give you koans."

"Back up," I say. "Tell us what happened."

"You think I remember? They've got me on Thorazine. I'm totally weirded out."

But slowly he pieces it together. On the second day of sesshin, a great contentment came over him. "I thought, 'Shit, I don't give a fuck about kensho. I just want to be a man, accept my place in the world.' But then the Roshi gave a talk about enlightenment, and I thought I'd better look into it again."

To inspire his students, Eido Roshi had a practice of pinning a teaching on the bulletin board at the beginning of sesshin. This time, he'd chosen the famous Engaku Sutra:

1. Do not be deluded.
2. If you can't help being deluded, do not judge others, and do not feel guilty.
3. If you can't help being deluded, and you can't help judging or feeling guilt, do not open your mouth.

Jamie says he didn't pay much attention to the sutra at first, but once his passion for kensho resumed, he found himself possessed by it. "It's like it hit me for the first time how judgmental I am, how arrogant and moralistic, and how it's just these qualities that block my kensho. I'm totally selfish, man. Nothing but ego, self-importance. The only reason I sit is to feel better, have a good time. No thought of others. No desire to help. Jesus, even when I realized these things, I was looking to benefit from them, hoping they'd make me feel better. Like, it's too painful to see your selfishness, so you want to fix it so you can feel better, be even more selfish than you were before." Furious at himself, he pressed harder and harder, sitting through rest periods and, several times, through the night, until another realization came to him. "Suddenly, I saw that everything is a reflection of my mind. Everything! Oh, I know we say this all the time, but this was different! For once I wasn't bullshitting myself! When a thunderstorm broke, there was no distinction between me and the storm. I was the thunderclap. I was the rain and the wind. Later, during dokusan, I told the roshi what was happening, and he said I was on the verge of kensho. Picked up the stick and whop, whop, whop, hit me really hard four or five times on each shoulder. 'Keep going!' he cried. 'You've got to get it!' I told him, 'I don't give a shit about kensho,

Roshi. It's just delusion.' 'No!' he screamed, hitting me again. 'It's you who delude yourself!' "

From that moment, Jamie says, a terrific vacillation ensued, waves of exhilaration followed by attacks of fear and paranoia. "I was terrified of my own thoughts. Like if I thought something, it would happen. I mean, if cause and effect are one, there's no separation between things, right? Me and you, here and there, now and then . . . those are false distinctions! But no, I don't want to talk about that. I can't live with that kind of wisdom."

Referring to another famous sutra, he says that he understands it for the first time: " 'Things are not as they seem . . . nor are they otherwise.' Do you understand? It's not just a fucking poem, you know. It means that nothing matters but what you think. We're all trapped in our own thoughts."

I have a mind to question him on that, but then I think again. He isn't looking at us. His eyes are fixed and bright as strobes. At the edge of his gown, I can see the varicose veins in his calves that have given him so much trouble over the years. Once, during sesshin, he tied rags around his legs in a vain attempt to control the pain they caused and of course was angry at himself for doing so because the pain, he said, was good for his zazen.

The last two nights of sesshin, he says, he slept and sat zazen in the cellar of the monastery. The link between thought and reality grew more vivid, more literal. As he saw it, mind emanated. Its effect on others was concrete. Thinking of Andra and me and the trouble in our marriage, he was convinced that his "bad energy" had caused our problems. Even now, there were moments of happiness, but his terror outraced it, becoming more global. "My mind was full of this amazing energy. I didn't know if it was bad or good. I was breathing very fast and my heart was pounding. One minute I thought I'd had kensho, the next that I was having a stroke or a heart attack. A voice in my head kept screaming, 'No separation! No separation!' When sesshin ended, I sought out the roshi and asked to speak to him, but he shook his head and turned away. 'Sesshin,' he said, 'is over.' I went back to my room and tried to sleep, but my mind was racing and my body so agitated I couldn't stay in one position for more than a few seconds. Then I remembered the third line in the sutra: "If you can't avoid delusion or guilt and you can't stop judging others, don't open your mouth.' I knew at once what I had to do."

He tied a rag around his head and chin and vowed he'd never speak again. "I went into the woods, took off my clothes and ran and danced among the trees. Buck naked, man! Spinning like a dervish! Jesus, it was beautiful! I was everything! Trees, grass, sky, wind! Separate from nothing! I wanted to eat rocks! Once I opened my mouth and a fly flew in and I swallowed it. I was the fly! I swear to God! I was the fly!"

But even now the fear of thought persisted, the sense that his "negativity" had the power to harm. "Like, if I had an angry thought about someone, it could kill him. I'm talking literally, understand? Like voodoo. Every second I was terrified of what would pop into my mind." For fourteen hours, he wandered naked in the woods until, at dawn, he found himself near the caretaker's cottage at the monastery's gate. "Lock me up!" he cried, pounding on the door. "Put me away before I kill them all!"

. . .

A few weeks later, Chang gives a lecture on the "fighting" form of tai chi, "push hands." This is a practice done in pairs, two people facing each other at slightly oblique but parallel angles, hands pressed together, shifting back and forth in response to each other's movements. It looks like a dance, but in fact it is tai chi's equivalent of karate sparring. In contrast to karate, the idea is to make oneself supple and pliable so as to deny one's opponent leverage. In effect, Chang explains, demonstrating with a senior student named Hawkins, strength in tai chi is softness, and weakness is rigidity, inflexibility. Fighting with a great tai chi master is like trying to grasp running water. "He makes himself empty. His opponent can't defeat him because there's no one to defeat."

He and Hawkins face each other with palms touching and knees slightly bent, shifting backward and forward and side to side as if their movements are synchronized, until suddenly Hawkins lurches backward toward the wall. The reasons for this are not apparent. I see no thrust by Chang, certainly none to explain the force with which Hawkins has been thrown. Chang explains. "The idea of push hands is to make yourself a mirror. Feel your opponent. Become him. If you do it right, it's not you he's fighting but himself." Taking hold of Hawkins's arm, he rotates it at the elbow and the shoulder like an orthopedist examining a patient. "If he's soft enough, there's no resistance, therefore nothing to fight against. What you're trying to do is find his resistance, and the only way to do that is to make yourself *completely sensitive,* a clear mirror, feeling and reflecting all his vibes. Feel his fear, his anger, his confidence, his self-doubt. Above all, feel his resistance." He works with Hawkins's arm until suddenly it's clear that he has found what he is looking for—a slight stiffness in the elbow that gives him leverage. Once again, Hawkins is thrown off-balance. "See, his arm was soft, but not soft enough. Suddenly, I felt resistance and that was it. Resistance is ego. Once you find it, the fight is over. And for the same reason, a man who has no ego will always be unbeatable."

This is a Monday night class before zazen. Eighteen students stand in a circle, viewing the demonstration. Andra is among them, but unlike me, she is no longer an observer. Last week, two days after we agreed to a trial separation, and I began my search for a new apartment, she decided to become a student of tai chi. Tonight, for the first time, she wears a gi rather than the black pants and shirt that in the past she's worn for zazen. Her decision has deepened the darkness in which I'm living these days, taken me back to a kind of fear and loneliness I haven't felt since I was a teenager in Memphis, Jewish in a non-Jewish world. Now, as then, I feel like an alien, almost a pariah, outside our marriage and outside the dojo too.

Jamie is the only other person here who is not studying either karate or tai chi. They kept him in the hospital for six days, and he appeared here the day after his dismissal. He has moved out of the zendo, found a tenement apartment on the Lower East Side, hired on as a mechanic in a garage near the dojo. He won't talk about what happened in sesshin, and he won't talk about Zen. He tells me that Chang—or "Master Wei," as now, like the martial-arts students, he prefers to call him—is the only authentic teacher he knows. All the others are phonies, powermongers who feed off the weakness and fear of their students. Energizing, he says, is restoring his health. If possible, he has a session every day. Awaiting treatments or zazen sessions, he takes his cushion to a far corner of the dojo and, while others practice karate or tai chi, sits on his own.

Now that Chang has "opened" him, he says, he's become supersensitive to others, his body a sort of antenna, picking up vibes like radio waves. Even strangers passing quickly on the street cause physical sensations in him. More than once, at the coffee shop we frequent after zazen at the dojo, he insists on changing tables because the vibes of someone sitting nearby become unbearable to him.

After the tai chi demonstration, we lay out our cushions for zazen. Chang gives a talk before we begin. The only reason for this practice is to make you feel better, give you energy, elevate you in a manner that he compares to jacking up a car. If your energy is right, he says, the car goes up as if levitating, but if you're weak at the center, no amount of force will get it off the ground. Once again, he places his cushion near the telephone. Facing the wall, I can't see him of course, but I hear him dialing and I know that he has placed the receiver on his low belly and that someone far away, perhaps in a hospital or a hospice, has placed another receiver on his or her belly in hopes of receiving the energy Chang is sending over the wires. He strikes the inkin with its wooden mallet, and silence descends on the room. I know at once that it will not descend on me. The waters are much too rough tonight. I can't stop thinking of Andra, who no longer sits next to me but on the other side of the room. Zazen is a power struggle, a war, my mind an unbroken horse I'm trying in vain to ride. A few minutes later, not ten minutes after we have begun, Chang hangs up the phone, rings the bell, and summons us to the front of the room. "It's no use sitting tonight," he says. "The vibes in this room are awful. We'll do ourselves more harm than good." For the next fifteen minutes, in a talk that strikes me as completely incoherent, he reiterates what he said before. We are jacking up the car. We are the car and we are the jack and we are the flat tire, etc. It's all so dumb and banal that I feel embarrassed for him. "How do you feel?" he cries. "That's all that matters! How do you feel?"

Later, when Jamie and I walk home together, I tell him what I felt about the talk. "I tried to concentrate on what he was saying, but it didn't make sense to me."

He walks a bit ahead of me. I notice that his limp seems worse tonight, his left foot dragging and angled sharply away from his body. "Sense? What's that mean? That's your trouble, Larry. You look for ideas and miss the energy. What are you? Fucking blind? Don't you see what's going down? The man is offering us his energy! What more do you want? Sharing the best vibes you'll ever come across! Don't you realize how lucky we are? How much he risks by coming down to our level?"

We walk for a while in silence, because I'm a little stunned by his outburst and because Jamie rarely talks these days unless he's asked a question. It is bitterly cold, a windy night in January, and I am bundled up—long underwear, heavy sweater, down jacket and woolen cap. Jamie is wearing jeans, no hat, a light denim jacket, and a ragged sweatshirt that reads NOTRE DAME ATHLETICS. Also, like others in the dojo, including Chang himself, rubber sandals without socks. It is Chang's view that martial-arts training improves circulation so that one becomes indifferent to variations in temperature, and it is also his view that one furthers such training by enduring physical discomfort. He has never explicitly directed them to do so, but all his senior students wear these sandals, and no one ever sees them in socks. In effect, they more or less go barefoot through the winter. "By the way," says Jamie. "Isn't it time you started calling him Master Wei?"

" 'Master Wei'? He's 'Chang' to me, Jamie. I can't do anything about that."

"Oh yes you can," Jamie says.

. . .

For the next three weeks, I avoid the dojo. Every time I think of the place, I remember Andra in her white gi or the isolation I felt there, my "Jewish" alienation. But just when I'm thinking I'm done with the place forever, I begin to miss it—the sitting and the energy, the sense of order and optimism it brings to my life. It's as if my brief experience there has, like zazen in general, exposed my tendencies toward laziness and self-indulgence, and I fear what I'll become without it. On a Wednesday evening early in February, I climb the stairs, remove my shoes and bow with gratitude, a rush of joy to be here again. The first thing I see is Andra on the bench getting energized. She's flat on her back with Chang kneeling beside her, one of his hands somewhere around her navel, the other more or less centered between her breasts.

Later, when sitting ends, we have dinner together. "What's going on?" I ask.

"You'll think I'm crazy," she says.

She looks younger somehow, also excited and slightly disoriented, like a tourist just arrived in a country where she doesn't speak the language. The thought that our separation seems to be good for her health inspires a fit of rage in me.

"Two weeks ago I sort of collapsed during tai chi class. That's when it began. Master Wei is giving a talk and we're all gathered around him and—"

" 'Master Wei?' Is that what you call him now?"

"Of course. It's not a matter of choice, you know. When I

started tai chi, he sent word through Jamie that I was not to call him Chang anymore."

"Why'd you collapse?"

"I don't know. It was one of those endless, boring talks he gives, and the room was hot and stuffy, like all the air had been sucked out. All of a sudden, my head is spinning. I go down to my knees, hoping it will pass. I don't exactly faint, but I feel like I'm on the verge. Everyone's gathered around me and some-one's wiping my face with a damp towel. When finally I can stand, I go to the bathroom and stay there for a long time with a terrible case of diarrhea. When I come out, Master Wei is furi-ous. 'Why didn't you faint? Why'd you stop yourself?' The rea-son I got dizzy, he says, is because I had an energy surge while he talked. If I'd given into it instead of copping out, I'd have broken through to a whole new level."

An event like this, Chang told her, could only mean one thing: it was urgent that she get energized. Her energy level had been increasing ever since she'd come to the dojo, but now, because of tai chi, and our separation, it was really taking off. Dizziness was typical of times like this because one had more energy than one could tolerate. It was like inflating a balloon or pumping water into a tank. That's why she needed energizing, to enlarge the tank. If she continued on this path without the help and guidance of his treatments, she was risking all sorts of physical and mental injury, but if she got energized while studying tai chi and continuing her zazen practice, her life would be transformed.

"You know Karen, that small, dark-haired woman who's always getting energized? When he sees that I am still resistant, he calls her over. 'Tell Andra about your treatments.' Karen takes me aside and tells me all about herself. She's been getting

energized for five years, and it's completely changed her life.
When she began, she was trapped in a bad marriage, working
as a bank teller. Now she's divorced, she's got a new lover,
she's an officer at the bank, and she's writing poetry. But the
big thing is what it's done for her sex life. In the old days, sex
was a hassle, something she did to please a man but never to
please herself. Now it's like over the top. Until five years ago,
she never had orgasms except when she masturbated. Now she
has them all the time. In fact, there are times, like right after
energizing, when she has them for no reason at all. 'After my
session last week,' she says, 'I was driving back home to Connecticut, and while I was on the highway, I started thinking
about Master Wei and I suddenly felt like I was going to come.
And you know what? I did!' "

It was this story that convinced her, Andra says. "Part of
me was shaking my head and pulling back, but I feel so lost and
desperate these days, I'll try anything to get strong. Suddenly,
Master Wei seemed sort of maternal to me, a tremendous
source of comfort. I thought, 'What's to lose? Where I am in
my life just now, I'd be a fool to pass this up.' Later, I told him
I'd give it a try. Tonight was my first session."

"How was it?"

"I don't know," she says. "To tell you the truth, I didn't
feel a thing."

.   .   .

Next day, with no little trepidation, and the sort of embarrassment that makes one pray that none of his friends are listening,
I tell Chang that I want to try a few sessions of energizing myself. Andra's story has made me admit my own desperation and

confusion. Most of all perhaps, it's made me see my loneliness. I'm not completely aware of it, but in the back of my mind is the hope that, even if energizing doesn't cure my malaise, it will make me part of the dojo again. Also operative, of course, is the reasoning that is central to relationships like the one I have with Chang, that in a practice involved with "surrender" and "relinquishing the ego," one can never underestimate the hope and freedom one comes to associate with indifference to one's critical intelligence.

"A few sessions?" says Chang scornfully. "Why not the whole course? You don't really get it until you've had fifteen or twenty treatments."

I tell him I'm skeptical by nature. I've got to test the water before I dive in.

"In other words, you're being cautious."

"Yeah, I guess so."

"You're scared."

"Maybe so."

"Fear is an energy problem, you know. It's just the sort of thing I treat."

But finally he relents. For a few weeks, we'll take it one session at a time, twenty-five dollars a shot. Furthermore, since he's just had a cancellation, I can have my first session immediately. "Lie down on the bench," he says. "Close your eyes and try to forget where you are."

The session is broken up into three parts, each about five minutes in length. First I lie facedown while he kneels beside me, placing one hand on the small of my back and the other between my shoulder blades. Then I lie on my back while he puts one hand on my lower belly and the other on my chest.

Finally, for the last five minutes, we sit facing each other and look into each other's eyes. When we're done, he slaps me on the back. "Well, that's energizing. What happened?"

I feel guilty, almost as if I'll hurt his feelings, but I have to be honest with him. "Nothing much."

"Well, you've got a lot of resistance, Larry. Some really tight vibes coming off you. We'll try again tomorrow."

The next three sessions are no more interesting. I'm thinking I've given it a shot and found it to be what I suspected all along—quackery and hype, a total waste of time. Then everything changes. Next time I lie down on the bench, I feel light-headed, almost intoxicated, as soon as I close my eyes. It's an uncanny feeling that seems to permeate my body. Waves of warmth come over me, a kind of tingling sensation in my hands, my feet and my forehead.

Chang is not surprised when I report all this to him. "The moment I put my hands on your back, I could feel you've opened up. But this is only the beginning! Now we'll go deeper!"

For the next few sessions, his prediction holds true. As soon as his hands are on my back, the tingling sensation resumes. Safe, comforted, I feel an amazing intimacy with him, a union that seems more global than personal. It's almost as if he's a conduit or a medium, as if I've discovered through him the freedom from self and ego that Zen has always promised.

But on the following Sunday, things change again. Before zazen, he gathers us around him. We think we understand energy, he says, but we don't appreciate how much it means to us. It can change our lives, open our hearts, protect us from danger. "Mary Jo, tell them what happened last week. It's a perfect example of what I mean."

Mary Jo is a small, blond woman who is a professional astrologer. She appears to be somewhat fragile, but having watched her spar, I know otherwise. With the exception of Hawkins, she is the most advanced of the black belts. Last week, she says, when Master Wei told her that he was driving up to the country, she decided to do his chart to see if he should go. "Every sign said 'Danger.' He's a Scorpio, you know, and that night, Pluto was conjuncting with his sun. I don't know how many of you understand astrology, but if you do, you know it was absolutely the worst time for him to travel. And as if that weren't enough, the next morning, when I got up, I saw that it was raining! With the weather we've had, the roads were sure to be slippery. I called him up and told him about my reading. How could I not? How could I let him go when the situation was so dangerous? I told him, 'You've got to listen to me. It's crazy for you to travel today.' Well, you know Master Wei. When he makes up his mind to do something, nothing's gonna stop him. He ignored my warning, went as he'd planned and . . . nothing happened! I couldn't believe it!"

Chang allows a long silence, then elaborates. Clearly, he says, it was his energy that protected him. If your energy is right, even destiny will bow to it! But if it isn't, it will make your fate even worse than it might have been! We must never underestimate the dangers we face or the power and protection that comes from the sort of energy practice we're doing here. He gives several examples of people who've left the dojo and fallen ill almost immediately. "You remember Frank Kelso? That tall fellow who studied tai chi here a couple of years ago? I ran into him yesterday—he looks fifteen years older! Talking to him cost me so much energy I slept nine hours last night."

When I arrive for my session a few days later, Mary Jo's

story is still in my mind. I feel absurd to be here and, once on the bench, impatient, embarrassed, even ashamed. The treatment itself has no effect at all. Gone is intimacy, the happiness I felt, the sweet sensation in my fingers and toes. It's as if I used to be a junky and I've developed tolerance for the drug he is dispensing.

I give it two more sessions, then tell him I need a break. If he is surprised, he doesn't show it. It's obvious what happened, he says. This is simply a case of too much too soon. My resistance is on the rise because he's pushed me too hard. "Don't worry! It's completely natural, like a backlash. The thing to do is rededicate yourself, sign on for a full course. What's the expression? Take the bull by the horns!"

"No, Chang, I'm sorry. I have to stop."

He still doesn't seem to get it. "Is it a matter of time? Are you too busy to get here? That's not a problem, you know. We can work by phone or even without it. There's a couple of people in China I'm helping on the astral plane."

"No, it's not about time. I just don't want to do it anymore."

"But how can you back off when we're finally getting down to business? I thought you had guts. I thought you were serious about your energy." He fixes me with a stare, as if waiting for me to find my sanity again. "Listen, Larry, it's times like this that people get strokes or cancer or Parkinson's disease. You've got to let me put a stop to it."

.   .   .

"Larry-san," says Roshi, "you have cow-shitting posture. Ha! Ha! Look like this." Rounding his back and dropping his chin toward his chest, he imitates an orangutan or someone with an intractable neurological disease. His laughter is so infectious that, even as my anger mounts, I find myself echoing it. "Larry-san cow-shitting! Ha! Ha! Ha!"

This is kansho on the third day of a seven-day sesshin. When I entered this room a moment ago, I felt extremely confident, almost cocky. I had an answer for my koan and had been feeling, for a change, a measure of stability on my cushion. Given our history, the endless collisions I have endured between his point of view and my own, I ought to have known I was headed for trouble. "Listen, Larry-san, what you doing on your cushion? Impossible you sit like that. Wasting lot of energy! Back bent, thought come. You know that! Head forward, mind become dark, discourage. Must straight! Must bravery on your cushion. Don't cheat yourself, Larry-san! Don't waste time!"

He laughs again, imitates me again, this time leaning so far to the left that he seems on the verge of lying down. How can I continue to speak to him politely when what I want to do is punch him out?

"C'mon, Roshi. You know I'm not that bad."

"Bad? Who say bad, Larry-san? You not bad at all. You thinking too much posture is all."

"I can't help it, Roshi. Sometimes I feel I'm suffocating on the cushion."

" 'Suffocating?' What's it mean, 'suffocating'?"

"I can't breathe!"

"OK!" he exclaims. "No need to breathe!"

It ought to be noted, I think, that my quest for a dependable meditation posture has by now been going on for more than twenty years. I've read every book I could find on the subject, tried yoga, rolfing, chiropractic, the Alexander and the

Feldenkrais techniques. An acupuncturist at one zendo placed needles in my ear and left them there through a seven-day retreat; a Zen student–chiropractor sold me a battery-powered device the size of a fountain pen that was supposed to cure knee pain by dousing it with negatively charged particles; another student, who was a specialist in shiatsu, tried to straighten my back by walking on it and pouncing like a tiger where he felt tension in the vertebrae. I've sat in front of mirrors in order to correct myself, assumed the lotus posture when reading or watching TV, sat with five-pound weights on my knees, tried higher cushions, lower cushions, even those cushions the size of orange crates, called "gomdens," which the Tibetan master Chögyam Trungpa Rinpoche, distressed by his students' posture problems, invented in Colorado. I've developed hemorrhoids from sitting too much, painful irritations of the coccyx. Once, attempting the kneeling, or "seiza," position, I turned my cushion on its side in order to gain height and, when the bell rang, found my penis and testicles numb because the cushion had either pinched a nerve or cut off my circulation.

Sometimes these problems are not so bad, but at others, like now, they take over my meditation. After Roshi laughs at me, I can't do anything on my cushion but adjust and readjust my posture. I feel as if my body is outside me. I'm like a sculptor trying to shape a piece of clay I can't quite see or get a grip on. Every time I begin to get comfortable, I shift just slightly, correcting or overcorrecting myself with maniacal attention. I feel tension in my lower back, my upper back, my neck, even my jaw. The slightest deviation from my idea of comfort, straightness, or stability seems like the sort of grotesque deformity Roshi has just enacted for me.

Sitting just behind me, Roshi is clearly aware of my struggle. Next time I go to kansho, he says, "Please, you bring me cushion."

I return to the zendo, get my cushion, bring it back to the kansho room. Taking it from me, he says, "I think maybe you sitting too far back." He draws an imaginary semicircle on it. "Look—you put anus here, cockix here. Push head up, make spine straight! Blood go down! Head become cold, feet become warm. Sometime sausage stand up!"

I take the cushion and put it beneath me and try to sit as he has advised. "Hmm," he says. "I think maybe book-writing you spend too much time in chair. Anus and cockix too close together. Maybe your ass pointed instead of flat."

"Well, what am I to do about that?"

"Maybe you try exercise. Look, I show you." Sliding off his cushion, he lies face down on the floor, clasps his hands behind him and lifts both head and feet to form an exaggerated arch in his lower back. "Twenty time every morning, every night!"

"Oh, Roshi, I've been doing that exercise for years. It doesn't help at all!"

He picks up his bell. "Well, don't discourage, Larry-san. Patience, patience. I tell you before, twenty-seven years I sit with pain, then one day, psht!—all gone!"

Another day passes before I see him again. If anything, my posture problems increase. Watching myself and conscious of him watching me, it's as if I've doubled my self-consciousness. When I go back to kansho, I'm so disgusted with myself that I'm thinking I ought to leave. Why should I come to sesshin if all I can do is obsess about my body? Why should I sit at all?

"Jesus, Roshi, I've never felt so uncomfortable on the cushion! I can't concentrate at all!"

Clearly bored with this level of discourse, he rings his bell at once. I stand and bow and turn to leave, but just as I reach to open the door, he takes pity on me. "Of course you not concentrate. You thinking too much posture. Making separation mind and body. Listen, Larry-san, when you laugh—ha! ha! ha!— what laugh, mind or body? If uncomfortable, must into uncomfortable! Understand? If tight, into tight! Mind make posture, posture make mind. Zazen make posture. Posture make zazen. Understand? Forget it! No more separation! No more posture! Breathe with whole body! In and out through every pore! Slowly, slowly, breath deep, mind calm. Soen Roshi, he say all the time: 'Calm mind, deep breath. Deep breath, calm mind. Who know which come first?' "

"But that's just it, Roshi! Which does come first?"

He fixes me with an angry stare. "First, second—no idea, Larry-san. No separation. Only you become sincere. Then, I guarantee: all your problems gone!"

"Sincere," of course, is a sort of buzzword for him, his all-purpose adjective. "Sincere mopping." "Sincere walking." "Sincere zazen." So often and in so many different circumstances has he equated Zen with sincerity over the years that I hardly hear him anymore. This time, however, is different. Returning to the zendo, I feel as if he's shot an arrow to the middle of my brain. I am suddenly convinced that all my posture problems are the result of insincerity, the fact that I've never really committed myself to Zen or, for that matter, to anything. Isn't it obvious? What I suffer from on the cushion is not these particular, localized problems in my body but the fact that I am outside myself, holding back, playing it safe! My discomfort is nothing but a metaphor for my insincerity, my divided mind!

But far from being upset with these thoughts, I am inspired by them. For the next few sittings, my mind is in a bookkeeping mode, tallying the price I've paid, over the years, for all my insincerities, and at the same time, of course, imagining how happy I'll be when I break this habit and become wholehearted, single-minded, pure in thought as well as action. I hardly think of my posture, but when I do, I feel completely stable and relaxed.

Needless to say, I can't wait to share my insights with him. It's all I can do, next time I see him in kansho, to hold off talking until I've taken my seat on the cushion. Unfortunately, he has other things on his mind. Lately, I've served as breakfast chef at our sesshins, and he is unhappy with the menu I am offering. "Larry-san," he says, "too much choice at breakfast! Cottage cheese, penis butter, two kinds bread. What you think, sesshin like luxury hotel?"

"What should I eliminate, Roshi?"

"How I know? Breakfast your job, not mine. Are you a child?"

"OK, I'll get rid of the cottage cheese."

"No, no. Cottage cheese very good." He puts his forefinger on his tongue and, using the Hebrew word, "Umm," he says, "*mitzuyan!* I love cottage cheese! You have answer for your koan?"

My present koan is called "Gutei Raises a Finger." I have struggled with it for months, and I am particularly galled by my failure with it because it has always been one of my favorites.

*Master Gutei, whenever he was questioned, just stuck
up one finger. At one time he had a young attendant,
whom a visitor asked, "What is the Zen your Master is
teaching?" The boy also stuck up one finger. Hearing
this, Gutei cut off the boy's finger with a knife. As the
boy ran out screaming with pain, Gutei called to him.
When the boy turned his head, Gutei stuck up his finger.
The boy was suddenly enlightened.*

"No, I'm sorry, Roshi. I have no answer."
He lifts his bell to dismiss me.
"Wait, Roshi. I want to talk about insincerity."
"Yes?"
"I feel as if I've never understood what it means. Never
seen what a poison it is."
"Don't worry insincere, Larry-san. Just concentrate one
finger, OK?" He wags his finger in front of my nose. "Cut off
my finger, nothing problem! *Essential nature* can't be cut! You
go back cushion, become one finger, nothing blame, nothing
problem. You beautiful human being." He rings his bell. Once
again, I bow and stand to leave and, once again, he speaks to
me when my hand is on the doorknob. "Larry-san—sincere insincere forget it! Sometime insincere better than sincere."

.   .   .

Several weeks after my last energizing session, as I walk downstairs after evening sitting, I hear a conversation between one of
the black belts, a fellow named Hertz, and a man who recently
began karate and has apparently decided to quit. The latter is a
successful sculptor whose work hangs in a number of prestigi-
ous museums. He seems to have known Hertz before he came

to the dojo. Walking behind them, I hear him explaining the reasons for his decision: the classes are too difficult, take up too much time, and leave him exhausted the next day, interfering with his work. Furthermore, he can't stand the way Master Wei orders him around. He has no intention, he says, of becoming a sycophant like most of the other students here.

By this time, we've reached the sidewalk. Hertz has listened in silence as we descended the stairs, but now he stops and looks at his friend and shakes his head with disgust. An advanced black belt, he is tall and wiry, with a skinhead haircut and long arms and legs that snap like whips when he kicks and punches. Even to me, his talent is obvious, but equally obvious is his lack of discipline, his bad temper, his inability to separate his emotions from his practice. I've seen any number of sparring sessions interrupted by punches he didn't pull, three or four when he and his opponent did not stop fighting when the bell rang. "Well, it's your decision," he says. "If you want to be a schmuck all your life, no one's gonna stop you."

His words stun me. I hear them all through the evening, and next morning when I wake up. It's as if he's made me realize what a schmuck I am myself. Ever since I gave up energizing, I've been apathetic and distracted, caught up in self-pity and endless, circular obsession about my marriage. I still attend the dojo regularly, but, feeling like a pariah there again, I derive no pleasure from it at all. Now, suddenly, it occurs to me that Hertz has not only diagnosed my problem but shown me its solution. Karate! I can't imagine I have much talent for it, but I know at once that I must try. Here's a chance to get my body in shape, strike a blow against depression, and deepen my spiritual practice. Later that morning, I telephone Chang to tell him of my decision.

Nonplussed as usual, he says, "It's about time. Got a pencil?"

He gives me the address of the shop where I can purchase my gi and my white belt and tells me to bring him a check to cover the first three months of classes. Along with several other beginners, he says, I can start the following Monday. He is distant and matter-of-fact, but suddenly he brightens. "Tell you what. If you sign on, I'll let Jamie begin as well. Maybe the two of you can settle each other down."

Needless to say, it doesn't surprise me that evening when Hertz takes me aside. "Your name Larry? Master Wei asked me to give you a message. You're not to call him by his first name anymore. You're his student, and he's your master. From now on, he's 'Master Wei' to you."

In addition to Jamie and me, there are four others in the white belt class—two men and two women, none of them older than twenty-five. At forty-one, I feel almost geriatric among them. Chang says little to us this first evening, assigning our orientation to Hertz, who instructs us in such matters as how to tie our belts, how and when to bow on entering the dojo, and finally, the two cardinal rules: "One: Under no conditions are you to lean against the wall, lounge about on the floor, or display any other form of laziness in the dojo. Two: If Master Wei calls, you drop whatever you're doing, run to him quickly, and bow—like this—before you speak." After that, he demonstrates the "forward punch" on which we'll be working for the first two classes. It's a straight punch that seems simple enough, but it has a number of components and, like everything else in karate, infinite room for polish. Along with the "forward kick" and a couple of blocks that we will learn tomorrow night, this punch, says Hertz, is the basis of all karate and, in all probability, all one needs to know to win a street fight. From now on, he says, we're to practice it constantly with both hands, at home or in the dojo. It's a good idea to do it in front of a mirror in order to correct one's mistakes, and it's very important to be aware of your breath, so that exhalation occurs at the point of contact. "Don't ever think you've got this punch down. Even Master Wei works on it every day."

He directs us to find ourselves a mirror and spend the rest of the evening practicing our punch. We have about an hour, and this is all we have to do—step and punch, step and punch. Within ten minutes, I am sweating profusely and, despite the fact that I've been running five miles a day, reaching for my breath. Already, it is apparent to me that karate is more like sprinting than distance running, that I am not therefore in shape for it at all. More than the exertion, however, what strikes me about this simple, repetitive practice is that, like zazen, it is never far from desperate, hair-raising boredom. I'd like to *use* this boredom, treat it, as one treats boredom in zazen, as a means of going beyond the need for entertainment and escape, but all I'm doing is watching the clock, counting the minutes till this will be over, wondering how the schmuck in me can be defeated by this exercise in drudgery and self-punishment.

· · ·

When he learned that Chang had decided to permit him to study karate, Jamie's excitement verged on hysteria. Slapping me on the back, he cried, "You and me, man! We're gonna turn this place on its fucking ear!" Between zazen and energizing, he was already giving most of his spare time to the dojo, and once our classes begin, he gives it the rest. He takes it for

granted that I will be here as often as he is, and though I'm well
aware of his tendency to abuse himself, I can't resist his challenge or, more important perhaps, the bond that's grown between us. From the beginning, we follow a six-day schedule,
attending all four karate classes (Monday, Tuesday, Thursday
and Friday evenings from six to eight) as well as Wednesday
evening and Sunday morning zazen. We work out before zazen
and, though we are not yet allowed to participate, attend all
sparring sessions in order to study the techniques we're learning in class. Throughout tai chi classes, which are conducted
before zazen on Wednesday night and after it on Sunday morning, we stretch, do calisthenics, and practice our punches and
kicks before the mirrors. Demonstrating his forward punch,
Jamie likes to say that it teaches him more about Zen than he
could learn from all the roshis in the world. "This is all the
zazen you ever need. Breathe into it, focus your mind and body
at the point of contact, every punch a matter of life and death—
if this doesn't wake you up, what will?"

Sports have always come easily to me, but karate is an exercise in humiliation. I can manage the rudimentary kicks and
punches, but there are certain moves that demand an elasticity
I can hardly imagine, much less achieve. In one kick, the so-
called "roundhouse," the foot describes a wide arc that termi-
nates, ideally, at the head or neck of one's opponent. The idea
is to pivot on your opposite foot, make your hips a fulcrum,
develop centrifugal force that snaps your foot like a whip at the
point of contact. When Hertz demonstrates, his foot ends up
maybe eighteen or twenty inches above his head. When I try it,
I feel a sharp pain in my hip socket and my foot snaps lamely at
the level of my waist. I am not inexperienced at getting into
shape, but with karate, my limits seem absolute, as if it is not

my physical condition that's being challenged but my body type, my age, my psychology. Desperate to be done with my ineptitude and determined to keep up with Jamie, I make no dates that interfere with our schedule, and every morning I try to work out for at least an hour before I start my work. What it amounts to is that my life begins and ends with the dojo. Forget movies, theater, dinner with friends. More important, forget thinking about myself or writing in my diary. It may be the most important attribute of this sort of life that it leaves no room for introspection. Most evenings, exhausted from class, I am asleep by ten o'clock. A few months later, when I take a weekend trip to visit my parents, and Jamie accuses me of "copping out," I feel a lot more guilt than irritation.

Classes begin with about half an hour of calisthenics, followed by another half-hour in which we run through our kicks, blocks, and punches, twenty to fifty repetitions of each. These include not just the basics but more sophisticated techniques like the "knife hand," which is usually aimed at the Adam's apple, the backhand thrust that can paralyze an opponent if you catch him in the temple or the neck, and an elegant pincer-like thrust that is particularly effective against the eyes. In praise of the last, Chang says, "I'd rather put out an eye than break an arm any day." He can't remind us often enough of our basic maxim: A good fighter must be able to kill with a single punch. In fact, he says, if your first punch doesn't do it, and if your opponent is a fighter himself, you can automatically, given the impeccable logic of karate, consider yourself dead.

When calisthenics end, we work on forms, or "kata." These are ritualized progressions in which kicks, blocks and punches are linked sequentially. For the most part they trace their lineage to the late nineteenth century, in Okinawa. Karate

was invented by Ch'an monks in China, as a means of defending themselves against marauders without violating their religion, but it was not until a few of these monks had passed it
along to the king's guard in Okinawa that its modern form
began to evolve. Kata become, of course, more difficult and
complex as the ladder toward black belt is climbed. Some of
the more advanced involve sticks, swords or other weapons.
Each has its own rhythm and pace, a flow pattern the purpose
of which is to breed these moves into the body so that response
to attack is correct and spontaneous. Kata are beautiful, no less
a dance than the tai chi form, but they are definitely, if my experience is any guide, an acquired taste. The elementary ones
consist of twenty-five to thirty moves, the advanced more than
sixty. They can only be learned, of course, by endless repetition. Even the simplest are demanding and, like the forward
punch, subject to infinite polishing. I try my best to treat them
as meditations—actually, there's no other way to approach
them—but when I fail, they become oppressive, claustrophobic, even, quite literally, a source of nightmares.

What I'm discovering, of course, is that practices like karate are no less profound in their effects on the mind than on
the body. My moods are as volatile as they are in sesshin. Rare
is the day my heart doesn't sink as I head off to the dojo or that
I don't, at one moment or another, accuse myself of masochism
for being here. Equally rare, however, are days when class
doesn't leave me exhilarated. It's not just that I haven't been in
this sort of shape since I was eighteen or that, for the first time
in my life, I feel I might be able to handle trouble on the street.
I sense subtle but fundamental changes in myself—as if I'm
more assertive, more comfortable in space, more at home in my
body. As I walk home after class, I can hardly remember the

dread I felt a few hours before. But of course, it always comes back. And next day, when I head off to class again, it is last night's exhilaration that baffles me.

. . .

Calisthenics, kata and individualized practice take up an hour and a half of the two-hour class. At this point, Chang rings his bell to announce the beginning of sparring. Until this moment, the atmosphere of the dojo has been serene, almost meditative, but now it shifts as in a zoo in which the cages have been opened to give the animals a bit of exercise. Contact is prohibited, but Hertz is not the only student who seems to forget this rule as soon as fighting begins. As white belts, we haven't sparred for the first four weeks, but tonight our holiday is ended. I am thrown to the floor twice, struck very hard in the chest, and lightly brushed in the groin by a kick that Hawkins pulls at the last second. On succeeding evenings, there will be blows to the face and neck and now and then a kick in the groin that will double me over. Worse than any punch or kick, however, is the state of panic that sparring induces in me. My opponent seems like a windmill coming at me. I can't find my concentration or my balance. Often, I feel as if my vision is impaired. Advanced students fight like long-distance runners, adjusting their pace so that they never go into oxygen debt, but I am sprinting from the start, gasping for breath within two or three minutes.

At first, of course, these problems seem reasonable. Even my panic can be explained by the fact that I haven't been struck in the face since my last street fight, more than twenty years ago. But as the months go by, I don't improve. Sparring gets harder, not easier, and there's rarely a week when I don't add another injury or symptom to my chart: two bruised ribs, both feet swollen, chronic headaches, insomnia, nightmares, breathing problems so severe that I wheeze when climbing stairs. After six months of sparring, I feel like a ninety-year-old.

"What do you expect?" says Chang, when I describe my symptoms to him. "Karate is purification practice. All your poisons are coming out."

"Well, I just want to be sure I'm not hurting myself."

"The only way you'll hurt yourself is by backing off or feeling sorry for yourself, like you are now."

.   .   .

There are very few Rinzai Zen masters in the world right now, fewer still who speak English and pay visits to the West. Furthermore, only five members of this select group are Dharma heirs of Soen Roshi. Thus, it is no surprise that the Zen grapevine has brought me news for years about a Dharma successor of Soen, a roshi called Kyudo, or Dokyo, or Doshi, who has a Zendo in, of all places, Jerusalem. Several friends of mine have made special trips to meet with him, and from what they tell me, he's no less wild or unpredictable than Soen himself. For the last five years, working on a difficult book, I've been promising myself that when I'm done I'll go to Israel and seek him out. Now that time has come. I turned in the manuscript last week, and tonight will be my last at the dojo for nearly a month. For once, I'm free of dread as I don my gi. It is many months since I felt so relaxed and lighthearted. Between work on my book and my six-day karate-zazen regimen, not to mention my breathing problems and my injuries, I've begun to feel like a rat on an exercise wheel. Furthermore, Andra and I have just endured another failed attempt at reconciliation. The trip to Israel seems less vacation than a matter of survival, an urgent bit of ventilation in a life that's come to feel almost suffocating in its constriction.

Chang was annoyed when I told him of my plans, but to my surprise he softened rather quickly. After all, he's heard of Kyudo Roshi too, even met him once when Kyudo came to the states for the opening of Dai Bosatsu in 1976. Without exactly encouraging me to go, he cautions me not to get out of shape and outlines an extensive routine of kata and exercise that I am to follow, at least once a day, in my hotel room. Jamie, of course, is less sympathetic. For the last three classes, he hasn't spoken to me, and when he sees me come in tonight, he jerks his head away as he used to do when I tried to talk to him during sesshin.

As it happens, Hertz has a sort of going-away present for me. Always particularly dangerous on Wednesday nights because he shows off for the female tai chi students watching us spar, he lands a straight punch to my right eye that almost puts me down. It is the hardest blow I've taken since I've been here. By the time zazen begins half an hour later, my eye is almost closed. Later, I ask Chang to take a look at it, and while a number of students, including Andra, gather round to watch, he "heals" me with a technique he calls "Okinawan acupressure." It requires that I kneel on the floor between his legs, tilting my head upward while he grips my head at the temples and, with tremendous force, almost as if he means to remove the eye completely, grinds his thumbs into the socket. I'm nauseous, near to fainting from the pain, but while upbraiding me for "whining," he assures me that I'll thank him for this tomorrow. Without this treatment, my eye would be closed for a week at least, but now that he's "extracted the poisons," I'll wake up with nothing but a shiner. In fact, my eye will be even more swollen tomorrow, and what little I see will be a blur. My vision won't be normal for at least three months, and the inflammation caused by this punch will lead to a chronic iritis which, even today, seventeen years later, flares up periodically.

. . .

On my first morning in Israel, after a ten-hour flight from New York, I set out in search of Kyudo Roshi's zendo. Allowing an hour's travel time, I take a five o'clock bus from Central Station in Jerusalem to the last stop on the Mount of Olives, in East Jerusalem. Following a rough map drawn by a friend in New York, I find my way to a narrow, unpaved street, a succession of small, unnumbered houses with red tile roofs and blue or yellow doors. From a stoop fronting one of the houses, four Arab children eye me carefully as I search in vain for signs of Zen or Buddhism. Finally, one of the boys approaches. He is seven or eight, short-haired and dark-skinned, wearing khaki shorts, no shoes, and a yellow T-shirt with arms cut off at the shoulders. I think he means to ask for money, but walking past me in the direction from which I have come, he motions for me to follow. Near the bus stop, he points to a house I passed before. No less innocuous now that my attention has been directed to it, it borders on a small, fenced playground with a single basketball goal, several swings, and a jungle gym. "Zeen," says the boy, and walks away. It is not at all surprising that he understands what I am searching for, but at the moment he seems an auspicious confirmation of the karma which has brought me here.

Even on the stoop, I smell the incense. Inside, there's a vestibule with a shoe rack and a coat stand, the door to the zendo opening to the left. The room I enter is about twelve by fifteen feet, with a low ceiling and small windows facing the playground. The floor is speckled-grey linoleum, the only light a pull-chain fixture hanging from the ceiling. Eight sets of brown cushions are arranged in two rows on walls to the left and right of the door, and Roshi, facing out, sits at the head of the room between them. He is the only person in the room. There is a clock on one side of his cushion and, on the other, a bell and a set of wooden clappers like those at Dai Bosatsu. Beside him is a small altar on a low wooden table—a small sitting Buddha, a vase of yellow tulips, a water bowl, incense burning in a three-legged copper bowl—and on the wall behind there is a long scroll with a red stamp and the signature "Soen" in the lower left-hand corner. Despite these familiar objects, the room seems tacky, a zendo for losers or dabblers, completely devoid of the energy I've come to associate with Zen. Everything looks secondhand, scavenged from the city dump or purchased from the Israeli equivalent of Woolworth's. Even the cushions are tawdry. As for Roshi himself, he has long ears, a nose too big and a mouth too small, the face of a peasant or a farmer but not by any means, according to my images and expectations, a Zen master.

Without speaking, he motions me to take a cushion next to him and, with a rotating finger, to face the wall. The cushion is uncomfortably thin, maybe half as thick as the one I sit on at home, but a moment later, it doesn't matter where we are. Thousands of miles may separate me from the dojo, but the mind I face is the one I faced when I sat there, and this practice offers me the same detachment from it that it offered in New York. Excitement straightens my back and deepens my breathing. I feel my mind settling, going quiet, and finally, along with the expectations I brought here and the disappointment to which they led, dissolving. When I stand for kinhin thirty minutes later, the room looks familiar and homey, and everything that bothered me before seems perfect, just as it ought to be.

Four other students have joined us. There is a short fellow about my age who answers any sort of noise from the street with a frightening, convulsive grunt; an elderly, heavyset man whose breath sounds like an exhaust fan; a plump, grey-haired woman in her fifties; an even plumper woman in her twenties. By now, the playground is active. Squeals and shrieks and a constant babble of Arabic have filled the room since we began our second sitting.

After the third sitting, all except the younger woman depart. Heading for the kitchen, Roshi prepares tea which, with a bowl of nuggets that look like corn chips but taste like miso, he serves up for the three of us in a small room off the zendo. We sit on our heels at a wobbly table covered with a yellow oilcloth. Like the bell and the clappers, the green tea is familiar to me from the monastery. Filling my cup, Roshi says, "You coffee this morning before zazen?"

I am a little stunned by the question because it actually occurred to me during sitting that the cup of coffee I had before boarding the bus had caused me to be agitated and distracted on my cushion. When I confess that I did drink coffee, he says: "No good! Coffee too much excite. Much thought come. I can tell! Your mind much busy on your cushion! Better you green tea. Tea make settle mind, deep breath, give energy. Coffee make energy more worse. You wasting time! Where you from?"

"New York."

"Why you here?"

"Well, to be honest about it, I've mainly come to meet with you."

"Why you want to meet me? Many teachers in United States. You have teacher?"

"Yes, I study karate at a dojo where we also practice zazen. Our teacher is named Chang Wei."

"Chang Wei? I know him! Fat man! Nice man! I meet Dai Bosatsu Zendo! He study Soen Roshi! His students wonderful posture! Best full-lotus! I can tell! Any student from America, I can tell by posture. That one Dai Bosatsu. That one Chang Wei. Maezumi Los Angeles, Suzuki San Francisco. Master Wei very good. Why you come here? You honey bee student? Flower to flower, tasting, tasting, American students always shopping around! Pepsi-Cola, Coca-Cola, pizza, sushi. What you think, Zen like supermarket? You wandering! Wasting time! Better you go back Chang Wei. You getting confused! What's your name?"

So it goes. He fires off questions so fast that I have to answer at once if I answer at all: my age, my work, what size apartment I live in, whether I do my own laundry or take it to a laundromat, how often I cook for myself and how often I eat in restaurants, whether I eat meat, whether I'm married, have a girlfriend, etc., etc., and finally, "You often conshtipation? Diarrhea? No? Very good! You healthy man. When you shit, what come out? Little pieces or one long banana?"

I shrug my shoulders, embarrassed not by the question itself but, for reasons unclear to me, the fact that I cannot answer.

"Best healthy, one long banana. Shit one piece, mind one piece, all your organs healthy, all your pores open. How often you take shower? Every day? Very good! Shower very important. Especially feet. Must feet clean if you want to study Zen."

His voice is thunderous, a palpable force that makes the room feel smaller. At first, it intimidates me, but once I'm used to it, it gives the room a sort of party atmosphere. Soon I'm speaking as loud as he is and laughing for no reason whatsoever. He pauses a moment to light a cigarette, then continues his interrogation. Where am I staying in Jerusalem? Where did I eat last night? What did I order? He lists tourist sights I have to visit, food I have to try. He wants to know if my parents are alive and if I take care of them. "Must gratitude your parents. They give you most precious gift. If you not gratitude parents, you not gratitude Buddha." In addition to being fragmented, his English is peppered with Hebrew and spoken at such speed that his sentences often seem like single words. It's as if he joins words together to hide the fact that he is missing the ones between them. His concentration reminds me of Soen Roshi's. Whatever he does—pouring tea, lighting a cigarette, eating a corn chip—seems almost maniacally focused, as if there is no time beyond the present.

"What happen your eye?"

"I got punched in karate."

"Swolling. Very red. Must take care, Larry-san. You go Arab vegetable store Old City. By Damascus Gate. Sell ginger, Japanese miso. Make how you call it, like bandage, put on your eye. Only Japanese miso! No Korean! Terrible taste Korean! One spoon ginger, one spoon miso, two spoon water, very much mix. Two days, completely swolling gone, I guarantee!"

Until now, he hasn't said a word to the young woman. In fact, he has barely looked at her. In future years, I'll learn that this is characteristic of him, partly shyness and partly a by-product of a life spent in monasteries, temples and all-male

educational institutions. Whatever the reason, his relations
with women are anything but straightforward. Zen monks do
not take vows of celibacy, but he abstains because of a personal
vow to Soen, who appears himself to have been celibate all
his life.

"How you, Yael-san? OK?"

Yael has short red hair, green eyes, a face that's almost
perfectly round. She's changed from her robe into military kha-
kis. Later, when we ride the bus together, I'll learn that she's a
career officer, a captain assigned to a radar unit on the Golan
Heights. Speaking an English that is perfectly grammatical but
thickly accented by the harsh gutturals of the native Israeli, or
Sabra, she confesses to Roshi that she's feeling frustrated with
her practice. "I've been sitting for six years now, every sesshin,
every day for at least an hour, but as far as I can see, I've realized nothing."

Roshi giggles for a moment, but then his face turns grim.
For the first time, he looks into her eyes. "Realize nothing?
Great realization, Yael-san! Greatest Zen realization—nothing
at all! Understand? Nothing to worry! Must cheerful! Must patience! You become patience, you become enlightenment!"

"Patience?" Yael sighs. "I don't even know what patience
is, Roshi."

"Patience? Very simple! Patience Buddha. Understand?
Patience Buddha, Buddha patience! Buddha Yael, patience
Yael. You and Buddha not separate, you and patience not separate. You become patience, you become yourself. All connected, understand? Already I tell you famous Zen proverb:
'Buddha cannot become Buddha. Only he who is not Buddha
can become Buddha.' "

While he speaks, something extraordinary happens to

me: suddenly it is clear that I am finished with the dojo. I don't know why I've come to this decision, but it seems completely inarguable. Sitting here with Roshi, Zen seems easy, almost carefree, the dojo a dark, airless place that made the practice an exercise in masochism. Indeed, it strikes me that for the first time since I began to sit, Zen actually seems *possible*. Was it only my deluded, puritanical mind, with the help of people like Chang Wei and Eido Roshi, that made it so joyless and inaccessible? Later, when I return to New York, I'll find all the familiar arguments waiting for me, but the conviction I feel at this moment will never leave me. It's as if Roshi and this little flea-market zendo have forced me to consider the terrible possibility that when the Buddha said "All beings, as they are, have the Buddha nature," he was speaking of me as much as anyone else.

A few minutes later, Roshi stands and gathers the dishes together. When Yael and I attempt to help him, he declines our offer. "No, no. Thank you, thank you. I do myself!" Before leaving, I bow to him and shake his hand and tell him I'll be back tomorrow morning. Only then does he tell me that he is leaving this afternoon for three weeks in Japan. This is the only time I'll see him until, four years from now, I meet him in New York.

5   *Longing the so-said mind long lost to longing. The*
so-missaid. So far so-missaid. Dint of long longing lost to
longing. Long vain longing. And longing still. Faintly
longing still. Faintly vainly longing still. For faintest. Faintly
vainly longing for the least of longing. Unless enable least of
longing. Unstillable vain last of longing still.

   Longing that all go. Void go. Longing go. Vain longing
that vain longing go.   —SAMUEL BECKETT

Two months after my return from Israel, six weeks after I've resigned from the dojo, I receive an announcement of a seven-day sesshin to be conducted by a man named Bernard Glassman, Sensei. Glassman is familiar to me as the coauthor, with his teacher, Taizan Maezumi Roshi, of several well-known books on Zen practice. He is also the administrative director of the Zen Center of Los Angeles, which Maezumi founded in 1969. Still in his forties, he's considered something of a prodigy in the Zen world, but as a product of the laid-back, California style of practice, he is not much admired by hard-liners like Chang Wei. I heard him speak last year, when I was still under the spell of the dojo, and found him an almost perfect opposite of Chang—weak energy, bad posture, long on thought and short on spontaneity. Now, isolated in my practice, bereft of my marriage, and totally disenchanted with Chang, I am surprised to find that I remember him almost fondly—a brooding, talmudic sort of fellow with an enthusiasm for subtle distinctions and slightly heretical definitions. It occurs to me that it might not be completely uninteresting to study Zen with him—a man who speaks my language and is not afraid to entertain an occasional concept. Is it because of this—the fact that he's a product of my culture rather than an Oriental import—that, as I send off my deposit, I feel no trace of the terror I usually associate with sesshin?

This is winter, 1978, and, in addition to innumerable small zendos, there are at least four large Zen centers operating in the United States. Not one has avoided the sort of scandal that struck Dai Bosatsu. In fact, one would be hard-pressed to find a spiritual group—Zen or Tibetan or Theravada Buddhist, Hindu, Sufi, etc.—that hasn't crashed on the shoals of its own politics, the moral failings of its teacher, bewildered disappointment with the teachings themselves, or all of the above. Still, more teachers are arriving, more centers and ashrams and zendos being formed, and the pace at which spiritual books and articles are published increases all the time. In the eight years since it was published, *Zen Mind, Beginner's Mind* has sold between 35,000 and 50,000 copies per year. I have myself joined the parade, writing an article on Dai Bosatsu for the *New York Times Magazine* which has attracted large numbers of prospective students to the monastery and, according to Eido Roshi's detractors, who will never forgive me for writing it, revalidated his credentials. It has also given me a few credentials of my own. Nowadays, I am invited to every Buddhist function in New York, and when I attend, I am often received like an advanced practitioner. Certainly, I'm not the first to discover that it's a whole lot easier to write about Zen than to practice it.

My father was upset by my article, especially its descriptions of sutra chanting and the orioki style of eating. It appalled him, he said, that I'd allowed myself to be "seduced by the silly rituals of organized religion." How could anyone in his right mind connect Zen with such "superstition," such "neurosis"? Maybe it was time for me to reread Krishnamurti.

Kelman too has taken note, but like everything else in his life these days, his response is colored by the fact that he has recently been diagnosed with a malignant brain tumor. Doctors give him, at best, another six months to live. In fact, he'll be dead in five. He has given up his practice, of course, spending most of his time at home in pajamas, where he is constantly visited by ex-patients and -colleagues, many of whom he tries to bill for the time they spend with him. When I go to see him, he gives no sign of recognizing me, but the magazine in which my article appeared is rolled in the pocket of his bathrobe, and three or four times, while we sit together, he takes it out and waves it, crying, *"This* is our work! *This* is where we have to go!"

.   .   .

Instructions for Glassman's sesshin, arriving a few weeks after I send in my deposit, contain much comforting information. The sesshin will be held at a Catholic retreat house attached to a convent in eastern Connecticut. We won't need our special eating bowls because the nuns will cook for us and meals will be taken in the dining room, and we won't need sleeping bags because we'll each have our own beds and the nuns will furnish bedding. There is also a schedule which, indicating as it does that we'll be able to sleep until the luxurious hour of 5 A.M., have two long rest periods every day and sit only two hours in the evening, pleases me more than I care to admit to myself. I can already hear Chang and Jamie sneering at such comforts, but in my present state of mind, that makes them all the more attractive to me.

In early June, we meet and board a bus at a loft building in Lower Manhattan. Sitting in the front seat, Glassman is the first person I see when I climb aboard. I am about to introduce myself, but to my surprise he grips my shoulder and slaps me on the back as if we've known each other for years. He asks me about my writing, the dojo, mentions several people I know who will participate in this sesshin. How he knows so much about me is a mystery now, but when I get to know him better, I will find that this is characteristic of him—extensively wired into the gossip that circulates through the American Zen community, he probably knows this much about almost everyone who's attending this sesshin. Moon-faced, slightly pudgy, he wears baggy chinos and a white button-down shirt that look like relics from his college days. His lips are thick, his shaved head round and shiny as a Christmas ornament, his brown eyes hooded, elusive, impossible to read. They blink but rarely, and when they do, it is a lengthy, deliberate affair, as if the lids are so heavy and fatigued that they may never rise again. One is almost surprised when the pupils, more or less unchanged, reappear.

By now, from his books and the same flow of gossip that has informed him about me, I know a bit about him. He was born in Brooklyn in 1939. That makes him three years younger than I, thirty-nine at the present time. Until a few years ago, he worked for McDonnell-Douglas as an aeronautical engineer. Like many of his contemporaries, he had developed an interest in Zen through college philosophy courses, and he began to sit after reading Philip Kapleau's *The Three Pillars of Zen* in 1967. Apparently, the practice obsessed him from the moment he discovered it. When he learned of the zazen meetings that Taizan Maezumi, then a young monk just a few years out of his monastery in Japan, was leading at his small house in Los Angeles, he attended morning zazen almost every day. Two years later, when Maezumi acquired a building, and his zendo became a residential center, he made Glassman its chief administrator. In 1970, while McDonnell-Douglas was sponsoring his doctoral work in mathematics, Glassman shaved his head and—just three years after beginning to sit—took monastic vows. He maintained his secular life for the next five years, but after he'd been certified a teacher by Maezumi, he resigned from McDonnell-Douglas and devoted himself to the center. Nowadays, he is the driving force behind an expansion that has turned the Zen Center of Los Angeles into one of the largest such establishments in the United States. It has more than two hundred members, offers a full schedule of workshops and residency training programs, operates several businesses, and owns several buildings on the block that surrounds its offices.

It is a beautiful summer day, and traffic is light. In a mat-

ter of minutes, we're on the parkway, heading for Connecticut.
There are thirty of us aboard the bus, with fifteen more expected at the convent. The group is a little older, a bit more
conservative than most Zen groups I've known. College teachers, psychotherapists, artists, writers—all of us white and most
of us working at jobs that permit the time off we're taking this
week. One of the constraints of Zen and other spiritual practices is that few people can take seven days off from work without at least giving up vacation time, and fewer still would
choose to spend their vacations staring at a wall. Since family
life is another constraint, the preponderance of students are
single, widowed or divorced, and most of the couples are child-
less or old enough that their children have left home. Given the
fact that loneliness and psychological desperation are two of
the best catalysts for practice, one of the largest contingents
around Zen or other spiritual centers will often be drawn from
the recently divorced.

Two other monks and a nun have accompanied Glassman
from ZCLA. The nun is his wife, Helen, who goes by the
Dharma name Yuho. She is a plump, spirited woman with an
attractive face and a high-pitched laugh, an interesting comple-
ment to her husband's melancholy and detachment. A rabbi's
daughter who resisted Zen in the early years of her marriage,
she has developed a passion for it now that is almost the equal
of her husband's. Her shaved head attests to the fact that she
was herself ordained last fall. Maezumi remains her primary
teacher, what in Dharma is called her "root guru," but recently, despite the fact that many consider this an impossible
combination, a contradiction of marriage as well as the practice, she has become her husband's student too. She suffers
from rheumatoid arthritis that requires her to sit in a chair,

with one cushion beneath and another behind her. Though she remains close to her parents, she has never told them of her ordination or, for that matter, of his.

The convent is a white two-story wood-frame building with green shutters and chimneys at either end. The wall we face as we enter the driveway is a riot of blooming wisteria. There is a meadow just inside the gate, a large, manicured lawn between the meadow and the house and, out back, surrounded by another lawn, a swimming pool close to Olympic size. Such beauty seems incongruous with the austerities of sesshin, but we are not by any means the first to explore this contradiction. At least two other Zen groups have made use of these facilities, one of them led by Soen Roshi.

Like a traveling theatrical troupe, we've brought all the props we need to stage our production: fifty sets of black cushions; incense and incense bowls and sand to fill them; candles and candleholders; an inkin and a gong, a drum for chanting; the large bronze standing Buddha that will remind us where all this began. In the large meeting room on the first floor, we set up an altar on a folding table borrowed from the nuns, install Glassman's cushion to the left of it and then, on either side, arrange two long, precisely straightened rows of cushions about six feet away from each wall. Cushions are marked with name tags, a bouquet of flowers collected for the altar, incense lit, drum and gongs arranged before another cushion, to the right of Glassman's, where the head monk will lead us in chanting. This is an unattractive, featureless room with a tacky, emerald-green carpet, fluorescent lighting and pale yellow walls, but suddenly we find ourselves removing our shoes and pausing to bow before we enter.

Across the hall from the zendo, two other rooms are refitted for our purposes. One is set up with a pair of cushions and its own small altar for private interviews—here called "dai-san"—with Glassman, the other equipped for the lesser plea-sures which, in the context of sesshin, can assume the urgency of a Heimlich maneuver—coffee machine, hot pot for tea, sev-eral large jars of peanut butter and jelly, etc. When one of the monks explains that sesshin participants will be permitted to partake of such refreshment whenever they wish, my mind spins out in a mix of anger and relief. Even as I attack myself as a traitor to the cause, I'm joyous with the thought that two days from now, when pain and fatigue begin to mount, I'll be able to refuel with caffeine or a hit of peanut butter and jelly. Zen is hard to beat when it comes to bottom-line ambivalence. Am I angry at Glassman for giving me what I want or angry at myself for wanting it?

.   .   .

Glassman's revisionism is apparent in every aspect of sesshin. Sittings are never more than thirty-five minutes long, and those who move—no small number in this permissive atmosphere—are never reprimanded. Attended by the nuns, sitting on chairs rather than on our heels, we eat gourmet vegetarian meals, des-serts like coconut cake or apple pie. During breaks, we swim or sunbathe on the lawn and, at night, before going to bed, we take long solitary walks in the moonlight. It is not awfully hard to suspect that one has stumbled upon the ideal luxury vaca-tion—absolute quiet and solitude, first-rate food and congenial company, accommodations that rival a first-class hotel. But after all, this is still sesshin. Coconut cake cannot erase the fact that we're spending nine hours a day on our cushions, and no amount of sunbathing can protect us from the bliss or terror

that emerges in the silence. I am amazed to find my knees hurting no less than they did at Dai Bosatsu, my mind no less prone
to seizures of panic, anger or, for that matter, equanimity. The
big difference now, however, in addition to all the other support systems here, is Glassman himself. This is actually the first
time I've ever worked with a Zen teacher, and I quickly understand why spiritual practices place so much importance on this
relationship. His talks and advice and, most important, the witness he offers in daisan give the practice shape and objectivity,
a kind of motivation I've never known before. He laughs at my
pretensions, scolds me when I'm shirking, flatters me when I
sink too low. Most of all, he dangles before me the dream of
making the sort of commitment he has made, the hope that if I
go but one step further, manage but one more lurch of renunciation, I will be liberated from my self, my ego, and most of all,
perhaps, the endless disappointment which derives from this
sort of fantasy.

"All of us who come to Zen," he says, "have a yearning to
let go. Naturally, we want to be free of the self, free of the ego,
attain the mind that Shakyamuni attained under the bodhi tree.
But what is letting go? I think we don't understand it at all.
We've got this idea of something trapped that we've got to set
free. Like there's a bird in your hand, and what Zen is about is
spreading your fingers and letting it fly away. Whoosh! I'm enlightened! But you and the bird are the same! You and your
hand are the same! Nothing needs to be opened! Nothing
needs to fly away! Realize this and you've automatically let go!"

These words are delivered in the course of a teisho on my
old favorite, the koan about the flag and the wind from *The
Mumonkan*. Glassman offers us a perfect example of letting go
by taking it forward in time and turning it on its head. "Two

hundred years after this event occurred, seventeen monks, taking refuge at an inn while on a pilgrimage, were caught up in earnest discussion of it. 'Which is moving—the flag or the wind? It is not the wind that moves; it is not the flag that moves. It is the mind that moves!' As it happened, the old lady serving them dinner was an enlightened being. After eavesdropping on their debate for some time, she could not contain her impatience with them. 'You fools!' she shouted. 'Don't you understand? It is not the wind that moves; it is not the flag that moves; and it is not the mind that moves!' At this point—a world record, for sure—all seventeen monks were enlightened."

·   ·   ·

Visiting New York for a few days, my father wants to meet "your friend the Roshi." I arrange for him and Mother to come to the zendo soon after morning sitting a few days later. Mother is a bit ambivalent about the meeting. She is not averse to meeting Roshi, but in addition to being skeptical about Dad's enthusiasms, she has a tendency to injure herself whenever, as she puts it, she "traipses after him." She threw out her back once doing Feldenkrais exercises—with Feldenkrais himself—in Tel Aviv. Another time, she pinched a nerve in her neck trying to stand on her head in a yoga class Dad had arranged, just for the two of them, with a teacher who'd just moved to Memphis. Despite her reservations, however, she offers Roshi her cheek to kiss and doesn't seem embarrassed when he declines the invitation. "Hi, Kyudo," she says, "I'm Dorothy." Social encounters have always had an independent momentum for her, transcending any mood she brings to them. Like Dad, she is seventy-six years old now, but she looks ten years younger, and her voice and manner are younger still. The "cuteness" which irritated me so when both of us were younger strikes me, these days, as "spirited" and "feisty." She still persists in her unfortunate tendency to catalogue her pains and illnesses as if they are both the axis of her life and a matter of consuming interest to everyone else, but she's become more independent as Dad has aged and become more dependent on her.

Dad has lost more than 80 percent of his hearing and with it most of what little interest he ever had in conversation or social intercourse. Brow furrowed, feet raised in his recliner, he spends most of his time reading or encased in a cloister of introspection. Actually, I've seen evidence that he can hear if he pays attention, but listening—especially to someone who might offer him something he doesn't know—has never been his habit, and he is not about to cultivate it now. These days, he turns his head away the moment you address him, saying "What? What?" with irritation and impatience, as if it's not his hearing but your voice that is impaired. Yesterday, in a coffee shop, I wanted to move because the Muzak was at high volume, and we were sitting beneath the speakers. "Why move?" he said. "I can't hear it at all!" He retired ten years ago, and now, living half the year in Florida and half in Memphis, he devotes his time to reading, managing his money, golf and painting. With regard to the last, he is not altogether untalented, but he never works for more than an hour before calling Mother to see what he's produced. His reading is still voracious—everything from best-sellers to Wittgenstein—and he continues his early-morning Krishnamurti habit, reading him for thirty minutes to an hour after he's finished his other rituals: thirty sit-ups, thirty minutes on the treadmill and, ever since reading my article in the *New York Times,* fifteen minutes of meditation. For the last, he sets a timer, lights incense I've sent from New York, sits on the edge of a bed, and practices "choiceless awareness," as he learned it from Krishnamurti. As always, his letters to me are about spiritual issues, but despite the fact that his interest in such matters has persisted for almost forty years, he is almost always argumentative. He has never quite decided whether my involvement with Zen is admirable or pathological:

> *Dear Larry,*
>
> *Since writing to you yesterday, I have been concerned as to whether or not I was clear to you about my feeling about all this guru business. I just did not nor do not want you to misunderstand me. What I am trying to convey was the dangers involved for all of us neurotic and disturbed people in selecting—in the course of our desperate seeking—the wrong direction.*
>
> *Again I would emphasize my firm convictions: that we are all born with what evolution has endowed us with. That we are all conditioned by the field in which we happen to come into this world. That being the case then we are in a sense victims—having to use these capacities to adjust—adapt—find a place for ourselves— somewhat conducive to survival.*
>
> *Fortunate ones find a harmonious situation—but the overwhelming majority have to adapt by distorting most of their basic needs and capacities. As you know— in the process all kinds of confusion tensions fears etc are the result.*
>
> *There is desperate need to find relief for all these inner tensions—and most of us fantasy all kinds of solutions—following this one—or that one—imitating this*

or that—etcetera. Organized religion offers Jehovah and the saints—and monasteries and some folks do find a relaxation of their tensions by submerging themselves in those patterns. Some take to Dope—to sexual excesses— and these work too—albeit temporarily—but at a terrific price—some take to meditation—which also works—and the best of all understanding I am convinced is to be found in the teachings of Krishnamurti— and ZEN—with their approach of NO GOALS—just unwind and face the Truth of what one is doing with their capacities—and with enough insight maybe intelligence will indicate the problems—and that there is no need to seek a goal or other solution.

As far as I'm concerned—it seems to me that all my moves—into analysis—interest in Zen—interest in Krishnamurti, originally imitating those elders around which I was raised—my jealousies—envies—greeds— were all done (i.e.) directed my energies) was basically to assuage the anxieties in me. So I conformed out of pragmatism, rebelled when threatened—dreamed of solutions—and most times in desperation used the opportunities of the moment—those present to alleviate the tensions of the moment.

So this is also the whys and wherefores that I am basically cynical about organizations—for in retrospect I find that I used all of them that I associated with for this same purpose. And that is why tho I am fascinated by Krishnamurti Zen etc—I leave them at the point where they talk about the "beyond"—the "ineffable"—the Mystic—Gods and all that—for somehow or other I feel that all these images words—are one more attempt to

assuage this anxiety we all have about being temporary
abode on this earth.
     anyway I love you and admire your dedication—
and will go along with most of your doings.

                                                              Dad

Will not read over for fear will tear up

We take our seats around Roshi's table, in the small room
adjacent to his kitchen. It is separated from his windowless
bedroom by sliding glass doors and vertical blinds. This is the
room and the table where our food is set out during sesshin.
Opposite the table are two large dressers. One holds his TV
and VCR (both, as usual, covered with a yellow brocade altar
cloth), and the other has been set up as an altar with a picture
of Soen Roshi, a vase of flowers and an incense bowl where
even now a stick is burning. Every morning when Roshi gets
up, he bows to Soen and then to the Buddha on the altar in the
zendo, and then—reading their names from a list he keeps behind the Buddha—offers prayers for all the members of our
zendo and the two zendos, in Jerusalem and London, where he
conducts sesshin every year. Since Buddhism is unqualified in
its rejection of theism, I was somewhat surprised when he told
me of this habit. "What does it mean for a Buddhist to pray,
Roshi?"

"I have no idea," he replied. "When I pray, I *just* pray."

In addition to his usual pot of green tea, he has prepared
coffee and set out a bowl of grapes and a plate of cookies. He is
wearing a freshly washed black robe rather than the slate-blue
Ryutaku-ji work clothes he usually wears around the zendo.
Since hospitality always takes precedence for him over his own

habits and taste, he does not ask my parents to remove their shoes on entering.

Mother keeps touching Roshi on his arm or shoulder, once even on his cheek. I am a little embarrassed by her behavior, but as it turns out, he is enchanted with her. After today, he will always inquire about her health, send his regards to her, and admonish me to spend as much time as possible with her because "she very wise lady" and there is no end to what she can teach me.

It is clear from the outset that I must serve as translator of these proceedings. Roshi's speech is hard enough on good ears, much less Dad's, and my parents' southern accents make their English, for him, a language he has never heard before.

"What he say?" he says.

"He says, 'What is your background?' "

"What means 'background,' Larry-san?"

"Your past. He wants to know about your past."

"Tell him monk six years old. Seventeen years monastery, thirteen Israel, New York four years ago."

"What's he say?" Dad says.

"He became a monk when he was six. Spent seventeen years in the monastery, thirteen in Israel. He came to New York four years ago."

"In other words, his experience is completely narrow, just like mine. Tell him I said his mind is just as limited as mine."

"No!" cries Roshi, when I've translated. "His mind not limited! Please you tell him: his mind unlimited!"

"What's that?" Dad says.

"He says your mind is unlimited."

"Unlimited? Impossible! How can my mind be unlimited? I am the product of my conditioning, my psychology. My *fundamental anxiety!*"

"No, no. You tell him unlimited! You tell him please I guarantee! His mind unlimited!"

"But how can I know that? Ask him how with my limited vision I can see what's unlimited?"

This time, Roshi doesn't wait for me to translate. "Must find out himself!" He brings his fingers to his lips and makes a smacking sound. "Tell him, sugar sweet. Umm! Does it help I tell him? No, must taste himself! Yes! Yes! Completely unlimited!"

Shaking his head, Dad lowers his voice and speaks to me confidentially. "If you ask me, that's a lot of who-shot-John. I know the Zen lingo. Koans, irrational, confusion. They're always trying to turn you inside out. But how can I know what I don't know?" Leaning across the table, he lifts his fist as if he means to pound the table, but Mother reaches for it and lowers it quickly without a sound. "How can I know what I don't know?"

"Yes, yes!" Roshi cries. "Know what you don't know! Therefore unlimited! Formless mind! Therefore unlimited! Listen, Larry-san, you tell him Coca-Cola cannot Pepsi and Pepsi cannot Coke. But formless can any drink! Can Coke! Can Pepsi! Your hand empty, can take whatever put in it. Your mind like mirror. Gorilla come, reflect gorilla. Miss Universe, reflect Miss Universe. Because mirror itself, don't hold any attachment. Clear! Unlimited! Ask him does he have camera. OK. Your lens clean, you make clear picture. But if lens dust, you want nice photograph, no, no, impossible! Understand English, Larry-san? Poor Japanese accent, I'm sorry."

Dad looks at me blankly when I relay all this to him. For a moment, he seems almost a child. There seems to be no mid-point for him between certainty and helplessness, absolute authority and absolute confusion. I've seen this expression before, of course, but it never fails to make me feel as if I'm falling apart myself. It's as if I can't bear to see him frightened or, more to the point perhaps, as if my brain is wired to guarantee that I'll never be less frightened than he.

Mother says, "Will you please ask Kyudo if he's bald or does he shave his head?"

"Plenty hair!" says Roshi proudly. "Shave every three four days! If hair more than a week, catch cold!"

"What's that?" says Dad.

"Roshi says he catches cold if he goes more than a week without shaving his head."

"If he's unlimited, how come he catches cold?"

"He wants to know how come you catch cold if your mind is unlimited."

"I catch cold—therefore unlimited! Understand? Today mirror reflect cold. Tomorrow reflect healthy. Mirror itself—always unlimited!"

A silence ensues, all of us sipping coffee or tea and nibbling on our cookies. Dad's eyes are fixed on Roshi as if he means to see into his brain. If the past is any guide, I know that he is engaged in a flight of comparison, measuring his life against Roshi's and coming up short at every point. Since fantasy and self-criticism always go hand in hand for him, he is also imagining himself living in a monastery, teaching Zen, surrounded by disciples and receiving their parents in a zendo he has founded. And finally, yes, of course, imagining himself "en-

lightened." Free of pain and confusion, free of the mind that is
torturing him now. How could I be wrong about such things
when my tape loops are almost duplicates of his?

"Ask him where does he get his flowers," Mother says.

"I buy myself!" Roshi says. "Twice a week, for Buddha!"

She tells him she grows flowers in Memphis—roses, lilies,
dahlias, not to mention dogwood and magnolia. Maybe one
day he'll come and see for himself! Roshi is delighted with the
invitation and promises to take her up on it. She asks questions
about his domestic arrangements. A little surprised to find that
he cooks for himself, she is incredulous when he tells her he
doesn't have a cleaning lady. "A place this big you clean yourself?" She nods in Dad's direction. "If I could get him to close
the refrigerator, I'd think I was a genius."

Conversation turns to Israel. Being longtime Zionists,
supporters of Hadassah and the United Jewish Appeal, they are
delighted to find a bit of common ground with him. As they
drift off into talk about the Wailing Wall, the Dead Sea, and
Masada, I find it harder and harder to pay attention. My eyes
are shifting back and forth between Roshi and my father. It is
as if both of them are changed for me by their being here together, as if they're real—ordinary—in a way they've never
been before. I can see them as children, I can see them awake
and frightened in the middle of the night. Maybe too I can see
them dead. What I cannot see is the abstractions they have always been for me, the preternatural authority figures. It is
beyond my efforts of comprehension to remember the power
I invested in them or the self-consciousness I felt in their
presence.

When finally it is time for them to leave, Roshi invites
them to look at the zendo. Mother wants to know which cush-

ion I sit on, which cushion he sits on, what actually goes on in here. "You sit and look at the wall," I tell her.

"What happens then?" she says.

"Well, among other things, you see how stupid you are."

"Well, who needs meditation for that? I see it all the time!"

Meanwhile, Dad is silent, eyes roaming the room. As she and Roshi move toward the door, he lingers behind. Once again, I can hear his thoughts, and the sound is anything but pleasant. He's envious of me for sitting here, he's angry at himself for not sitting here, he's dismissing the act of sitting here as futile and neurotic. Joining us at the door, he asks the question I've expected since the moment they arrived. "Ask him has he read Krishnamurti."

"Yes, of course," says Roshi when I've relayed the question. "Very intelligent. Beautiful words!"

"Tell him Krishnamurti hates spiritual practice or any kind of formal meditation."

Laughing, Roshi offers him a friendly pat on the shoulder. "Yes, yes! Very intelligent. I feel same!"

"Then what's all that about?" says Dad, waving his hand in the direction of the zendo. "The cushions! The altar! The Buddha and the flowers and the candle. How can he maintain this establishment if he doesn't believe in formal meditation?"

Once again, Roshi doesn't wait for me to translate. "Please you tell him—I have no idea."

· · ·

Two weeks after sesshin, I receive a letter from Glassman. Like any great Zen master, he says, Maezumi Roshi knows he has to let go of his student, allow him to develop on his own. For this reason, he wants Glassman to leave Los Angeles now and establish a Zen center in New York. He and his wife and several other monks and students from Los Angeles will make the move as soon as possible. The new center will be called the Zen Community of New York—ZCNY—and he would like me to serve on its Board of Directors.

Later on, when we put the chronology together, many of us will be shocked that Maezumi, who comes from a tradition in which some teachers train for forty years or more before being granted permission to teach, sent Glassman out to start his own Zen center just ten years after he began his studies and eight years after he became a monk. For the moment, however, there are no such reservations. I am excited by this news and flattered by his request, and I write at once to tell him so.

Another letter follows quickly. "Roshi thinks it might be a good idea if someone wrote a book about me. I can't think of anyone better qualified to write it than yourself. What I'd like you to do is come out to Los Angeles, live with me and my family, write a book about us as well as the center. I want you to see the good and bad in me. Tell the truth, warts and all. Don't leave anything out!"

At one time, I might have been shocked by such pushiness and lack of humility, but I've learned to smile at such matters or, like Jamie with Chang Wei, treat the urge to criticize him as a weakness in my practice. Later, I will discover that this book, which will never be written, is only one of many steps he's taking to pave the way for his move to New York. By the time he arrives, at least thirty other students will feel the sort of bond with him that I feel now, their practice and their relationship with him already intermingled, and each will be, as I am myself, positioned to make specific contributions (financial, clerical, legal, etc.) to the community he is forming.

A few months later, he returns to New York for an organizational meeting. The scene is a loft in Chelsea. Notified by means of the telephone tree that Helen Glassman has organized from Los Angeles, fifty-eight people attend. Everyone from sesshin is here, plus a number of students who are disaffected from their own zendos (at least ten former students of Eido Roshi and three or four of Chang Wei's). The meeting begins with thirty minutes of zazen and concludes with a highly emotive, California-style "sharing" session in which each of us presents our vision of the community we're about to form. Some envision ZCNY as a monastery, some as an austere city zendo devoted exclusively to zazen, some as a sort of New Age commune where we can divest ourselves of private property and get high on meditation. As for Glassman, the excitement circulating in the room inspires the CEO in him. When "sharing" is over, he appoints a Newsletter Committee, a Telephone-Tree Committee, a Fund-raising Committee, a Real Estate Committee to seek out property, and a Legal Committee to investigate the matter of incorporating us and obtaining our tax exemption.

Three months later, back for another meeting, he surprises us by announcing that the community will be located not in Manhattan, where most of us live, but in the small section of the Bronx called Riverdale. The reasons for the change, he says, are mostly economic, but he admits to being influenced by Dennis Huebler, a member of our board who happens to live in Riverdale. A well-known figure in the New York spiritual world, Huebler is a man of wealth who, as we will discover, has already made a $250,000 contribution to the community. He has published a number of books on Eastern religion and has a local radio show on which he discusses spiritual matters and interviews teachers and gurus who live in or visit the city. Last month, Glassman himself was featured on his show. As it happens, Huebler has already located property for us—a seven-room apartment with a living room large enough for fifteen to twenty meditation cushions to be arranged along the walls. On the day after this meeting, a group of us head off to Riverdale to investigate it, and not one of us finds it suitable. It is accessible from Manhattan only by car or a bus which, depending on traffic, takes anywhere from an hour to an hour and a half. Glassman, however, likes the safety and quiet of the neighborhood, and he admits to being pleased by the fact that there is a Hebrew day school two blocks away where his kids can get the sort of education he and his wife prefer. Before any of us can process this odd conflation of Zen and Orthodox Judaism, he proceeds to the larger question of inconvenience. Those who care about Zen practice and ZCNY, he says, will find a way to get here, and those who don't—why should we accommodate them? What better way to practice "letting go of self" than by the sacrifice and inconvenience involved in reaching the place by bus?

. . .

Three months after he returns to Los Angeles, the telephone tree informs us that Glassman and his entourage, in four cars and two vans, are driving across country, heading for New York and the formal launching of ZCNY. On the second evening after they arrive, fifteen students make their way to the Bronx for two thirty-minute sittings followed by a potluck dinner. There are no community cushions yet, so we carry our zafus along with the plastic containers of pasta or beans or salad we balance on our knees throughout the ninety-minute bus ride. Needless to say, the air is filled with a sense of mission, our zazen so excited it's almost impossible to concentrate. On the following Sunday, at the first meeting of the Board of Directors, Glassman announces that, in addition to the apartment, the community needs an office and a larger zendo. Despite the fact that we can barely afford the rent on the apartment, the Real Estate Committee is directed to initiate a search. Within two weeks, they've found a "perfect" four-story building in a commercial neighborhood six blocks away from the apartment. Its asking price is $175,000, 25 percent up front. With Glassman himself at the helm, an emergency fundraising campaign is launched. Tapping the mailing list that Helen Glassman has gathered over the past three years, we solicit foundations, members, friends of members, anyone we know with Buddhist sympathies and money to spare. By now, with zendos and centers all over the country, there is no small amount of competition for the Buddhist dollar, but the product we're selling is in our view unique: an American teacher, Zen as community, Glassman's vision of Zen as no less consistent with Judaism, Catholicism, or any other religion than it is with Buddhism. Like his Dharma talks and, for that matter, his general demeanor, Glassman's attitude toward raising money is at once reticent and aggressive. As one student says of him, "He's a man who always gets what he wants but sees himself as wanting what he gets." Even as he makes it clear that it pains him to ask, that he would never concern himself with such matters were it not for the needs of the Dharma, he notes that Zen is about "giving" and "letting go," and thus, that there is no better way to realize oneself than by giving money to one's sangha. Within three weeks, we've got the downpayment, and two weeks later the deal is closed.

. . .

The new building is dilapidated, but in a couple of months our pool of skilled and unskilled—and unpaid—labor has whipped it into shape. Tools and materials are donated—desks, chairs, typewriters, lamps, an old Ping-Pong table, two radios, a phonograph, four or five telephones. We haul rubbish, sand floors, install Sheetrock, paint. There are sixty members now and more arriving all the time. Our spirits are high and the work takes them higher. Some who insist on making Zen self-conscious refer to our labors as "work practice" or, even more pretentiously, use the Japanese word, "samu," but our excitement is such that even piety cannot diminish it. We're always laughing and embracing, heading out for beer and pizza when the work is done.

The first floor contains our new zendo, the second our offices, the third and fourth, apartments that will be rented out to members. There are two public bathrooms, a small communal kitchen we'll use for sesshin, a library of religious books donated by members of the community. In a small room adjacent to the zendo, Glassman envisions a bookstore and an outlet for the meditation cushions we will manufacture in our soon-to-be-established stitchery. We've got a four-line telephone system with intercom, and a graphic artist in the community has designed stationery worthy of an international corporation. A car is bought on credit and, until we talk him out of it, Glassman wants the license plates to read ZCNY. He appoints one student his secretary, another as a receptionist, another to assist Helen with the children and the housework. He is on the phone most of the day, and his appointment book is filled with lawyers, accountants, and potential donors. When a veteran student, at one of our board meetings, complains that all this activity may be "too much, too soon," Glassman reminds him that in Zen there is no separation between the relative and the absolute. "Everything we do to make this community happen—that's our practice!"

"Still," says the student, "I'm worried about the tail wagging the dog."

"The tail," says Glassman, "is the dog."

. . .

After his teisho one evening, Roshi asks if anyone has a question. "Yes," says one student. "I'm having a lot of trouble concentrating during zazen. What can I do to settle my mind?" "Of course you not concentrate," Roshi replies. "You trying to concentrate! When you reading newspaper or watching TV, you not tell yourself 'Concentrate!' *Just* you reading paper! *Just* you watching TV! Zazen same! Just you sitting! Forget concentration, no trouble concentration at all!"

. . .

Six months after the christening of our new zendo, Glassman phones to invite me, along with several others, to an "urgent" meeting in Riverdale. In a minivan driven by one of his monks, we are taken on a fifteen-minute ride to an exclusive neighborhood that might be on another planet. It is mid-January, a luminous day, bitter cold. A recent heavy snowfall has left these narrow suburban streets almost impassable. Our destination is a three-story mansion that might be a setting for a novel by one of the Brontë sisters. It is called "Greyston" after the fieldstone which forms its exterior walls, and it is for sale for $600,000. We park in a circular driveway beneath a monumental oak tree that is listed, according to Glassman, in the "national registry of botanic treasures." To our right, across a sweeping, descending half-acre lawn, we see the Hudson River. The building has a gabled, tile roof and arched windows and is half-encircled by a screen porch. It has twelve bedrooms, an institutional kitchen, winding staircases with mahogany balustrades. For a down payment of only $150,000, Glassman says, ZCNY can have the home it deserves, a space in which to realize "the infinite possibilities of community practice." Here is our chance to build an "ecumenical temple" where we can jettison our absurd parochial concepts of Zen and explore its commonality with all religions. Two huge rooms on the main floor will be our zendo and our "Dharma Hall." Two large rooms on the ground floor will be used for seminars and workshops, a "seminary" where one can study Mahayana and Theravada Buddhism, Tantrism, Vedanta, Sufism, Jewish and Christian mysticism. And why not a yoga class? Why not a soup kitchen for the poor? And while all of this is going on, students in the rooms upstairs will be forced by communal life to "let go of selfishness and privacy, possessions, fixed ideas—all the conceptual baggage that blocks the Enlightened Way."

.   .   .

Two weeks later, Glassman's teacher, Maezumi Roshi himself, makes the transcontinental trip to attend another emergency meeting that Glassman has called, for the entire community, to discuss the matter of Greyston. Maezumi doesn't speak, but his imposing, concentrated presence dominates the meeting, especially so because there is no doubt about his views. When I am introduced to him—for the first time—before the meeting begins, he fixes his eyes on mine and addresses me in that fierce, guttural whisper that Zen Masters use when exhorting students during sesshin: "Get that building!"

Of those who attend the meeting, all but a few endorse the venture with enthusiasm. There is much impassioned talk about "karmic coincidence" and "Sensei's vision." Dissenters—a group that includes myself—worry that we'll be "politically compromised" by locating in a wealthy, upper-class neighborhood or that the financial pressures imposed by the building will distract us from our practice, but Dennis Huebler silences us by laying our fears to lack of confidence in our teacher. "Don't you realize that this is no ordinary man? What do you think we've got here? Some two-bit guru with nothing to offer but a mantra? Sensei is a biggie! I'm talking Dogen Zenji! Martin Luther King! If he thinks Greyston is right for us, how can we question him?"

When Huebler is finished, Glassman stands. After a long silence in which he gazes at us as if we are a single individual, a lover whose eyes and mind are linked in perfect intimacy with his own, he speaks of the "miraculous dialogue" in which we've just engaged. It doesn't matter if we buy Greyston— we've already received a precious gift from it! Still, we live in the Relative World as well as the Absolute. We have a difficult choice to make and we mustn't be impetuous. We need a committee to investigate the pros and cons. Two weeks from now, when we have all the facts, we will arrive at our decision.

Despite the fact that I have been the most outspoken of the dissenters, it comes as no surprise to me when he asks me to chair the committee. When it comes to wayward sheep, there is no better shepherd than he, no one more skillful at tapping the inherent need that exists in me, as it probably does in most everyone here, to be a member of the family, not to mention a loyal son to its patriarch.

.   .   .

Friday evening, the first night of sesshin at the Soho Zendo. The weather outside is perfect, but that's bad news for us. Since it is too warm to close the windows and too cool to use the air conditioner, we will be at the mercy of sidewalk and traffic noise as well as the clamor our neighbors send through the walls. The balmy conditions have filled the streets with strollers, musicians and vendors, and the crowd will expand dramatically if the weather holds through the weekend. More ominous than anything outside, however, is the sound of our upstairs neighbor's vacuum cleaner. Since he never cleans except when he has parties, and since his parties usually begin after nine o'clock, when we are going to sleep, and end around the time we awaken, at four-thirty, the roar above can only mean that we will get no sleep tonight.

I have never approached sesshin with enthusiasm, but my resistance this time is at an all-time high. For the last four months, I have had little to do with Zen. I've been sitting on my own, but I haven't been to the zendo at all, and I've kept my contact with Roshi to a minimum. The reason? Last February, I met Samuel Beckett. I had sent him a book of mine, and he had responded cordially; after several further exchanges, he invited me to meet with him in London and sit in on rehearsals of *Endgame* for a production he was directing. Given the expectations I took to these meetings, it was hard to believe that Beckett would not disappoint me, but in fact he was more than I expected—warmer, more inspiring, and more disconcerting in his effect upon my life. Though I still found his work closer to Zen than that of any other writer I knew, he left me disgruntled about my practice, resentful of Roshi's influence on me, fearful of zazen's effect on my writing. What moved me most about Beckett was the urgency one sensed in him. One could not doubt that his work was his primary means of survival or that this was the source of its immediacy and authenticity. I was not so foolish as to equate myself with him as a writer, but whenever I thought of Zen in his presence, I felt a little embarrassed. It was as if by offering an alternative to writing, another means of bringing order to one's life, the practice provided a sort of cushion which protected me from the desperation I needed to produce a valid work. Writing was Beckett's spiritual practice, but I had zazen. I had Roshi. How could I tap anything like the urgency I needed as long as Zen continued to offer me sanctuary and relief? When I returned from London, I vowed to avoid both Roshi and the zendo. I would continue to sit on my own, but for now, my work would be my spiritual practice. What I could not find through it, I would not find at all.

Among the people who attended the *Endgame* rehearsals were two puppeteers, a married couple, who cast their puppets in Beckett plays. At a cast party one night, they gave a performance of *Act Without Words I,* a silent, Keatonesque drama about the futility of hope that may be, of all Beckett's work, the most "Buddhist" in its vision. A man sits beside a barren tree in what seems to be a desert, a blistering sun overhead. Suddenly, offstage, a whistle is heard and a glass of water descends. He reaches for it, but it rises beyond his outstretched hand. He resumes his position beneath the tree, but the whistle sounds again, and a stool descends. Mounting it, he reaches for the water, and it eludes him once again. A succession of whistles and offerings follow, each arousing his hope and dashing it until at last he ceases to respond. Like so much else in Beckett, it is a vision of almost unbearable bleakness rendered in comedy nearly slapstick, and that evening, with the author and a number of children in the audience and an ingenious three-foot puppet in the lead, it had us all, children included, laughing as if Keaton himself were performing it. When the performance ended, Beckett congratulated the puppeteers, offering—with his usual diffidence and politeness—but a single criticism. "The whistle isn't shrill enough."

As it happened, one of the performers, the woman, was a practitioner of Tibetan Buddhism. As a devotee and a Beckett admirer, she was understandably anxious to confirm what she, like many people, took to be his sympathies with her religion. Beckett responded to her as he always did to such assertions. "I know nothing of Buddhism. If it's present in the play, it is unbeknownst to me." Once this had been asserted, however, there remained the possibility of unconscious predilection, innate Buddhism, so to speak, so the woman had another question, which had stirred in her mind, she said, since the first time she'd read the play. "When all is said and done, isn't this man, having given up hope, totally liberated?" Clearly, she was familiar with the Second Noble Truth—if desire is the root of suffering, and Beckett's character is free of it, is it not reasonable to assume that he is free of suffering? Beckett looked at her with a pained expression. He'd had his share of drink that night, but not enough to make him discard his vision or his profound distaste for hurting anyone's feelings. "Oh, no," he said firmly. "He's *finished.*"

When I returned to New York, I found myself haunted

by this exchange. It showed me, I thought, a fork in the road, the point at which Beckett, for all his putative Buddhism, ceased to be a Buddhist. You could say that he embraced the First and Second Noble Truths—the inevitability of suffering and the fact that it springs from desire—but not the third and fourth, which point the way beyond desire and, thus, out of the human quagmire. There is no salvation for him. He embraces his dilemma, and his greatest work derives from it. Some might say that he is a nihilist, but to me he seems a warrior who goes into battle without his shield. In contrast, I felt that Zen had been a kind of shield for me: it weakened my work because it offered me a way out of my quagmire. I had to throw away my shield, turn away from everything that promised a way out. I was well aware that there was no better definition of Zen than this—throwing away one's shield—but it seemed to me that this was Beckett's Zen, not Roshi's. Implicit, not explicit, it was the sort of Zen that came through living rather than from sitting on a cushion. That's what Beckett had shown me then— that I had to escape explicit Zen. If implicit Zen turned out to be truer Zen—how many times had we been told that knowledge of Zen can only interfere with it?—this paradox would have to remain, as it had remained for Beckett, "unbeknownst to me."

So what am I doing at sesshin? For that matter, why do I continue to practice Zen in spite of all the obstacles I've encountered? Why do I interrupt my life and my work, invite the torturous pain in my legs, the sleepless nights, the rage I feel at the rigidity of the schedule? Ever since I placed my name on the sign-up sheet that Roshi posted on the bulletin board, I've been asking myself these questions, and I've not come up with an answer. Of course, the answer will be clear when sesshin is

over. Why is it unavailable now? I think it's because sesshin
alone unearths the mind that is its justification. It is that
mind—tougher and less self-absorbed; less involved with conceptual distinction, not to mention the sort of comparative
mind that has been plaguing me since I returned from London—I seek now, but until I actually reach it, I am acting on
faith alone.

The party begins a few minutes after we turn out our
lights. Our neighbor's music is so loud and his sound system so
powerful that the floor beneath my sleeping bag is shaking as if
in an earthquake. Roshi always keeps a supply of earplugs on
hand, but one would have to be stone-deaf to sleep beneath
this barrage. At eleven-thirty, he taps me on the shoulder and
asks me to go upstairs and see what I can do. It is an unusual
request from him, the first time I have known him to concede
to external circumstances. I put on my street clothes and
mount the stairs through a haze of smoke and a blast of mari-
juana. Two women smoking on the landing awaken a yearning
I can do without just now. Are they as beautiful as I think they
are? Is it desire for them I feel or desire for anything outside the
tight, grey world from which I have just escaped? I open the
door on a huge, smoke-filled loft, a dimly lit space the size of a
small factory with very high ceilings, exposed beams and sprin-
klers, virtually no furniture, people wall-to-wall. On a table to
my right is a well-stocked bar, on one to my left a spread of
cheese and cold cuts, peanuts and potato chips. Talkers cluster
near the tables, but the music is loud and the walls are shaking,
and most of the crowd is dancing. Searching out the host, I am
thinking about following my breath, pain in the knees, watching my mind, transcending desire and impermanence, "letting
go" or, as Dogen puts it, "body and mind falling away." God

knows that Zen, if I give it anything like serious thought, remains inarguable to me, but why do I feel such envy for these people?

The host is a tall, thin fellow in his mid to late twenties with a thick mustache and a dangling cross for an earring. He seems to be under the influence of alcohol or some other chemical, but he is cheerful and friendly and, since he knows Roshi and likes him, not unsympathetic to my request for protection from the noise. But after all, what can he do? "We've got, what, a hundred fifty people here and I promised them dancing. They'd kill me if I turned the music down. You can call the police if you want, but I can tell you it will take them a couple of hours to get here. Even if they make us turn the music down, we'll turn it up as soon as they leave."

I know it's useless, but I reason with him, explaining that we're trying to sleep and have to get up early, that the schedule we face tomorrow is something of an ordeal. Halfway into my argument, I realize that our conversation is being monitored by another fellow, a short, heavyset man somewhere in his forties, dark glasses pushed up onto a bald streak that runs the length of his head. "Hey," he says, "did I hear you say you're into Zen downstairs? How can you come up here and ask for quiet? Haven't you read D. T. Suzuki? Real Zen people, they don't ask for silence, man. They create it! Put them in the desert, put them in Times Square, shit, put them on the fucking beach at Normandy, it's all the same to them! I don't know what sort of Zen you're doing, but it can't be real if a little noise gets you uptight."

As expected, the party is just winding down a few hours later, when Roshi turns on the lights to get us up for morning sitting. Like everyone else, I suspect, I haven't slept at all. Expecting to be dozing and fighting off sleep, I dread the cushion more than ever now, but just before he rings the bell, he makes a statement that changes everything for me: "You think you tired, you 'fraid, what happen? You make pictures, thinking, 'What shall I do? How can I sit? All night I not sleep! What shall I do?' You making pictures of your energy! You creating your world! Don't make any pictures! Every sitting fresh! If you holding onto picture, you escaping! Zazen not escape! Understand? Don't escaping on your cushion! Whatever comes— this moment! this moment!—just you take it!"

"Zazen not escape." Maybe it's my fatigue, and the desperation it breeds in me, but despite the fact that I've heard these words countless times before, they enter my brain and explode. I am seized with energy and attention, not just resolved against escape, but—truly, unequivocally—not escaping. Every second is a matter of curiosity, an urgent need to see and taste whatever arises in my mind. But it's not like "I" feel this curiosity. I'm not here. Nothing is left of me but that which registers what I see. It's as if I was nothing more than the habit of escape which has suddenly dissolved. This state of mind will persist throughout the morning, eight half-hour sittings passing so quickly they might be compressed into an instant. In all my time in Zen or, for that matter, all the time I've been alive, I've never known a more precise attention or a greater indifference to discomfort.

It is impossible to remember, much less articulate, the experience of zazen, what one sees when the mind begins to slow down and gaps in thought become more frequent and expansive, but this moment surely offered one of my greatest revelations—the degree to which my mind is *always* involved in escape, lurching toward the future or clinging to the past, generating concepts that obscure reality, seeking relief or cessation, a way out, any time but this, anywhere but here. Now, for this moment, the grabbing has stopped, and it seems that this is all I've ever wanted, from Zen or anything else.

Joyous though it is, there is a kind of hopelessness about this state of mind. If I have embraced what might be called an attitude of no escape, the attitude itself is driven by the certainty that no escape is possible: *things will never be different from this moment.* Nothing will change. The sound of my mind won't change, my ignorance, my pride, my confusion won't change, impermanence won't change, the imminence of my death won't change, even the hope that all of this will change won't change. Like the character in Beckett's play, I am totally *finished*: no desire, no possibility, no hope—therefore absolute and perfect freedom to accept the present moment as it is. How can I doubt that the prison in which I've been trapped was composed of nothing more than the persistent hope of escaping it? That "liberation" consists in nothing more than accepting one's incarceration? Have I not, at this moment, dissolved my Roshi-Beckett polemic, the conflict between Zen and writing that has nagged at me since I began to sit? How can any writer imagine his work to be in argument with what I see now except one who seeks nothing more from language than perpetuation of his suffering? Who but someone completely ignorant of Zen would say that it offers "a way out?" And who, having experienced what it means to be "finished," would say of Beckett that he rejects the Buddhist path? The Buddha's teachings—what else does the First Noble Truth assert?— begin with "finished." To deny this fact is to turn his vision into therapy, self-improvement, an explicit, institutional religion that subverts itself.

Every day, after the rest period that follows lunch, Roshi gives his teisho. It is always based on a koan which, according to Zen tradition, is read aloud before his commentary begins. Since he struggles with written even more than spoken English, he usually asks one of us to read it for him, and today he chooses me. I stand and take the book from him and, reading from the page to which he's opened, find myself in familiar territory:

> *"The wind was flapping a temple flag. Two monks were arguing about it. One said the flag was moving; the other said the wind was moving. Arguing back and forth they could come to no agreement. The Sixth Patriarch said, 'It is neither the wind nor the flag that is moving. It is your mind that is moving.' The two monks were struck with awe."*

When sesshin ends six days later, I am so exhilarated that, for the first two nights, I cannot sleep at all. I have but limited access to my brief no-escape experience, but I cannot doubt that it has left me transformed. As usual, my elation lasts two or three days before I crash. The recoil seems worse than ever this time, like coming down from a drug. I can't even think of working. The insights I gained in sesshin are vague and intellectual. Once again, I'm angry at the practice, angry at Roshi, angry especially at myself, that I've allowed myself to be seduced yet again by Zen and its vaporous dream of equanimity. In a fit of despair, I write Beckett a letter, describing both the experience of sesshin and the understandings to which it's led me, arriving at last at the same, plaintive question I have been asking for years: "Why should an act so simple and logical as looking at a blank wall have such a paralyzing effect on writing?"

He replies by return mail: "When I start looking at walls, I begin to see the writing. From which even my own is a relief."

.   .   .

Four months after my committee concludes that we cannot afford Greyston, the deal is closed. A large part of the down payment comes from Dennis Huebler and a couple of other members who share his enthusiasm, the rest from several, like myself, who feel guilty about our skepticism. As far as I can see, there is no great panic about the fact that we have no money in the bank and no conceivable means of paying our mortgage or utility bills. As Glassman likes to say, "An organization without a cash-flow problem is one that isn't growing." Within three months, essential repairs have been made, and our first contingent—the monks who came from Los Angeles, our cook and her fiancé, our principal handyman—is in residence. On a Sunday morning in May, we have an inaugural sitting in the morning, a community meeting in the afternoon, a party in the evening. I cannot overcome the suspicion that this building is the end for us, death to any chance at simple Zen practice, but all around me joy is so ubiquitous that my skepticism feels perverse, mean-spirited, cynical in a way that reminds me of my father.

Toward the end of the evening, Glassman offers a toast: "There are lots of ways to look at this practice, you know. You can sit and derive a kind of serenity from it, come to the zendo once or twice a week, even every day, then leave it all behind when you go home. That's what I call 'Parish Zen.' Nothing wrong with it, of course. There's a lot of it in Japan. But it's not what I'm interested in. I can't imagine a serious practice that doesn't get into your life and affect the way you live. That's what this building offers us—a chance to let the practice into our lives, actualize the Enlightened Way instead of merely talking about it."

Later, going home on the subway, his words haunt me as Hertz's words once haunted me several years ago. It's as if they've reconnected me to "real" Zen as opposed to the ideas and fantasies with which it's come to be surrounded. Suddenly, it's not Greyston or Glassman I doubt but the mind in which doubt originates, the mind which, like my father's, takes refuge in its cynicism. Exhilaration rises in me, a rush that ought to be familiar but, as always, seems unique. My old Zen voice addresses me: "What will it be, Larry? Parish Zen or a Zen that permeates your life? Dreams of letting go or letting go itself? Have you ever had a better chance at this than Greyston offers you now? How better to challenge your stubborn ego than by giving up the bourgeois-bohemian comforts of your life in New York and moving into a building that contradicts not only your vision of Zen but your sense of proportion and taste? How better to express your devotion to your teacher than by supporting his enthusiasm at the expense of your own?"

. . .

Located on the third floor, my room is a garret overlooking our federally protected oak. It has a mattress on the floor, a small table on which I've placed my typewriter and my papers, a tripartite window with a broad ledge where I can stretch out and gaze over the tree canopy at the rooftops of neighboring mansions.

Among other things, my decision to move here makes it necessary for me to buy a car. Glassman suggests that, if I allow ZCNY to purchase and hold title to it, I can finance it with tax-deductible contributions. Since I'll often use the car for community business, we are adhering to the letter of the law though both of us know we're fudging a bit. We also know that it is not exactly good karma to use a spiritual community as a tax loophole. But after all he is a man who loves such schemes, and being my father's son, I cannot help but share his enthusiasm, so there's no question that we'll go through with his plan.

Within a few days, I've settled into a sweet routine. Up at four-thirty for morning service, zazen from five to seven, a yoga class led by one of the monks, hearty breakfast in the dining hall. Since most of the residents work at outside jobs or at the office building, Greyston is quiet throughout the day and, with no schedule until evening zazen, a perfect place to work. It is also, on these hot, midsummer days, perfect for long, melancholy walks by the river and reading on the lawn. Not for nothing do some of the residents call it the "Zen Hilton" or the practice we pursue the "Upper Middle Way." Most days, I work until three-thirty, go for a run or a walk by the river, return in time to do my chores—kitchen work or building maintenance. Dinner at five-thirty, evening sitting from seven to nine, a couple of hours' reading before I go to sleep. It's true that Chang and Jamie continue to hover and condemn my decadence and betrayal, but their potency is so diminished by now that I smile at their arrival, thinking back to a statement by the Buddha that Glassman quoted last week: "The first mark of an enlightened man is the ability to be content." For the most part, it seems to me I've never had a better chance at such contentment: no television, no phonograph, the only telephone a pay phone in the basement, four hours of zazen every day, my legs in such good shape that I sit with no pain at all. The practice has never been such an intrinsic part of my life, and sesshin, which occupies one week out of every month, differs so little from our daily schedule that I am hardly conscious of its approach.

One day, after I've been here a couple of weeks, it occurs to me that my zazen has changed. Unless I'm mistaken, I am less involved in a power struggle with my thought, less engaged in resisting or containing it. I'm simply observing its movement, watching it come and go, and discovering in the process what so many teachers speak about—that thought dissolves in the light of awareness. It's as if attention empties my mind or, more precisely, reveals the essential emptiness that thought obscures. Until now, I've understood "emptiness" in terms of absence of thought, but it strikes me with the force of revelation that the empty mind and the thinking mind are no different from each other. What zazen dissolves is the separation between mind and thought and the attachment and distraction— the urge to hold on to thought or push it away—separation creates. For the first time since I began to practice Zazen, I feel that I can actually *see* this separation occur, subject and object emerging from their single source like a pair of cells issuing from mitosis.

When I see Glassman again for daisan, I describe these observations. "What is this 'I' that registers these changes?" he says. "Isn't it thought as well?"

.   .   .

It doesn't take long to discover that the most difficult and instructive "practice" at Greyston is communal living itself. My life in New York is controlled and insulated, idyllic for a writer, a sort of privileged isolation. Now, since there are always chores to do, guilt is factored into the choice to read, even to write. There is constant social demand as well. In this highly charged, self-conscious atmosphere, psychological crisis is virtually a constant, and being one of the older residents, I am more or less on call as therapist or confidant. When one of the younger students has problems with his girlfriend, he knocks on my door at midnight, and I find it impossible to turn him away. Glassman loves this sort of communal pressure and the way it jars the quiet and solitude of zazen. What happens off the cushion, he says, is much more important than anything that happens on it. Zen is not about achieving serenity and spiritual depth, but understanding that the whole universe is "one body." "Don't you see? There is no point where you stop and the rest of the world begins! When we understand this, we can truly see the functioning of wisdom, compassion. It's no longer possible to be small-minded or selfish."

This is the point he hammers at—"one body," the extension of identity, in space and time, beyond what is known through consciousness, dualistic thinking. The limited self or ego is "form," a function of subject-object separation, the vast, all-inclusive self a union of subject and object, therefore non-conceptual, "empty." "We think of 'emptiness,' " he says, "as absence of content. What it really means is absence of description. What we're doing in zazen, all the time, is simply recognizing the constant, inescapable fact that there is no separation between subject and object. In other words, that description is not reality." If the self is empty, he says, there are no limits to it, nothing outside it, and nothing inside. There is no separation between self and other, therefore none between existence and its opposite. "Look around. You see things that seem different, separate, outside you, but it's one body, see, with different qualities, different features. We cultivate the soil, and it affects the flowers. We take care of the flowers and it affects the soil. Flowers and soil are one body with different features. You and the universe are one body with different features. Hurt another being and you hurt yourself. Ignorance distorts our vision so that we see ourselves as fragments of the whole, subject perceiving objects, but there is nothing beyond us and nothing beyond the moment in which we live. It's all here, all present. This is it! There is nowhere to go, nothing to achieve, no other shore we have to get to. How can there be another shore when there is nothing outside of us?"

Perhaps if I better understood this point of view, I'd not be bothered about my car, but I don't, and I am. Though Glassman assured me that the community's ownership would be nothing more than nominal, word gets around that I donated it, and people stop me in the halls to enthuse about my "generosity" for an act which, as noted, was nothing but a tax dodge. I am constantly besieged by people who want to borrow it and, of course, constantly reminded by my Zen voice that, if I am sincere about "letting go" of my ego, I cannot refuse. The car is used for pickups at the airport, emergency visits to parents in New Jersey, grocery-shopping in Manhattan, a Saturday afternoon picnic for the cook and her fiancé. Within a month, the odometer has passed 1,000 miles, and so many duplicate keys have been made that often, when the car is gone, no one knows who's taken it. I try to "practice" with my "clinging" and my "selfishness," but I check the parking lot five or six times a day and never fail to be annoyed if the car is gone. I am also beginning to get requests for use of my apartment on weekends. Thus far, I have rejected them, but it won't be long before I reverse myself on this as well.

. . .

Every couple of months I return to the city for a weekend of R&R, and every time I do so, I go through the same lunatic vacillations. Though I've not been conscious of any particular deprivation or desire, I feel an unnatural excitement as I approach the time of departure. My piety weakens as I drive out of the parking lot, and by the time I'm on the highway, heading for the city, it disappears entirely. Like a veteran Buddhist, I try to reflect that this is all about the grasping of my ego for that which ZCNY is taking away, but suddenly I am astonished, even embarrassed, by the life that I've been living. Chanting, menial chores, communal meals, all this earnestness and self-effacement—the man who loved this life just an hour ago is completely unrecognizable to me. As for Glassman himself, the faults I've used as a measure of my devotion have such validity now that I feel nothing but anger at him.

Over the next two days, the city seems a sort of hospital where I've come for rehabilitation. I eat and drink as if I've been fasting or living in the desert. Shop windows, restaurants, women—I want everything I see. It's as if Zen, far from helping me master my appetites, has destroyed what little self-control I had. It seems impossible that I will ever go back to Greyston, but that is exactly what I do. The vacillation continues, the old Zen pendulum swinging as it always has, and even as I indulge my desire, I begin to remember the relief I felt to taste a bit of freedom from it. Back on my cushion a few days later, I tell myself that there is nowhere else I want to be.

. . .

Here is Roshi on the flag-or-the-wind koan.

"What you think, flag move or wind move? Listen." He picks up his wooden clappers and strikes them against the floor. "What is this? You soon associate, no? I think you intelligent! Thinking 'He moved by hand . . . sound come from three hundred forty meters . . . enter through ear, make ear vibrate.' Oh, no! Too late!

"OK—flag move? Wind move? Mind move? Don't keep any point. Then nothing move! Understand? Don't keep anything! You holding, you making measurement, you keeping point . . . therefore move! Death and birth, poor and rich, you keep point, but without point, nothing move! Flag not move, wind not move, mind not move! Simple! If you move, whole universe move, understand? If not move, even one piece of dust not move. If you truly discover move or not move, you can discover death and birth. Everything in your daily life, from morning to evening, settle down."

. . .

It is more than a year since we purchased Greyston. So much in flux is Glassman's vision of the community that our monthly newsletter is out-of-date by the time it arrives in my mailbox. Committees are formed—"Finance" and "Maintenance," "Publicity" and "Translation," "Public Relations" "Grounds-keeping," etc.—then bifurcated, renamed, dissolved, and revived. Originally, he divided the membership into three groups—"Friends of the Community," "Extended Community" and "Active Community"—but the most recent issue of the newsletter informs us that "our Mandala" will now consist of five "paths"—"confirmed member," "active member," "staff person," "monk" or "monastic." Each of these paths involves seven levels—"candidate," "novice," "apprentice," "senior," "successor," "teacher" and "master"—and each includes training in the role of "meditation hall monitor," and "beginners' instructor." Each path has its own director, assistant director, and committee, its own representative on the staff, its own reading list, its own schedule of classes, workshops and retreats, and of course its own notebook filled with pages rolling off the copying machine.

In addition to Glassman's seminars, there are classes or workshops in "Mahayana Buddhism," "Hinayana Buddhism," "Zen and Western Philosophy," "Zen and Kabbalah," "Zen and Ecology," "Zen and Go," "Zen and Healing," "Seeing and Drawing as Meditation." Every Sunday there is a beginners' class, a Catholic mass, and a Quaker meeting and, every Friday evening, a ceremony to commemorate the Jewish Sabbath. Arriving one night for evening sitting, we find Rabbi Schlomo Carlbach playing his guitar and singing Jewish folk songs in the zendo, and afterward we dance the hora on the porch.

We have 150 members, including several rabbis and a number of Catholic priests and nuns, a permanent staff that fluctuates between fifteen and twenty, all receiving room, board, medical insurance and, when funds are sufficient, $100 a month. We've given up our first apartment, but we've rented another for Glassman, his family, and the student who serves as his attendant. We still own the office building. Our assets are close to $1 million, our total debt a little more than $800,000, our monthly expenses $20,000, our income, $9,800, our deficit never less and often much more than $10,000 a month. The building is always crowded. To express his conviction that Zen is nonsectarian, Glassman has removed our Buddha from the zendo. He's also cut down on the number of our retreats. "The Zen I want to practice," he says, "is all the things that people say are not Zen."

After breakfast one Sunday morning, he asks me to take a ride with him. We follow the winding roads of Riverdale to a small estate a few blocks away. On one side of the driveway is a white clapboard cottage with a shingled roof and green shutters and, on the other, a two-story, three-car garage with aluminum siding. The main house, at the end of the driveway, is a modern, red-brick monstrosity just slightly smaller than Greyston. The property is for sale, he says, and he wants the community to buy it. "Just five hundred thousand! One twenty-five down!" Never mind that ZCNY has not been able to pay its staff for the past three months. He and his family and a couple of students will live in the main house, several other students in the apartment over the garage, and I will live in the cottage. Taking me by the arm, he leads me across the driveway to look through the windows. "Is this a perfect place to write, or is it? You'll be near Greyston, near me, and yet you'll have your privacy! Every morning and every evening, you can walk to Greyston for zazen, and during the day, you'll work. What more could you want? All day, you'll be alone here. Listen! Not a sound except the birds!" Arm in arm, we cross the enormous lawn that stretches toward the river. "Over here, we'll build a swimming pool. Over here, a small gymnasium, a sort of dojo. We'll teach tai chi, aikido, karate, acupuncture, shiatsu. The Zen world is full of people with skills in these areas! Mark my words! Once they know we can offer them this sort of space as well as a ready supply of students, they'll flock to us, rent apartments in the neighborhood. Soon they'll be sitting with us at Greyston. Slowly but surely, all of Riverdale will become saturated with Zen practice, a great mandala with Greyston at its center."

Heading back to the car, he asks if I'll be attending his seminar next week on the "Maha Prajna Paramita," or "Heart Sutra." "I think you'll be interested. I want to examine the language we use in our translation. Think of the title, for example. The whole sutra is contained in the first word. 'Maha' is usually translated as 'great,' but the real meaning of the Sanskrit word is 'greatness' in the sense of infinity: there is nothing it does not contain. 'Maha' means one body, unlimited in size. It's us, all of us, the whole universe. One body! Nothing outside and nothing inside! This sutra is simultaneously a reaching for the Absolute and an acknowledgment that, since the Absolute is nothing but ourselves, our reaching is itself absurd. The Heart Sutra negates everything about Buddhism, and it negates the negation too!"

By the time we reach Greyston, I've almost forgotten the estate we've been to see. In fact, I will never hear it mentioned again. Later, during afternoon sitting, it's the Heart Sutra I'm thinking about, or trying to think about, but what I actually experience is vertigo, bewilderment, a sense almost that my brain is dysfunctional. Isn't this his greatest pleasure, to generate such disequilibrium? Isn't this why I persist with him, even when, as now, I suspect he's gone completely around the bend?

. . .

Eighteen months have passed since we moved into Greyston. Newspapers litter the dining hall, dishes are piled in the sink.

So many people come and go that the building feels like the student center of a small college in which meditation is but one of many classes offered. A number of our original members, including most of the monks who accompanied Glassman from Los Angeles, have left in anger or frustration. For daily zazen, there are rarely more than three or four people in the zendo, and Glassman is seldom one of them. He leaves one retreat in the evening, just before his scheduled talk, to go to a movie with his son. The community itself is awash in endless discussion about his latest paradigm, the meaning of "Zen community" or "true zazen," or more prosaic matters like whether we'll fast on Yom Kippur or serve turkey at Thanksgiving dinner.

One evening, angry, I seek him out to complain about the distraction. He argues that I am "holding onto a fixed idea of Zen." Who knows what Zen is? Who creates the definitions we hold sacred? Isn't it precisely this sort of attachment we're trying to dissolve? "Listen, Larry, anyone can sit in a zendo. The trick is to sit in the world. You think Zen is about nonmovement, but it's really about stillness in the midst of movement. When you get a top spinning just right, it looks as if it isn't moving at all. It only wobbles when it's off-balance. That's what we're trying to do here—find the axis that lets us spin without wobbling."

He allows a minute for this to sink in. "Want some advice?"

"Sure."

"Instead of worrying about other people's practice, why not push harder into your own? What you need right now is a solitary retreat! Cut off from the world for three or four weeks!

It's time to connect with things as they are instead of whining about how they ought to be."

I take him up on his suggestion. Beginning on Easter Sunday, I retire to my room for thirty days. I bring no books with me, and I make it a point to be on my cushion at what he believes to be the most critical moments of the day—dawn, dusk and midnight. I get up at four-thirty, sit until breakfast at seven, sit again from nine to one, two to five and seven to nine. I go to sleep at nine-thirty, set my alarm for eleven-thirty, drag myself out of bed to sit for another forty-five minutes. It is a rough schedule that quickly comes to seem idyllic. Meals are brought to my door. Every day I go for a swim (Glassman's instructions again—he calls it "body practice") at the local YMCA. By Buddhist standards, thirty days is but a hint of retreat, of course (I once met a Tibetan monk who'd just done thirteen years), but this is the longest solitude I've ever known and by far the deepest immersion in zazen. My mind grows quieter day by day. At times, it seems to disappear entirely. At least once or twice a day, I feel as if I've finally begun to practice Zen or as if I haven't the least capacity for it. There are many dark moments, but as time goes on, they become less frequent. Also less overwhelming. For the most part, I have never known such contentment or equanimity or such a sense of good will toward other human beings. This is an eerie, almost preternatural feeling, as if my mind has become more spacious, thoughts and sensation smaller and less significant by comparison. So often this practice has made me earnest and pious, more inhibited and puritanical, but I am beginning to feel that its principal effect is to enlarge one's sense of humor. It's as if I am actually breaking the habit that led me, in the past, to take myself so

seriously. As if *nothing* is serious, or dangerous, or unforgivable. Who knows—maybe the piety and puritanism are de-
fenses against such changes—as if one fears to break too many
habits, cast oneself into unmarked space, and is suddenly desperate to regain control and a viable sense of direction.

What makes all this especially strange is that it occurs in a
social context. I can hear but not participate in conversation.
People in the building have been instructed not to look at me
when they meet me in the halls. It is an eerie, almost occult
experience, not a little like being dead. Needless to say, Glassman is delighted when I mention this to him. Maybe, he says,
I'm finally making progress. A few days later, when I describe a
panic attack I had the night before, he interrupts: "I thought
you were dead. Why should panic bother you?"

He promised to meet with me twice a week, but after the
first week, I rarely catch up with him, and when I do, he usually
talks business. It seems we're in the midst of another financial
crisis, unable to pay our mortgage. Broaching these matters, he
seems, as usual, painfully shy, almost helpless, his face a mix of
embarrassment and sadness. Forgetting the questions I've
brought to our meetings, I find myself solicitous and protec-
tive. It's as if our relationship has reversed itself, and all the
authority resides in me. In our last meeting, halfway into my
fourth week, he asks if it might be possible to approach my father for a loan. Of all the requests he's made to me, none has
seemed so ill-timed or insensitive or evoked in me such a sear-
ing sense of betrayal. How can he speak of such things when I
am nearing the end of a thirty-day retreat? Leaving the room, I
think, what else but my dependency, my lifelong need for tran-
scendent, all-knowing authority, has led me to consider this
man a teacher?

. . .

A few weeks after I come out of retreat, Glassman announces "the first ZCNY Novitiate Program." Eleven students will participate, and he invites me to be one of them. He also wants me to take notes so that, when we've completed our studies, I can write a "training manual" for use by future novices. Four days later, we have our first meeting. This is a crucial moment, he says, in the history of ZCNY. We're embarking on a two-year course of practice and study that will "form the center of our mandala." All of us will be required to make four basic vows: (1) to realize and actualize the Enlightened Way; (2) to live a life of stability; (3) to live a life of simplicity; (4) to live a life of service. We'll have a novitiate meeting once a month and an annual three-month intensive training period. Since no one has defined what it means to be a Zen monk in the context of American Zen, we will be involved in a kind of research as well as training. Is it appropriate for us to take vows of celibacy? Poverty? What do such vows mean? Come to think of it, what is a vow? He distributes a reading list that includes more than fifty titles—Buddhist texts, Catholic texts, Jewish texts, Sufi texts, Vedanta texts. Zen and Tibetan monastic discipline, Buddhist ethics, Buddhist history, the Lotus Sutra, the Diamond Sutra, the Platform Sutra, the Life of the Buddha. We will learn to make our robes and mend them, memorize all the important sutras in English as well as Pali, study all "service positions" that are required for Zen liturgy. In addition to our four basic vows, we will take vows committing ourselves to ZCNY and to Glassman as a teacher. We will learn to be servants of our immediate community and the community beyond it, attending to chores such as cooking, cleaning and maintenance as well as working in soup kitchens in the neighborhood. In addition to our zazen practice, we will engage in a daily "bowing practice" of 108 prostrations such as that which is followed by Tibetan monks, and a "body practice" such as running, yoga or tai chi. Every month, on the day of the new moon, we will fast from sunup to sundown.

Excitement with the program makes me forget my anger at him. For the next three months I feel as if in a state of grace. Devoting at least four hours a day to zazen, I am diligent about my prostrations, my reading, and the daily recitation of my vows, and with regard to my fellow novices the comradery I feel is more powerful than anything I felt at Dai Bosatsu or the dojo. It seems to me that Glassman has brought me at last to the crux of Zen, the realization I've pursued since I began to sit. In so many ways, I've used the practice for selfish purposes, searching for insight, concentration, a means by which to alleviate anxiety. But far from being selfish, this practice is *entirely utilitarian,* a recognition that suffering and selfishness are identical and therefore, that the ultimate selfishness is nowhere distinct from altruism. "Selfishness" is not simply indifference to the needs of others. It is anger, loneliness, the tyranny of ego and desire, the mind that follows thought, clings to pleasure, avoids pain. This is the mind that Glassman's Novitiate Program will help me transcend. He's offered me the means to live the life I've dreamed about for years.

Once a month, we meet to study a text that one of us has prepared for discussion. The text I've been assigned is scheduled for the third month's meeting. Glassman does not show up for my presentation. A "personal crisis" is rumored, a romantic entanglement with a female student. Whatever the reason, this is the last such meeting we have. Our next two are canceled, and only three of us, not including Glassman, are present at the third. In fact, though it won't be acknowledged for many months, the Novitiate Program is finished, another casualty of what Glassman likes to call his "management by meandering."

. . .

Six weeks have passed since my profound "no escape" experience, and another sesshin is looming at the Soho Zendo. Caught up once again in a fever of resistance, I seek out Roshi for advice. I've lost the logic of the practice, the understandings of self and ego which on good days make its austerities seem luxurious. Today they seem compulsive, neurotic, a masochistic interruption of my normal life, a hopeless pursuit of unattainable ideals. Is any desire more virulent than the dream of no desire at all? For years, I've steeled myself against feelings like these, but maybe they're telling me something! Maybe it's time I backed off a bit and examined my motivations.

Serious as usual when I've asked his advice, he closes his eyes and sits erect in his chair as if doing zazen. "Larry-san, you rich man's son. Live most luxury life. Never have to do anything you don't want."

"So what?" I snap. "What's that got to do with sesshin?"

"OK you say no to sesshin, but what you say when cancer come? Everyone want bad feeling go away, good feeling stay, but cannot always choose. You running, Larry-san! Wandering! All your decisions emotional. Today much excite, you decide. Tomorrow no excite, decision gone! Forty-nine years old! Still wandering! Like baby! Listen, sesshin easy! Zazen easy! Can up from cushion but cannot up from cancer!"

Like Glassman's ideas ten years ago, his point is not unfa-

miliar to me, but it seems to me he is playing one more counter-
phobic card, offering sesshin as a sort of medicine against
weakness and self-indulgence. I've lost my appetite for this sort
of reasoning. Maybe I am weak. But isn't it time I accepted my
limitations and got on with my life?

A silence ensues between us. After a while, Roshi stands
and puts the kettle on for tea. He sets out a plate of cookies,
spoons green tea into a bamboo strainer, sets the strainer in a
ceramic pot, pours the water through it, and sets the pot between us. After both of us have stared at it for several minutes,
I begin to feel uncomfortable.

"So, Roshi, how are you today?"

"Fine! Fine!"

I'm not sure why, but his answer annoys me. "Come on,
Roshi, you always say that. Nobody's fine all the time. Don't
you ever have bad days?"

"Bad days? Sure! On bad days I fine. On good days I
fine."

.   .   .

After his personal crisis, Glassman takes a month off. He wants
to reassess the community and his personal priorities, he says,
reconnect with the essential energy of his practice. A few days
after his return, I run into him at breakfast. After reminding me
that there is a meeting tomorrow morning of the Translation
Committee (presently working on a new version of the Heart
Sutra) and a Board of Directors meeting this coming Sunday,
he talks about the Lotus Sutra seminar he's giving next month.
Am I coming? Yes, yes, I must be there! He needs my input!
"Have you read Dogen's 'Genjokoan' recently? I'll be using it
more than anything except the sutra itself. Try to review them

both, OK?" He speaks a little about the sutra, quoting several lines with some emotion, then shifts with barely a pause to community business: the possibility, using several doctors and nurses who are ZCNY members, of starting a free medical clinic on the ground floor of the office building; an empty lot adjacent to Greyston where, if he can raise the money to buy it, he wants to build "townhouses" for members; a $100,000 loan he is negotiating with a rich Texas family and his plans to ask them, a few months later, to make it a gift; two new members he is excited about because one is a trained accountant and the other a professional house painter who has promised to repaint the zendo. Finally, ignoring the fact that there hasn't been a Novitiate meeting for more than six weeks, he asks if I would mind advancing the community $500 for my monk's robes. It is true that they won't be ordered (from a special shop in Kyoto) until two years hence, when I have completed my training, but the community is in urgent need of money to pay its staff.

He is drinking coffee and eating oatmeal with raisins and brown sugar. Pausing a moment, he takes out his handkerchief and blows his nose with the gooselike honk he's famous for. He has gained a bit of weight. I think we could safely call him "portly" now. When he first came to New York, he told me he wanted to run with me, but it never happened. Now I'd be shocked if he made such a promise because, knowing him better, I cannot imagine him doing any sort of physical exercise or even, for that matter, seeking for time outdoors. Beneath his black monk's smock, he wears the same khaki pants and white button-down shirt he wore the first time I met him, on the bus to sesshin in Connecticut. In daisan, his eyes are dark and brooding, trancelike, but now, as always when he is in his managerial mode, they are vibrant and restless and charged with a kind of madcap inspiration that reminds me, not for the first time, of Van Gogh's eyes in one of his self-portraits.

Sunday's board meeting, he says, will be "a humdinger." He plans to make a surprise announcement that will "push everybody's buttons." Making me promise to keep it a secret, he describes a venture which, if it works out, will solve the community's financial problems as well as offering endless opportunities for "work practice" and "service." For many years, upper-income residents of Riverdale and northern Manhattan have maintained a yacht club at the river's edge about half a mile from Greyston. It seems to be more or less a country club for boat-owners and their friends. Surrounded by a chain-link fence, it looks a little like a prison, but as Glassman explains, it consists of a marina, a swimming pool, several tennis courts and a restaurant for indoor and outdoor dining that is said to have certain haute cuisine pretensions. Glassman has learned through the Riverdale grapevine that the club has recently lost its manager and chef and, as these two have been responsible for hiring, the majority of its staff. The club's loss, he explains, will be our gain, a karmic coincidence of the highest order. He wants ZCNY to assume full responsibility for the club, handling its cooking, cleaning, and maintenance, furnishing waiters, waitresses, and busboys from our membership. Even the most conservative estimate would figure us selling them three hundred man-hours a week. If we can charge them six dollars an hour, we'll be able to pay our monthly expenses!

Stunned, I point out that we are short of staff already. We can't even keep the zendo clean! How can we take on an operation of this size? Besides, how many of our members will be willing to wait tables? How many can handle a kitchen? Even if we can manage the job, won't it distract us from our practice?

Glassman smiles at me with that particular combination of impatience and sorrow I've come to expect when I balk at his enthusiasms. "How can you talk about distraction from the practice? The yacht club itself will be our practice! Every dish we wash, every table we set, every hour we give to the place will be a practice in serving, a practice in letting go. What are we here for, Larry? To serve an abstract Zen idea or to let go of ourselves? To sit like statues on our cushions or to realize and actualize the Enlightened Way? Take someone like you, with your uptight ego and your attachment to zazen, your middle-class background and parents who brought you up to think that you were God's gift to the world. What could be better for you than waiting on a bunch of rich people who treat you with contempt?"

Sipping the last of his coffee, he stacks his dishes and stands to leave. I notice that, in violation of his own frequently stated rules against shoes in the building, he is wearing them himself. I notice too that I don't particularly like myself for noticing it.

6   *Everything resolves itself in contradiction.*

—S∮REN KIERKEGAARD

It is early June now, three months after Glassman's yacht club proposal has been approved by the board. Returning home from Greyston one Friday afternoon, I find a message on my answering machine from a woman named Rose Jacobs. She is a well-known denizen of the spiritual world, a woman who has studied with a number of different teachers, and I know that over the last two years she has made several trips to Israel in order to sit with Kyudo Roshi. When I return her call, she informs me that Roshi is in New York, staying at her apartment, and has expressed a wish to see me again. Given the fact that we had but one brief meeting, four years ago in Jerusalem, I am astounded that he remembers me, much less wants to meet with me.

In any event, I am not particularly excited to see him. Despite the fact that I am still, as a monk-in-training, dutifully memorizing sutras, keeping up with the voluminous reading Glassman assigned, reciting my vows every morning, and sitting at least two hours a day, my Zen spirit is at an all-time low, eroded by yet another collision between Glassman's mind and my own. Three weeks ago, at a meeting of Greyston residents, he announced that he wanted to tighten the place up. "This building is disgusting! No one's sitting, no one's doing chores, there's so much noise you can hardly carry on a conversation, much less sit zazen. What do you think this is—a resort? I've seen people in the building with their shoes on! Yesterday, there were two people—two people!—at morning zazen! As of today, we're turning this place around. I'm appointing Larry to be 'director of practice.' He's gonna see to it that there's no movement or noise in the zendo, and he's gonna keep a record of attendance. If you can't be in the zendo, I want him to know why. And you better have a good excuse. Every week, he'll present the record to me so that I can see which of you is serious and which of you is not. If zazen is not the center of your life, you should be living somewhere else."

In spite of what I'd learned about him—his fickleness and his distaste for discipline—I was thrilled by his reversal, not to mention his confidence in me. So much so in fact that I contracted a very bad case of missionary zeal. I told myself that my job was a chance to renew my faith and revitalize my practice while helping others do the same. All that ZCNY was meant to be, it could once again become! I yelled at people who moved in the zendo, chastised those who slept through morning sitting and, now and then, when someone dozed on his cushion, I hit him with the stick. Several students expressed appreciation for my efforts, and one even asked me to pound on his door to wake him up, but for the most part, the result of my efforts was rage. In effect, I had become the zendo cop.

A week later, when I appeared, as arranged, to present my report to Glassman, he looked at me first as if he did not remember why I was there, and then with irritation and impatience. "Why all this concern with others? Is your own practice so perfect you can worry about them? Anyhow, why do we need a disciplinarian here? Our members aren't children. They shouldn't need anyone watching over them. If they can't discipline themselves, they shouldn't be here at all."

I reminded him that my job was his idea. Why had he appointed me if he had no intention of backing me up? "Damn it, Sensei, it's like we agreed to play tennis together, and you took the net away."

"Well," he said, "that's my job—to take the net away."

.   .   .

Roshi does not exactly embrace me—I've never seen him embrace anyone—but slapping me on the shoulder and clasping my hand with both of his, he offers me the most exuberant greeting I will ever receive from him. "Larry-san! How you? Looking young! Looking healthy!" This is an upscale New York apartment, and it is more than a little jarring to see him here. Remembering him in his simple zendo in Jerusalem, one could almost believe he's a sort of wild child captured by a group of anthropologists on a field trip. Wearing the blue out-fit that Japanese monks use for travel, he looks smaller and stockier than when I saw him in Israel, and as before, his eyes are so narrow that one can barely see the pupils. Tied around his forehead is a black bandana of the sort worn by sushi chefs, and perched at an angle just above it are the same cheap, horn-rimmed eyeglasses he wore in Israel.

I ask if he is excited to be in New York.

"Excite? Please, Larry-san, I am not a child."

"What brings you here?"

"Maybe I move here. Open zendo. Next week I Japan. Ask Soen Roshi permission."

"You're leaving Israel?"

"Maybe!"

"Why?"

"Why you ask so many questions? How I know that? Thirteen years Israel. Time for bar mitzvah."

The conversation continues in this manner until he in-quires as to my present circumstances. When I tell him that I am studying to become a monk, a look of incredulity crosses his face. Then he explodes with laughter. "You monk? Larry-san a monk? Ha! Ha! Ha!" For a moment, I think he'll never regain control of himself, but then suddenly his laughter stops and he fixes me with a stare. "No, Larry-san, you not monk. You *instant monk!* Understand? *Instant monk!* Listen: I monk. Become monk six years old. Four years temple, fifteen years monastery. Why you want to monk?"

Stammering slightly, I tell him I want to "take my practice to a deeper level."

" 'Deeper level'?" He laughs again. "What you mean 'deeper'? Zen practice only one level. No deep, understand?

No shallow. Listen, Larry-san. You book-writer! You want to Zen? You write book! Don't worry monk. You wasting time!"

Unfamiliar with his style, how often he erupts like this, and how quickly he forgets it, I am more than a little annoyed by his outburst. His laughter, it seems to me, is not without a touch of cruelty. Who asked you? I'm thinking. Who gave you the right to decide who should or shouldn't become a monk? But the nerve he has touched is very raw indeed. Even in the midst of my anger, a sense of relief is rising in me. How can this be? For all my disenchantment with Glassman and ZCNY, the community is still my family, and my monastic fantasies are very much alive. But the relief is undeniable. Indeed, half an hour later, when I take leave of him, it has grown and deepened into something very like exhilaration. Descending the stairs, heading back to my apartment, I feel like a schoolboy at the beginning of summer vacation. It will take me some time to put this together, but later I'll realize that both my discipleship with Glassman and my career as a monk ended at the moment Roshi laughed at me. A decision I've been trying to make for months has happened without my knowledge or volition. Just as he once diverted me from the dojo, he has diverted me now from ZCNY. For the first time in years, I am without a community, without the pressure and demands of formal Zen practice. Most important, I am without the sort of looming, oppressive authority figure who has so long been on my shoulder, and I am altogether certain that I will never allow such a figure to enter my life again.

. . . if we concentrate within,
And testify to the truth that Self-Nature is no-nature,
We have really gone beyond foolish talk.

The gate of the oneness of cause and effect is opened.
The path of non-duality and non-trinity runs straight ahead.

To regard the form of no-form as form,
Whether going or coming, we cannot be any place else.
To regard the thought of no-thought as thought,
Whether singing or dancing, we are the voice of the Dharma.
—HAKUIN EKAKU ZENJI, "THE SONG OF ZAZEN"

OCTOBER 1992. On a cool, sunlit autumn morning, I board the bullet train in Kyoto and disembark, an hour later, at the small town of Mishima. The town map, in the square outside the station, indicates the monastery called Ryutaku-ji with a childlike, cartoon drawing of a cross-legged monk who seems to be floating in midair. The monastery is only ten or twelve miles from the station, but traffic is heavy and it takes my taxi almost forty-five minutes to reach it. Leaving the narrow two-lane road, it climbs a steep, winding driveway to a graveled courtyard surrounded by four connected buildings. On first glance, the complex seems a scaled-down version of the great temples of Kyoto, but its relative smallness makes its function more apparent. One knows on first glance that this is not just a monument to Zen but an active center in which monks are trained, sesshin conducted, morning and evening zazen sessions held on a regular basis. A small open-sided building off to the right contains a bell some twelve feet high with the familiar hanging log for a striker. Behind the monastery, the snow-covered, cloud-encircled peak of Mount Fuji rises twenty-seven miles to the north.

Built in the fourteenth century, this venerable institution was a small, neglected temple until it was resurrected by the great master Hakuin in the seventeenth century, then renovated, enlarged and consecrated as a monastery in 1761 by Hakuin's successor, Torei Enji. Its ninth abbot was Gempo Yamamoto Roshi, who did weeklong, solitary retreats until a few weeks before his death, in 1961, at the age of ninety-six, pulling his arthritic legs up onto his thighs, crying "Son must listen to father!" with such "great decision" that he'd offer a lifetime of inspiration to his attendant, the monk Kyu-san, as well as the Israeli, English and American students to whom Kyu-san, now Kyudo Roshi, would one day relay the story in Jerusalem, London and New York. Gempo's successor, the tenth abbot of Ryutaku-ji, was the legendary Soen Nakagawa Roshi, who introduced Zen practice to a generation of American students in the sixties and seventies, became the first abbot of Dai Bosatsu Zendo in 1976, and swallowed the moon on the roof of our loft building in Soho in 1977. After Soen retired in

1973, one of his successors, Sochu Suzuki Roshi, served for eighteen years as eleventh abbot, and when Sochu died suddenly, last year, Kyudo Roshi took his place. Today will be our first meeting since he locked the doors of his bedroom in New York and left his empty cushion for us to contemplate when we came to the zendo for daily zazen and sesshin.

For all the honor and financial security offered by this position, Roshi had little enthusiasm for it. He had become, after all, a New Yorker—a curmudgeon who cherished his cable television, his walks in Greenwich Village and Chinatown, and most of all, after a lifetime of communal living, his privacy and solitude. The Soho Zendo, nine years old, had thirty members, and the steady group of nine or ten students who attended its sesshins was just the size he liked to work with. Now he is a prime-time Roshi, abbot of one of the most revered monasteries in Japan. Sesshins at Ryutaku-ji attract large numbers of students. He appears on television, commands $2,000 fees for his lectures, looks after several small temples in addition to Ryutaku-ji, and his appointment schedule—lectures, ceremonies, weddings, funerals, etc.—leaves him virtually no free time.

When he phoned in New York to tell me that a Japanese contingent—supporters and board members of Ryutaku-ji—had come to summon him back to Mishima, he was not a happy man. "I don't want! I happy here! But—no choice! Gempo Roshi tradition! Soen Roshi tradition! Sochu Roshi tradition! Understand? No choice!" After nine years in New York, he was packed up and gone in ten days. He has promised to return twice a year for sesshin, but even if he does, the Soho Zendo is our responsibility now. We clean it, conduct our sesshins, take turns watching the clock, ringing the bell and teaching classes for beginners, and every time we see his empty cushion, we are reminded that we are, as we have always been, alone on our own.

Though I was stunned, and not a little angry, at his departure, I have finally made my peace with it. There are even times, I must admit, when his absence makes me slightly giddy with relief. Along with him, my dream of monasticism has departed. I am no longer haunted by the belief that secular life at best permits a flirtation with Zen or that, sitting just once or twice a day, I am avoiding the breakthrough, the joyous mix of altruism and simplicity, one might find as a monk. I sit no less than I did before, and I go to the zendo almost as often, but I know now that the practice will always remain a part of my life rather than the whole. Finally, I am a writer who uses it. Even if I yearn to go beyond description into the union of subject and object, I will content myself with describing my desire and living it out, I hope, implicitly. Perhaps I've finally given myself over to the argument that Zen aspires to resolve. I can't say there is no sorrow in these realizations, but they have also helped me appreciate what Zen has meant to my life, the subtle accretions which even the most resistant student cannot fail to enjoy: an undeniable sense of wellbeing; more discipline and tolerance for pain; and—as I've seen in the last few years, when my father, my brother and my closest friend have died—a reasonable measure of equanimity in the face of death. I don't know that I'd be aware of such benefits if Roshi were still in New York. The monastic example is the dream of ultimate ego ablation—how can any secular attainment hold its own beside it?

Leaving the taxi, I remove my shoes and mount a short flight of stairs to a landing outside a wall of shoji screens that leads into the monastery. Kneeling and bowing before me is a young, black-robed monk who looks as if he's been waiting here all morning. "Mister Larry? I Kosho. Please you follow me."

I follow him down a long, shoji-bordered corridor, turn right and climb a flight of stairs. Finally, he opens another set of shojis and ushers me into a large, dimly lit room. Two long calligraphic scrolls face each other from opposite walls, the floor is covered with tatami mats, and the only furniture is a single, knee-high table. "Roshi busy now," says Kosho. "He join you ten minutes."

When I called from New York to make an appointment for this meeting, Roshi told me that the monastery is closed now, the monks out on the biannual pilgrimage—"takuhatsu" —in which, for ten days, they walk from dawn till dusk, begging alms. When he joins me a few minutes later, he apologizes for their absence, and then, as usual, inquires about my traveling arrangements—what airline I flew, where I stayed in Kyoto, what restaurants I've tried, etc. He does not inquire about our mutual friends in New York, other members of the Soho Zendo or, as always in the past, my mother. When I ask if he misses "Dallas," or Hulk Hogan, he shakes his head irritably and does not venture the slightest hint of smile. All his happy jokes about "ahmneejah"—is it possible he's forgotten who I am? His coolness reminds me that, when I wrote last year to tell him of my father's death, I received no answer from him.

His elegant black robe is neatly pressed and thin as gauze. Sixty-five now, he is thinner than I've ever seen him. He looks at least five years older than when I saw him last. God knows I've never been tempted to call him warm, but his formality and distance are so relentless that after a time they begin to make me paranoid. Is he angry at me? Have I violated some crucial tenet of Japanese etiquette?

"Well, tell me the truth, Roshi—are you happy here?"

"Busy!" he cries. "No free time! Every day appointment, morning to night!"

"If you had it to do over again, would you take the job?"

"Don't ask stupid question, Larry-san. No choice."

We fall into an uncomfortable silence. There are lots of Zen questions I've brought with me, quandaries I've accumulated since he left, but I can't remember any of them. I feel as if in kansho, once again unable to answer my koan. Not ten minutes after sitting down with me, he stands and moves toward the door. "Must go now, Larry-san. Monk Shoro, he show you room. Tomorrow I show you Hakuin grave, Soen Roshi grave. Then we trip together."

Downstairs, Shoro is waiting for me. He is a stocky fellow in his early twenties who looks like a Marine. He moves quickly, his walk almost a run, and he doesn't look me in the eye. Guiding me down the main corridor to a supply room, he issues me a futon, a blanket and a pillow, and then, still racing, leads me to a large tatami room at the other end of the monastery. In one corner is a drum and a large gong of the sort one sees in zendos. Sunlight filtering through the shoji screens illuminates a gilded Buddha on the altar. Clearly, this is no dormitory room but rather a formal hall used for ceremony and public functions. When I've deposited my gear, Shoro says, "Come," and I follow him along the corridor again for a tour. He shows me the kitchen, where cooking is done on two wood-burning stoves; a bathroom behind the dormitory which consists of a row of latrines and small cubicles where monks have stored their personal effects; several identical monks' rooms, each with a single futon on the floor. Finally, at the center of the complex, we arrive at the zendo. It is a rectangular hall some sixty or seventy feet long by forty or fifty wide, with hanging paper lanterns and three-foot platforms on which (I'll count them tomorrow) twenty-five sets of cushions are set out. Standing in the doorway, I am overcome with emotion. I haven't heard a sound since arriving at the monastery, but the silence seems thunderous, overwhelming. For more than two hundred years, monks have been sitting in this room. Hakuin sat here, Gempo Roshi, Soen Roshi. It is here that Kyudo Roshi finally saw "the roots of the tree." How is it possible that, after all these years of Zen practice, I have never sat here myself? Why have I not, once and for all, accepted the sanity of this path?

Back in my room, I find a cushion and spend the rest of the afternoon in zazen. For the past few months, my practice has been steady and unambitious, as close as I've ever come to the Zen ideal of "just sitting," but now the waters are rough again, my mind adrift between dreams of purity and the happy lust for its opposite, with a pause now and then to remember Roshi's vision of wholeheartedness—"one direction." Is it possible that ambivalence is a genetic disease? Could one embrace it, at least, wholeheartedly or is such embrace precisely what the genes do not permit? At four-thirty, Shoro calls me to dinner, and, sitting cross-legged on the kitchen floor, I share a bowl of curried rice with him and Kosho. Then I return to my room and spend the rest of the evening sitting. Now and then, my mind grows quiet, but I am never far from the vision of living here, free of telephones and media, desire and distraction, mounting at last an all-out attack on my stubborn, selfish ego, surrounded by monks whose commitment would encourage an

equal commitment in me. Next morning, I am awakened at
four o'clock by the great bell in the courtyard, and then I sit
again until Shoro calls me to breakfast. He and Kosho and I are
joined by another fellow, Kenjiro, who speaks a bit of English.
He is short and stocky, another Marine, with a sorrowful face
and thick, horn-rimmed glasses and a habit of shaking his
head—no, no, no—with everything he says. "Are you Buddhist?" he asks.

It occurs to me that I've never been asked this question
and have never actually defined myself as such, but how can I
answer in anything but the affirmative?

"Not me," he says.

"No? Why are you here, then?"

"Much trouble. My father have business, electronic, im-
port-export. I have gambling, how you say, debt? Borrow
money from company. Well, actually, maybe I steal. He give
me choice—go to monastery, or go to jail. Two more months I
stay here, then I work for him again."

Decidedly, another vision of monastic life. I wish I
found it less comprehensible than I do. When we've finished
eating and washed our bowls, Shoro gives me a rag and a
bucket of water and assigns me the job of cleaning the central
corridor. No mop—such tools are a luxury here. One cleans
as Roshi does—bending at the waist and running your rag
across the floor. Very shortly, I am panting as I haven't since
I sparred at the dojo. It is not for no reason that most of these
monks look like Marines. In fact, I've heard it said that, when
a large number of Japanese soldiers were stranded in the jun-
gles of Burma after the Second World War, those with Zen
training were the only ones who survived. There are twelve

monks in residence here, and they not only clean these buildings every day but work the ten surrounding acres on which
the monastery maintains a truck farm. They have sesshin
every month, they rise at four every morning (three-thirty
during sesshin), and, with the exception of the day after sesshin and one five-day period during the summer, when they
return to their home temples in order to help their temple
teachers, they have no time off. (Once I asked Roshi about
this. "Do you mean to say your monks have no vacation?"
"Larry-san," he replied, "does your heart take a vacation?
Your stomach? This is not the Soho Zendo here. We are pro-
fessionals!") Meals offer a total of 800 calories a day and,
though the climate here is more or less the same as New
York's, there is no heat in the building. It all makes sense, of
course, from the point of view of "ego-killing practice," but
as I push my rag across the floor, Kenjiro's vision of Ryutaku-
ji makes more and more sense to me. There are moments
when it seems to me the greatest stroke of luck and wisdom
that I've dodged the dread compulsion that almost brought
me here.

After cleaning, I return to my room and sit again until it's
time for lunch. Early in the afternoon, Kosho knocks on my
door and informs me that Roshi awaits me in the corridor. As
promised, he escorts me to the graves of Hakuin and Soen, and
then we climb into the backseat of a new Toyota, with Shoro at
the wheel. Roshi is no less cool, no more forthcoming. For
more than an hour, with almost no conversation, we drive
through densely populated suburbs, arriving finally at a hotel
which, he explains, is owned by a supporter of the monastery.
It is nondescript from the outside, but once the doors behind

us close, we might have entered a modern Zen temple. Walls of shoji screens, tatami floors, elaborate flower arrangements on every surface, exquisite calligraphic scrolls on the walls, a traditional tearoom, a museum with an extensive collection of antique pottery, a rock garden that is the equal of those I've seen in the great monasteries of Kyoto.

A striking young woman in a blue kimono introduces herself to us. Her name is Miyuki, and she is to be our servant while we are here. She ushers us into a large apartment—the Emperor's Suite, as Roshi informs me in a whisper. All expenses are on the house for us, but for ordinary guests the cost of these digs is $1,200 a night. Miyuki presents each of us with a flowered blue and white kimono, and then, when we've changed out of our street clothes, shows us around. There is a full, modern kitchen, a bathroom with wooden tub and sauna, two bedrooms, a living room some thirty feet square with a wall of glass facing onto the rock garden, an altar with a standing Buddha and a scroll by Soen Roshi. Crossing our legs, we sit at a low table where Miyuki serves us green tea and bean cakes. "This most special hot springs hotel all Japan," Roshi explains. "Later we bathe hot springs, then Miyuki serve us dinner. Now, Larry-san—today last game Japanese World Series. Please you watch with me." Opening a cabinet to reveal a huge television screen, he locates the remote control, and then, dressed in identical kimonos, drinking our tea and eating our cakes while he fills me in on all the important players, we enjoy a bit of baseball together. Roshi shows no particular excitement with the game, but it cannot be denied that he knows it thoroughly. In the commercial break between the seventh and eighth innings, I am suddenly overtaken with a rush of conviction which does not, however, prevent my being astonished, and not a little frightened, by what I say. "Roshi—I want to come to Ryutaku-ji!"

"Please anytime yes," he says. "You always welcome Ryutaku-ji. Maybe you discover something here."

As I write these words, it is April 1995, and I've still not accepted his invitation.

G
L
O
S
S
A
R
Y

BUDDHA NATURE   The formless spiritual principle, sometimes called "essential nature," which resided in the individual Shakyamuni Buddha, as it has in all other Buddhas who succeeded and preceded him. The Buddha's "enlightenment" consists in the realization that this principle is universal or, as Shakyamuni said, that "all beings, as they are, have the Buddha nature."

CH'AN   The Chinese equivalent of the Sanskrit word "Dhyana," which means "meditation." Generally considered the precursor of Zen ("Zen" also comes from "Dhyana"), Ch'an was the Buddhist sect that emerged in the sixth century in China and was much influenced by the native Taoism.

DAISAN   One of many words for the face-to-face encounter between a roshi and his student.

DHARMA (DHAMMA in Pali)   A word with multiple meanings. Its primary meaning is "phenomenon." Since phenomena are impermanent, according to the law of causation, its second meaning is "law." Since impermanence is a fact, the third meaning is "truth," and, since Buddhist teaching is based on truth, the fourth meaning is "teaching."

DOJO   A school in which a spiritual practice or a martial art is taught.

DOKUSAN   See **DAISAN.**

GASSHO   A form of greeting or an expression of gratitude, with palms pressed together at the level of the chin.

GI   An outfit consisting of tunic and loose-fitting trousers which is generally worn by students of the martial arts.

HARA   The abdominal area just above the navel, which is considered, from the point of view of most meditative practices, the vital energy center of the body.

HINAYANA BUDDHISM   "Hinayana"—Literally, "the Lesser Vehicle"—was originally a Mahayana term of abuse for the Theravadins, whom they held in contempt because they considered them conservative and doctrinaire. "Lesser Vehicle" refers to the fact that according to the teachings of this school, it is not possible for all beings to attain enlightenment.

INKIN   A small bell used to signal the beginning and end of meditation periods.

KANSHO   See **DAISAN.**

KARATE   Literally, "empty hands." A weaponless form of self-defense originally developed by Ch'an monks in China as a means of defending themselves against armed marauders without violating their religion. It primarily evolved in Okinawa, where Chinese monks taught it to the king's guard. It remained in Okinawa as a secret spiritual practice until the early 1900s, when it was adopted by the Japanese and the Koreans.

KATA Martial-arts forms; ritualized progressions designed to simulate combat, thus providing the martial artist a means by which to polish his skills. They are meant to train the mind as well as the body, to cultivate spontaneous response as well as technique.

KEISAKU A flat wooden stick used for encouragement and stimulation in zazen, also to ease tension in the neck and shoulders. For the most part, especially in the United States, it is offered only upon request.

KENSHO Literally, "seeing into one's own nature." The Rinzai term for enlightenment. Also called "satori."

KINHIN Walking meditation, usually practiced between periods of zazen.

KOAN A problem or dialogue used as a means of concentration during zazen. It is assigned by roshis to their students in order to help them perfect their understanding.

MAHAYANA BUDDHISM Literally, "the Greater Vehicle." One of two principal strands of Buddhism, mostly practiced in the northern countries: China, Japan, Korea and Tibet. According to its teachings, all beings are primarily Buddhas and can realize this in their lifetime.

MANDALA A geometrical form containing sacred imagery, most often associated with Tibetan and Shingon Buddhism.

MUMONKAN, THE Also known as "the Gateless Gate." A group of forty-eight koans collected by the Zen master Mumon Ekai of the Sung dynasty in China. It is widely used in Zen studies. See Zenkei Shibayama, *Zen Comments on the Mumonkan* (New York: Harper & Row, 1974). Also, Koun Yamada, *The Gateless Gate* (Los Angeles: Center Publications, 1979.)

RAKUSU A small embroidered cloth worn by all Zen monks; it is in fact an abbreviated version of the monk's or priest's robe.

RINZAI ZEN One of five schools of Zen that originated in China during the Tang dynasty; now, with the Soto school, one of the two principal sects in Japan and the United States. It derives from the teachings of the Chinese master Rinzai Gigen (?–867), who was a successor of Huang Po. Like Soto teachers (see below), Rinzai masters acknowledge universal enlightenment, but they are thought to place more emphasis on the direct experience of enlightenment, called "kensho" or "satori."

ROSHI Literally, "elder teacher." In the Rinzai tradition, the title refers to formal Dharma transmission; the Soto sect generally reserves the title for older teachers.

SAMU Literally, "work practice."

SANGHA In the broadest sense, any group of Buddhist students who gather to share their practice. Originally, it referred to the historical assembly of monks and nuns surrounding the Buddha Shakyamuni.

SEIZA A kneeling position in which one sits back on one's calves. Since it is generally assumed during the tea ceremony, it is also called "tea posture."

SENSEI Teacher. In certain Zen lineages it refers to one who has completed formal Zen studies and received Dharma transmission but has not yet received the final validation that conveys the title "roshi."

SESSHIN Literally, "to collect the mind." An intensive period of retreat, usually seven days in length.

SHIATSU A vigorous form of massage.

SHOJI A screen or room divider, common in Japanese architecture, composed of a wooden frame and rice paper.

SHUL A Yiddish term for "synagogue."

SOTO ZEN One of five schools of Zen that originated in China during the Tang dynasty. It was brought to Japan by Dogen Kigen Zenji. Generally believed to stress "shikan taza" or "just sitting" practice and original enlightenment; it is, with Rinzai, one of the two dominant schools in modern Japan and the United States. In contrast to the Rinzai emphasis on satori, Soto Zen teaches that zazen itself is the revelation of enlightenment.

SUFI TALE   Folk wisdom emerging from the Sufi religion (see below).

SUFISM   A sect of Islamic mysticism, dating from the eighth century A.D. and developed chiefly in Persia.

SUTRA   Literally, "threads." This term generally refers to the teachings of the historical Buddha. Many were not in fact delivered by him but written much later.

TAI CHI or TAI CHI CH'UAN   A weaponless form of self-defense developed in ancient China. Like all the martial arts, it is based in the idea of allowing the "ki," or cosmic energy, to flow through one's body. Emphasizing slow movement and sensitivity rather than aggression, tai chi is the most popular form of exercise in modern-day China.

TEISHO   The particular form of discourse used by Zen masters when addressing their students. The teacher tries to present the Buddha-Dharma directly and concretely without getting trapped in conceptualism. Literally, "tei" means "to carry" and "sho" means "to declare."

THERAVADA BUDDHISM   Literally, "Doctrine of the Elders." Originally, one of two offshoots of the "Old Wisdom School," which began about two hundred years after the Buddha's Nirvana. At present, along with the Mahayana, it is one of the two main strands of Buddhism, considered the orthodox form because its scriptures are in the original Pali. Because it is generally practiced in Ceylon, Burma, Vietnam, Thailand, Laos, and Cambodia, it is sometimes referred to as the Southern School.

YOGA   A Hindu discipline, aimed at training the consciousness; also, a system of physical exercises practiced as part of this disci-

pline. Its fusion with the teachings of the Buddha is believed to
have played a large part in the development of sitting meditation,
or zazen.

ZAZEN   Sitting meditation. Essentially, the unity of body, breath
and consciousnessness that reveals the fundamental union of subject and object.

ZENDO   The place in which zazen is practiced.

ABOUT THE AUTHOR

Lawrence Shainberg's previous books include *One on One, Brain Surgeon*, and *Memories of Amnesia.* He lives in New York.